IMAGES
of America

VAN ALSTYNE

On the Cover: Van Alstyne's railroad depot, visible in the background, was a symbol that the town was founded by the greatest industry of the 19th century. But once passengers stepped off the train, they entered the horse-and-buggy world of a classic American small town. (Courtesy of Van Alstyne Historical Society.)

IMAGES
of America

VAN ALSTYNE

Bill O'Neal with the Van Alstyne
Historical Society and Public Library

ARCADIA
PUBLISHING

ISBN 978-1-4671-3077-6

Published by Arcadia Publishing
Charleston, South Carolina

Printed in the United States of America

Library of Congress Control Number: 2013941694

For all general information, please contact Arcadia Publishing:
Telephone 843-853-2070
Fax 843-853-0044
E-mail sales@arcadiapublishing.com
For customer service and orders:
Toll-Free 1-888-313-2665

Visit us on the Internet at www.arcadiapublishing.com

Contents

Acknowledgments

Van Alstyne has been fortunate to have local historians who are proud of their town and who have worked to preserve records and artifacts, as well as photographs and interviews. Preeminent among the Van Alstyne historians is Julie S. Morris, who compiled a vast amount of material and who related her findings in a series of informative and well-illustrated articles in the Van Alstyne *Leader* in 1992 and 1993. Based on these articles, she published a fine booklet entitled *By the Banks of Sister Grove, A History of Van Alstyne, Texas*. These sources are essential to understanding the story of Van Alstyne, and I relied heavily upon her work.

Former mayor Benny Edwards is a native of Van Alstyne who served his hometown for two decades as city manager, as well as in a variety of volunteer positions. Twice he opened the Van Alstyne Historical Museum to me, permitting me to examine and photograph the impressive collections of the museum. He answered a multitude of questions and he opened the First Christian Church to my wife, my daughter, and me, so that we could explore and photograph the superb sanctuary.

Druggist David Schatz, owner of the historic City Drug Store and other venerable buildings, entrusted me with the keys to the old Carter Opera House. At the First Baptist Church, I was assisted by the minister to students, Griff Servati, who provided a number of photographs. Karen Barnes, genial employee at the Quilt Shoppe, informed me about the 1884 house where the business is located and gave me access to an archival photograph.

One of my first contacts was with Cheryl Snyder, president of the Van Alstyne Chamber of Commerce. Cheryl was immediately enthusiastic about this project, and she opened many doors for me. Kanita Adams, administrative assistant of the Van Alstyne Chamber of Commerce, provided me with useful material and stories about her town. Danielle Dorman-Chapa of the Melissa Area Chamber of Commerce was friendly and helpful when I looked for information about the town. At the Van Alstyne Police Department, dispatcher Beth Eggar assisted my search for information about Chief Will D. Echols.

My first research stop was at the Van Alstyne Public Library, where the capable director, Tracy Luscombe, familiarized me with the rich collection of local archives. Tracy and the Friends of the Library also arranged a signing to introduce the book to Van Alstyne. Becky Seevers, district librarian of the Van Alstyne schools, shared numerous leads and local stories with me. Laura Bruns, my efficient and tolerant Arcadia editor, was again a joy to work with on our second project together.

Four years ago, my youngest daughter, Causby Henderson, moved to Van Alstyne with her family, husband, Dusty, and their daughters, Bailey and Kendall. Causby was of invaluable help to me on the ground in Van Alstyne, and Dusty located several important items in libraries in Sherman and Texas Women's University. My wife, Karon, accompanied me on trips to Van Alstyne, helped with research, and expertly prepared the manuscript.

Introduction

Van Alstyne was born in an era when small towns formed the backbone of America. Throughout the Colonial era, more than one out of every 10 Americans lived on farms or in country towns. As late as 1860, four out of five US citizens remained on farms or dwelled in towns of 2,500 or less. After the Civil War, although industrialization and urbanization spread rapidly, the majority of Americans still lived, worked, worshipped, attended school, married, and raised children in small towns or rural homes. By 1873, when Van Alstyne was founded, the traditions and values of small town life were deeply ingrained in America. Van Alstyne, like small towns throughout the land, was close-knit, patriotic, religious, hard working, and progressive-minded. From its birth as a railroad town, Van Alstyne was part of the American mainstream.

The Houston & Texas Central Railway (H&TC), one of the most important Texas railroads, extended its main line from Dallas to the Oklahoma border in 1873. That year, a townsite, procured from the McKinney family (pioneer settler Collin McKinney was a noted patriot of the Texas Revolution), was surveyed and platted. Named after Maria Van Alstyne, whose deceased husband was a major stockholder and officer of the H&TC, Van Alstyne grew immediately. When the first train came through, on March 10, 1873, Dr. James Leslie had already moved his practice and his drugstore building from nearby Mantua to a corner lot in Van Alstyne. Oscar Riddle, a saloon keeper in Mantua, had transferred his business to a tent in Van Alstyne. Mantua, although less than two miles southeast of the new townsite, had been missed by the railroad, and Riddle and Dr. Leslie were the first of many to move to Van Alstyne. Other nearby rural communities also virtually disappeared when merchants and doctors and preachers joined the migration to the growing railroad town. The Van Alstyne townsite began to fill with frame buildings, and the population soon reached 400.

The new railroad town was surrounded by cotton farms. The region was part of the Texas Blackland Prairie, rich soil that was ideal for the plant that was king throughout the South and that was Texas's first cash crop. Cotton gins were erected beside Van Alstyne's railroad tracks—three, four, and finally five ginning operations. In the south part of town, the Van Alstyne Cotton Oil Company expanded into a complex of structures that became Van Alstyne's largest employer. Each fall, cotton wagons formed long lines in front of the gins. Farm families came into Van Alstyne every Saturday, and businesses stayed open late, enjoying their best day of the week. On Saturday, couples and families strolled arm in arm around the block enclosed by Marshall, Main, Jefferson, and Preston Streets, a promenade custom that the town enjoyed for decades.

A special census conducted by Texas in 1887 announced that the population of Van Alstyne had reached 1,000, and by 1900, the total had doubled to 2,000. Most of the commercial buildings were now brick, and many were two stories with decorative Victorian touches. Along tree-lined streets stood Victorian residences, from gingerbread cottages to substantial homes with soaring towers. There were three steepled frame churches with Victorian decorations, along with a three-story frame school, Columbia College. Historical architecture is our most tangible reminder of the past; throughout Van Alstyne are old homes and commercial structures that still provide eye-catching reminders of the community's Victorian heyday.

During Van Alstyne's formative years, the town progressively acquired the era's new inventions, such as telephones, phonographs, and electricity for commercial and residential lights. A volunteer fire department was organized, as well as a municipal water works. The town was linked to an electric interurban line, thereby enhancing transportation options. Early in the 20th century, Van Alstyne established a free public school and erected a brick school building. During the first decade of the century, 8,000 high schools were started across America, including Van Alstyne High School. The Panthers soon fielded basketball and football teams, among the first in the area. The Boy Scouts of America were created in 1910, and within just three years, school superintendent W.F. Barnett organized a Boy Scout troop—which is currently celebrating its 100th anniversary.

Baseball was America's first team sport, captivating the public and becoming the "National Pastime." As town teams and semi-pro clubs and professional leagues proliferated, Van Alstyne also embraced the game. There were sandlot games and town teams, and by 1902, the Van Alstyne Grays, a semi-pro squad, represented the town before avid crowds at weekend games against other community towns. The best Van Alstyne athletes played professional ball, either in the minor leagues or, in some cases, as big leaguers. In addition to flannel baseball uniforms, the young men of Van Alstyne donned khaki uniforms and marched off to the First World War. Lt. Hobart Burk was slain while leading a charge. During the Second World War, 27 Van Alstyne men died in uniform, and in later wars, there were other casualties.

In between the two world wars, the nation was ravaged by the Great Depression. Van Alstyne, which had reached a population of 3,000, dropped below 2,000 during these difficult years. But, thanks to the efforts of Congressman Sam Rayburn, who served as Speaker of the House for a record 17 years, the dusty streets of Van Alstyne were paved during the Depression, while another federal program produced a brick gymnasium on the school campus. Speaker Rayburn made numerous appearances in Van Alstyne through the years, but he was preceded in town by two even more prominent political leaders, Theodore Roosevelt in 1906 and 1912 and William Howard Taft in 1920.

A few years after World War II, the Van Alstyne Grays disbanded. But local sports fans could enjoy the high school football team, as well as Panther squads in a number of other sports. Youth baseball was played in the summers, and in later years, there were youth teams in basketball, softball, and football. By the 21st century, there was a splendid new high school and a fine middle school on a separate campus, both on the north end of town. South of town, a new elementary campus was built near a large city park that boasts tennis courts, a nature trail, and baseball fields. There are subdivisions with new brick homes. On Highway 75, west of the original town, there is a cluster of new convenience stores, restaurants, office buildings, and a campus of Grayson Community College, the successor to old Columbia College. The population has again passed 3,000. Van Alstyne is growing and thriving, just as it did 140 years ago when it was brought into existence by urban pioneers beside a new railroad.

One

Pioneer Beginnings

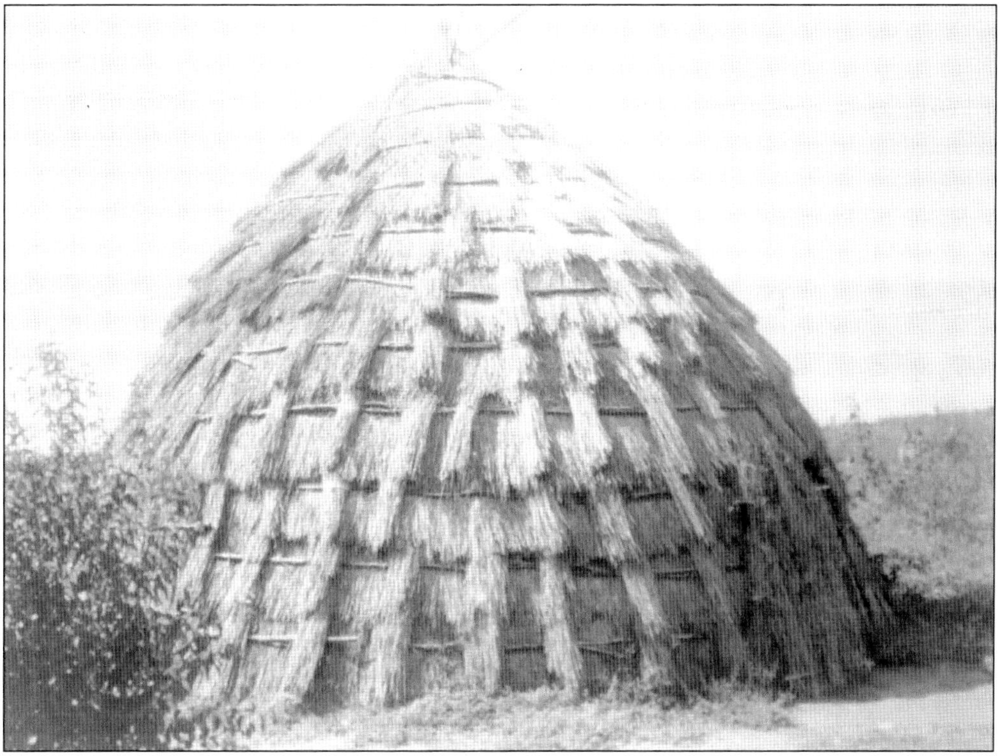

When settlers from the United States began to penetrate the region that would become Grayson and Collin Counties, the Native American inhabitants were Wichitas. The Wichita people were farmers who lived in beehive-shaped grass houses clustered in villages and towns. Wichitas had horses and were skilled hunters. In 1841, Republic of Texas surveyors appeared, connecting a north-south military road from Austin to Cannon's Trading Post at Preston's Bend of the Red River. The little community of Preston took shape (north of modern Pottsboro), serving as the location of an Army supply depot. During the 1850s, the Wichitas moved to the Brazos Reserve and then to a reservation in Indian Territory. Meanwhile, traffic on Preston Road passed a few miles west of the future site of Van Alstyne. (Courtesy of the National Archives.)

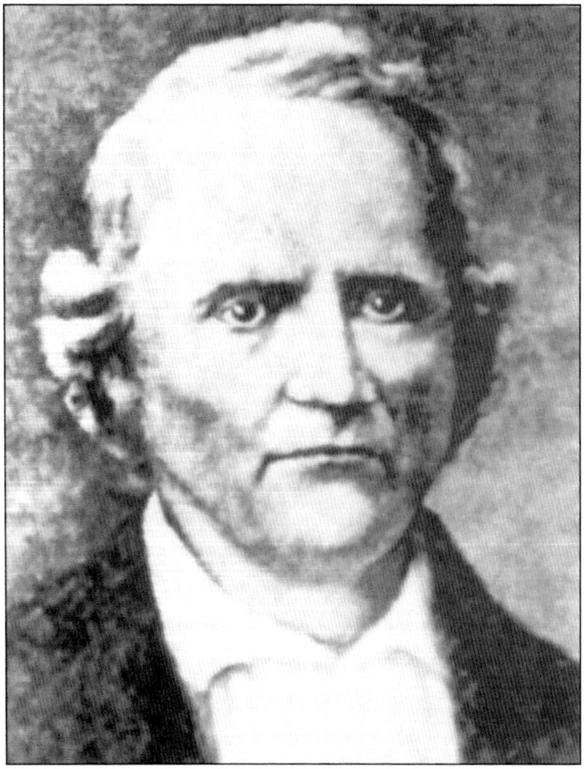

Collin McKinney was a restless, hardy pioneer who established frontier farms in Kentucky, Tennessee, Arkansas Territory, and, by 1830, northeast Texas. In 1836, McKinney was a delegate to the convention at Washington-on-the-Brazos. At 70, he was the oldest member of the convention, and he was placed on the committee to draft a Declaration of Independence and a Constitution for the Republic of Texas. He was presented the quill pen, which was used by the delegates to sign the Declaration. (Courtesy of Collin County Historical Society.)

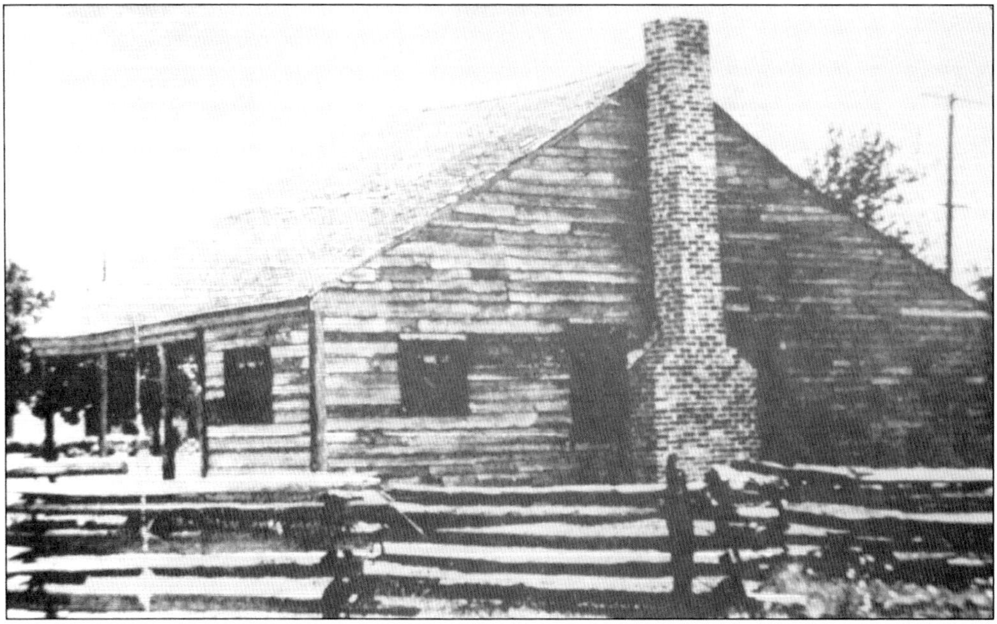

During the 1840s, McKinney, along with other family members, moved onto large Republic of Texas land grants around the future townsite of Van Alstyne. McKinney built his home in the midst of what would become the Van Alstyne Cemetery. Devoutly religious, McKinney was regarded by the Disciples of Christ as a "Christian patriarch" who helped organize the Christian Church at Mantua. (Courtesy of Van Alstyne Historical Society.)

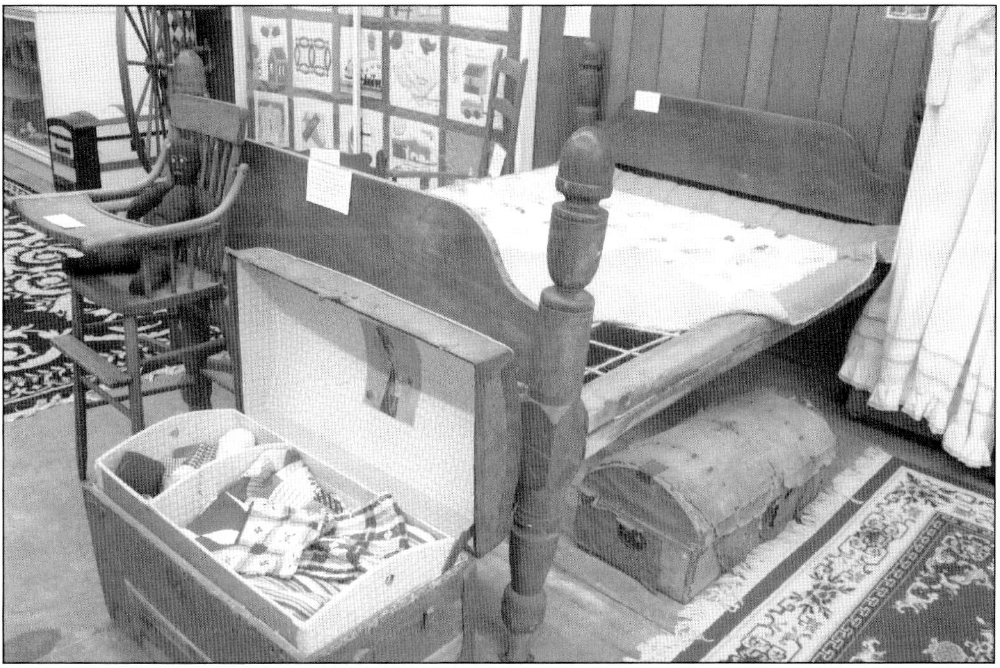

On display at the Van Alstyne Historical Museum is a bed made by Collin McKinney around 1830. The chair was fashioned by slaves. He took his trunk (beneath the bed) to Arkansas to settle his father's estate, and family members called it his "money trunk." (Photograph by the author.)

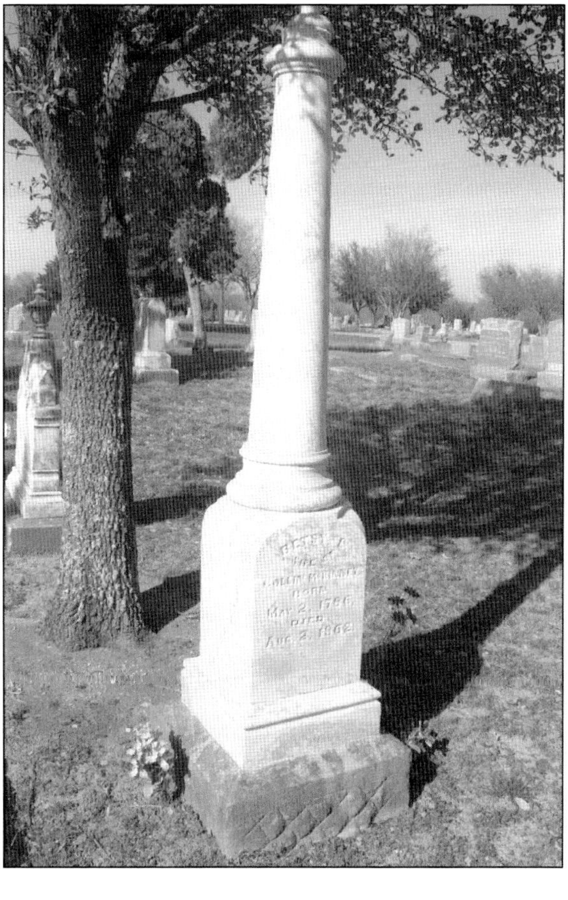

Organized in 1846, Collin County—and the seat of government, McKinney—were named after 80-year-old Collin McKinney. The Texas patriot died at the age of 95 in 1861 and was buried in the family cemetery near his home. McKinney descendants would later become citizens of Van Alstyne. (Photograph by the author.)

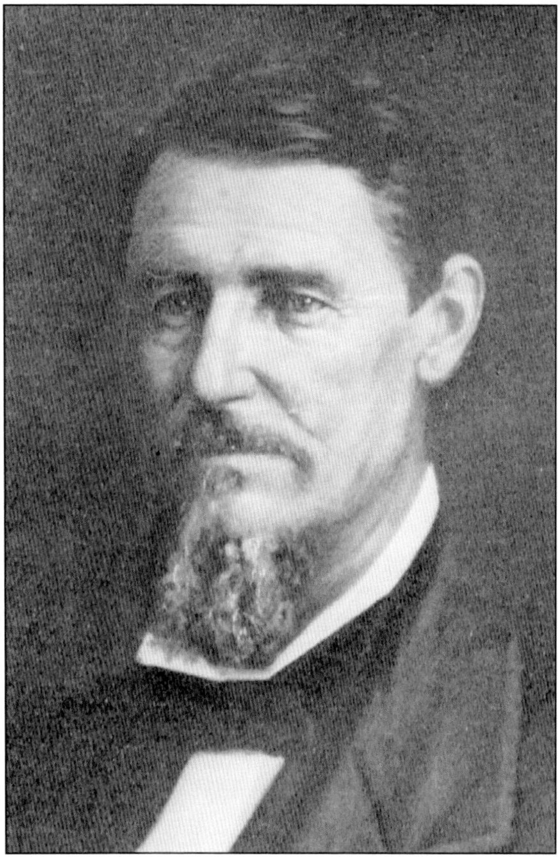

In 1854, William C. McKinney (son of Collin) sold 33 acres of land to future governor and congressman James W. Throckmorton (at left), John Throckmorton, and Joseph Wilcox. These men platted a townsite, intending to sell lots to finance a school, the Mantua Seminary. Within the next few years, businesses were established, as well as a post office and Masonic lodge. Two rural congregations organized churches, the Mantua Christian (below) and the Mount Zion Methodist. The two-story Mantua Seminary was erected in 1858. During the Civil War, many Mantua men joined James W. Throckmorton's company of mounted riflemen. The little town thrived until missed by the railroad in 1873. Businesses and churches moved to Van Alstyne, and today, no trace remains of Mantua. (Left, author's collection; below, courtesy of Van Alstyne Historical Society.)

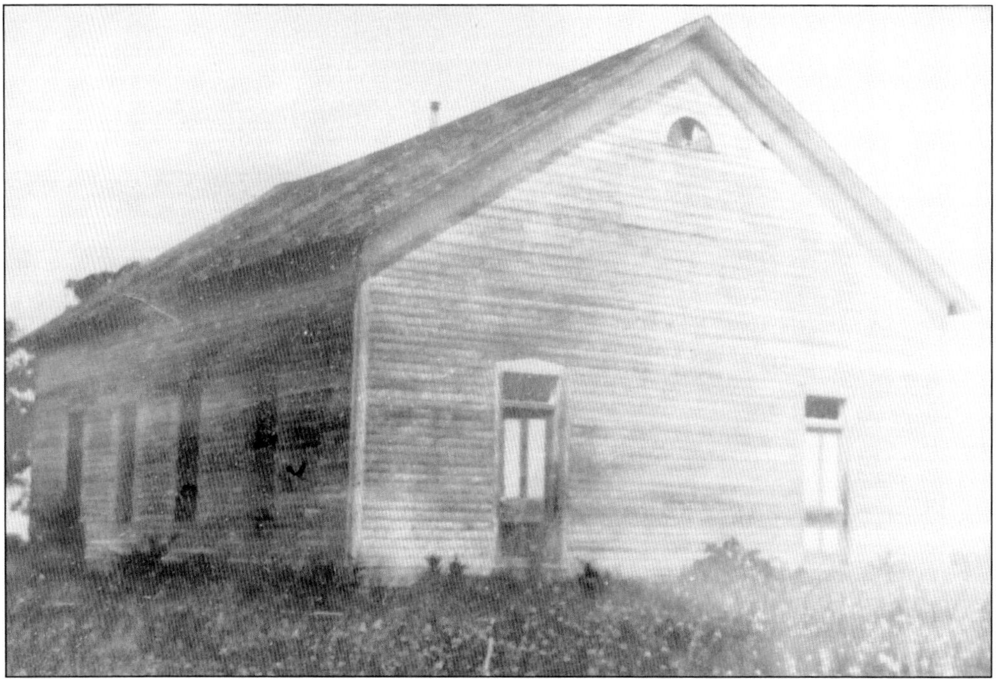

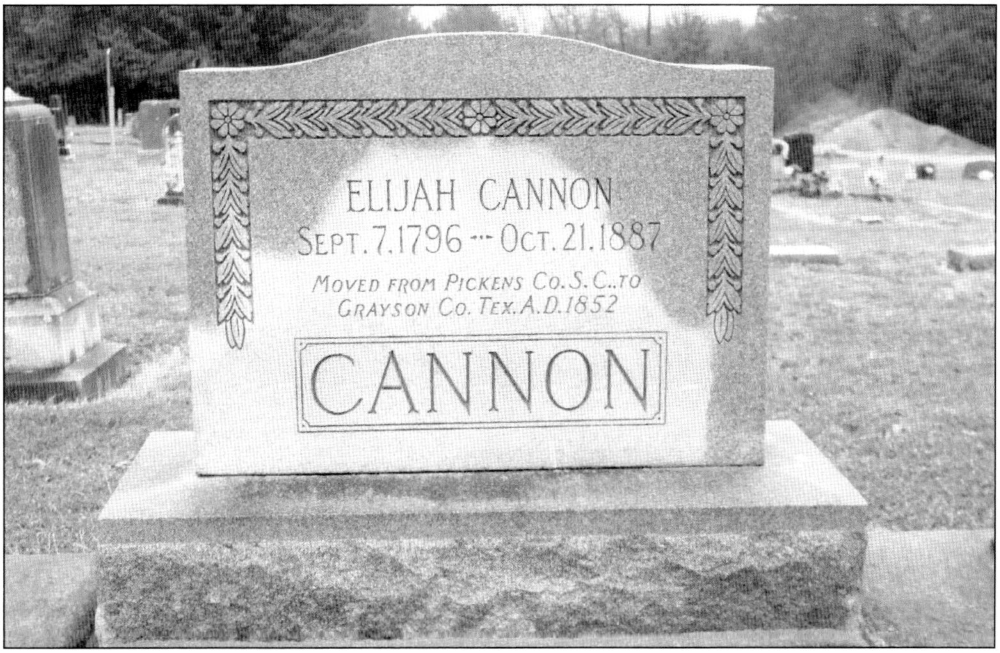

Texas was the fastest growing state in the Union during the 1850s. The population of Texas nearly tripled from 1850 to 1860, soaring from 212,592 to 604,215. Joining the parade in 1852 was Elijah Cannon, who came from South Carolina with his family and slaves to a 700-acre parcel of land a few miles east of the future site of Van Alstyne. (Photograph by the author.)

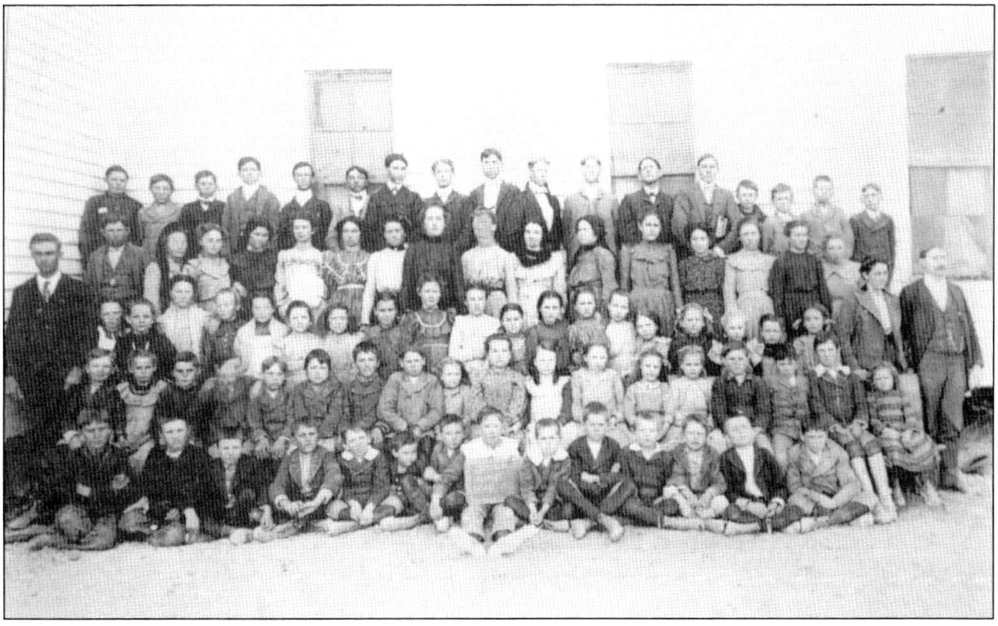

The region was part of the Blackland Prairie of Texas. The rich, loamy black soil was ideal for cotton cultivation, and cotton was king throughout the South. As Cannon thrived, other farmers moved into the area. Cannon built a cotton gin, a gristmill, and a church. The community was named Cannon, and the Cannon Academy taught scores of students. (Courtesy of Van Alstyne Historical Society.)

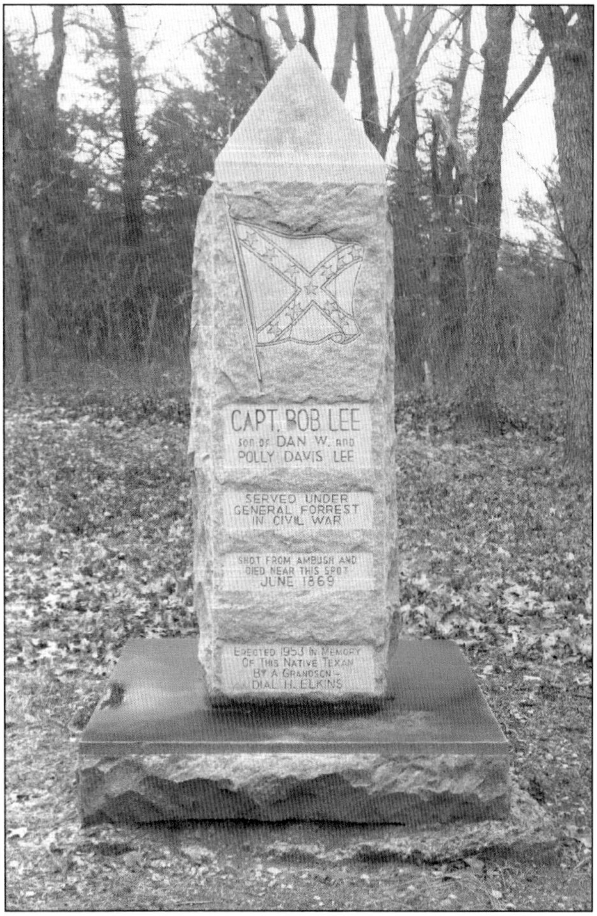

The post–Civil War years in Texas were torn by violence, gunfights, lynching, and blood feuds. There were more blood feuds in Texas than in any other state or territory, and one of the most vicious conflicts was fought east of the future site of Van Alstyne from 1867 to 1871. The Lea-Peacock Feud erupted at Pilot Grove when Lewis Peacock guided a faction of Reconstruction Union League gunmen against former Confederates led by Capt. Bob Lee. There were ambushes and skirmishes and revenge killings. Bob Lee was bushwhacked and slain near his Pilot Grove home in 1869. But the killing continued until Lewis Peacock was shot dead in 1871, two years before Van Alstyne was founded. (Both photographs by the author.)

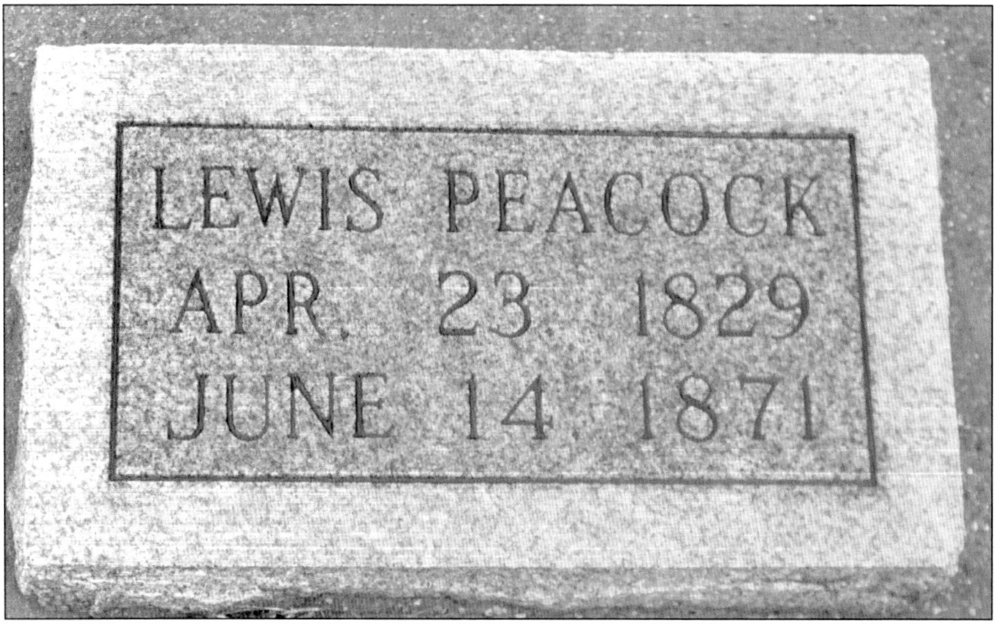

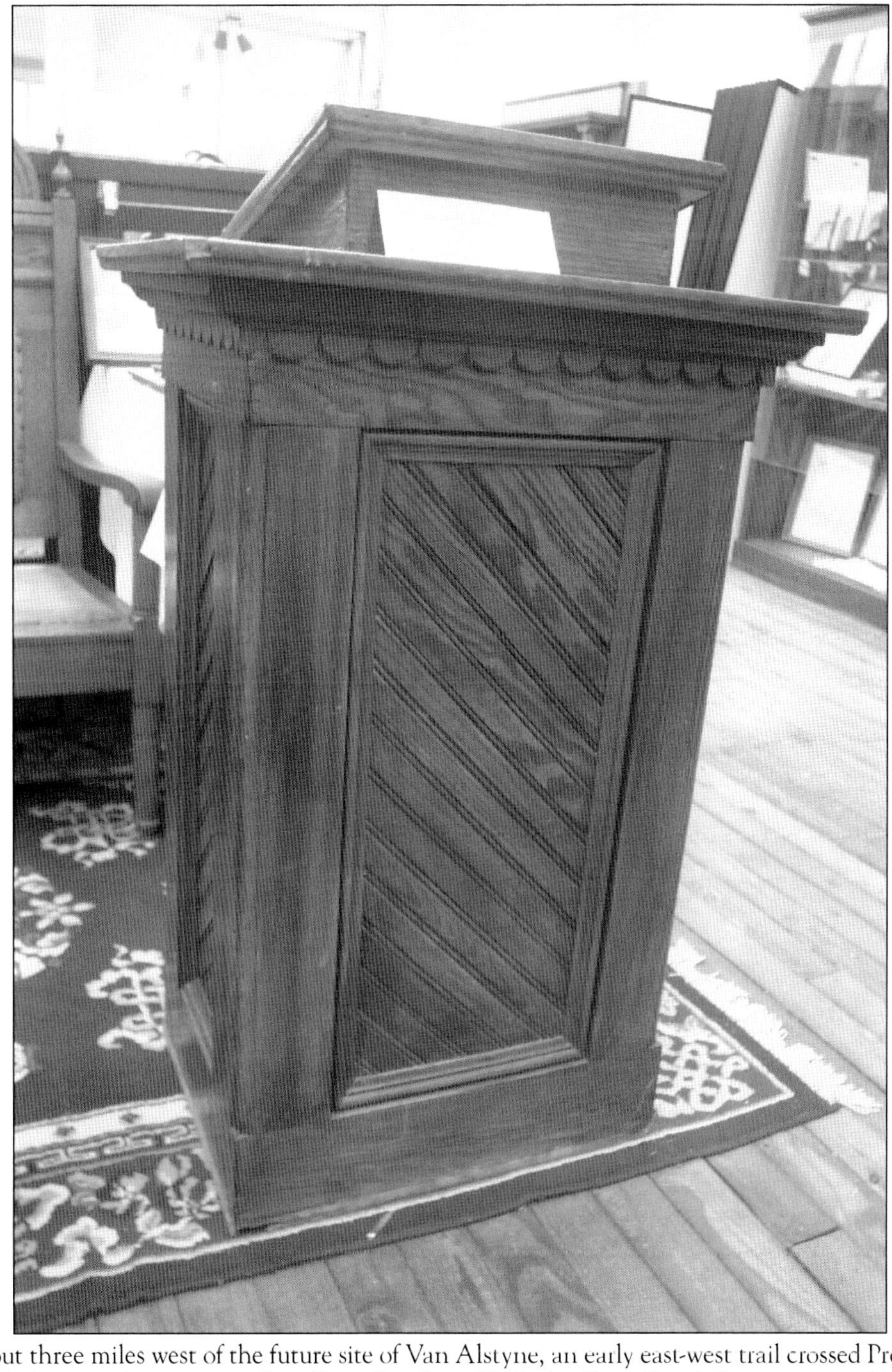

About three miles west of the future site of Van Alstyne, an early east-west trail crossed Preston Road. A general store opened at Cross Roads in 1845; the Cross Roads Institute was the best school in the area. The population of the Cross Roads community never exceeded 50, but there was a large farm population in the surrounding countryside. By the end of the Civil War, the village was called Elmont. The Elmont Baptist Church was founded in 1869 and still serves a vibrant congregation today. The Elmont Church of Christ donated its venerable pulpit to the Van Alstyne Historical Museum. (Photograph by the author.)

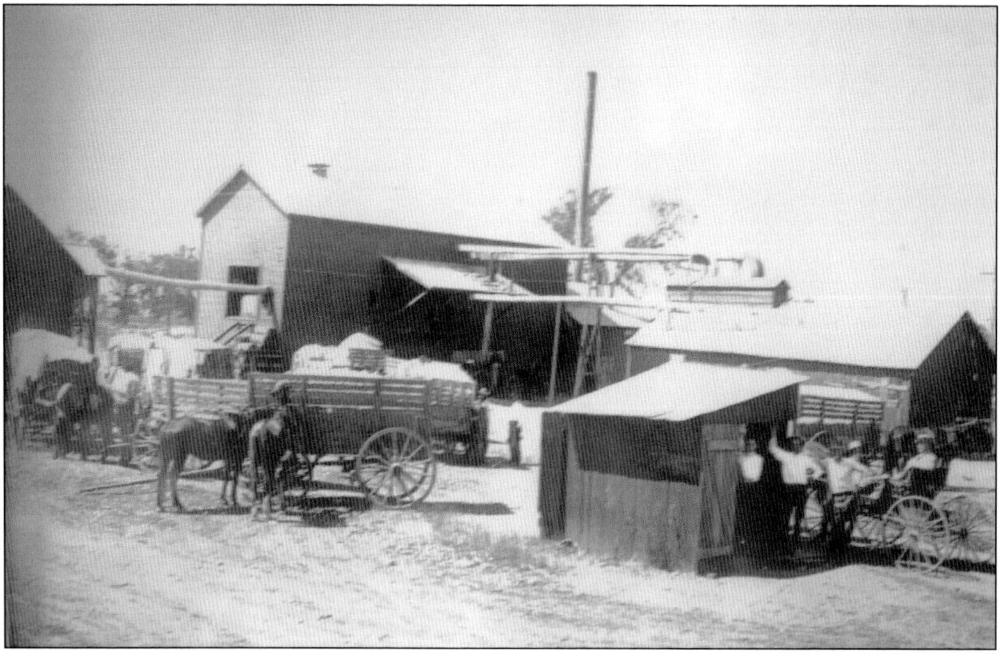

When the Houston & Texas Central Railroad built toward Sherman from McKinney late in 1872, Melissa was platted astride the tracks about seven miles to the northeast. A post office was authorized in 1873, and a couple of stores opened. The population did not reach 100 until 1884, but cotton flourished on nearby farms. Two gins were built, ginning 3,000 bales per year. (Courtesy of Melissa Chamber of Commerce.)

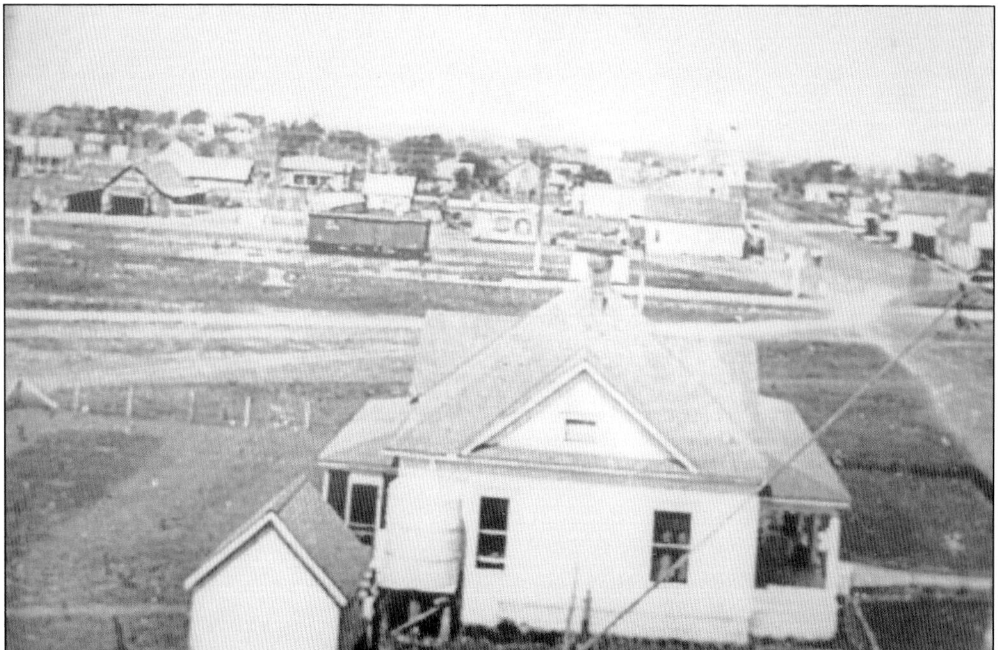

Looking east, the frame buildings of Melissa's early business section may be seen across the H&TC tracks at right. (Courtesy of Melissa Chamber of Commerce.)

In 1867, John F. Greer built a home and store four miles north of the future town of Melissa and four miles south of the future town of Van Alstyne, calling his town Anna. Greer's daughter was named Anna and probably provided the village its identity. After the railroad came through early in 1873, a second store was built, along with a steam gristmill and a Baptist church. In 1890, the First Christian Church became the town's architectural gem. (Photograph by the author.)

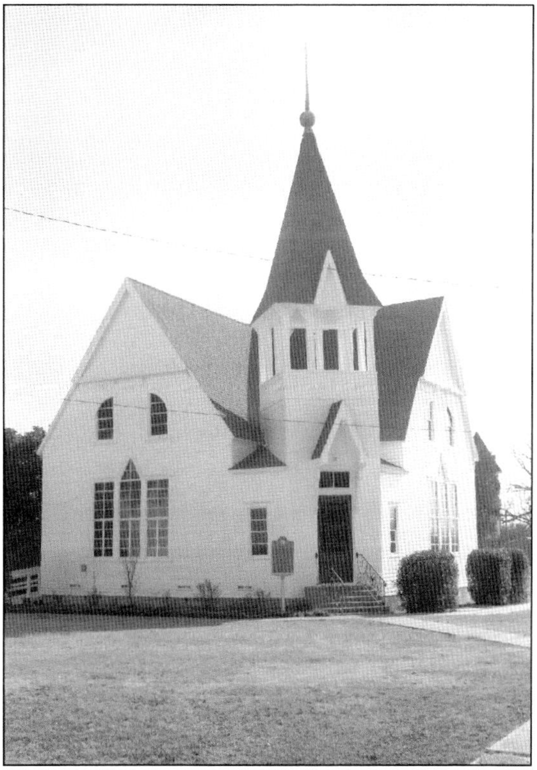

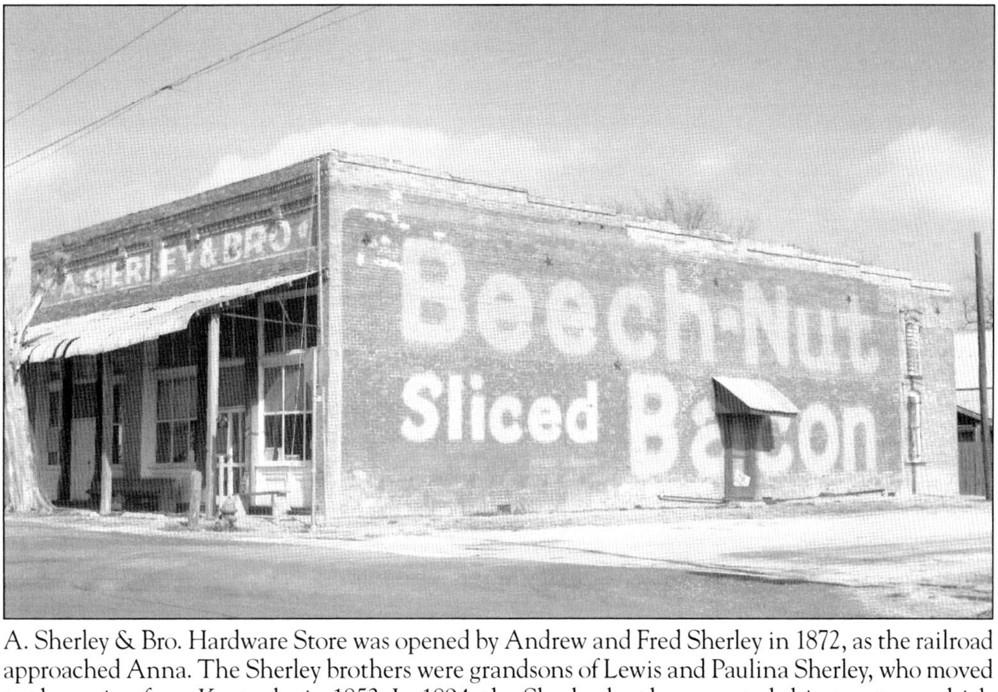

A. Sherley & Bro. Hardware Store was opened by Andrew and Fred Sherley in 1872, as the railroad approached Anna. The Sherley brothers were grandsons of Lewis and Paulina Sherley, who moved to the region from Kentucky in 1853. In 1894, the Sherley brothers erected this structure, which still boasts the original canopy. The business closed in 1979, but the old building remains full of inventory and can be toured. (Photograph by the author.)

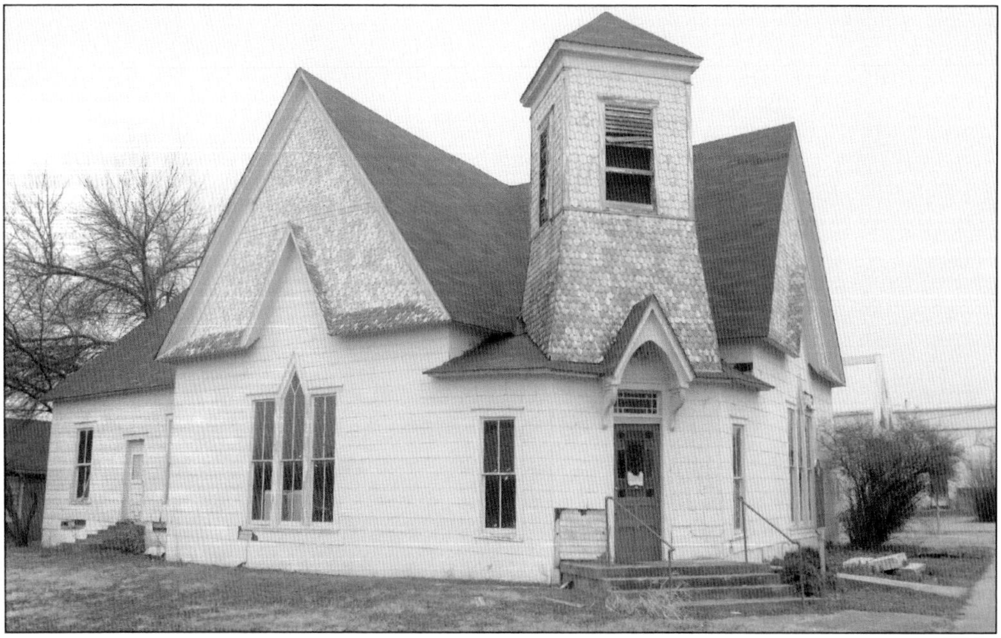

Six miles north of Van Alstyne, a rural community had developed known as Summit, because the elevation of 810 feet was thought to be the highest point between the Red River and the Gulf of Mexico. The last battle with Native Americans was fought in the area in 1843. Three decades later, the railroad reached Summit, and the name was changed to Howe, after H&TC official F.M. Howe. Victorian homes were erected (below), and the First Christian Church was built in 1893 (above) but finally closed in 1982 because of declining membership. Howe did not rival Van Alstyne in size, and neither did the other towns on the tracks to the south, Anna and Melissa. The nearby communities that were missed by the tracks—Mantua, Cannon, Elmont—lost citizens and businesses to Van Alstyne. (Both photographs by the author.)

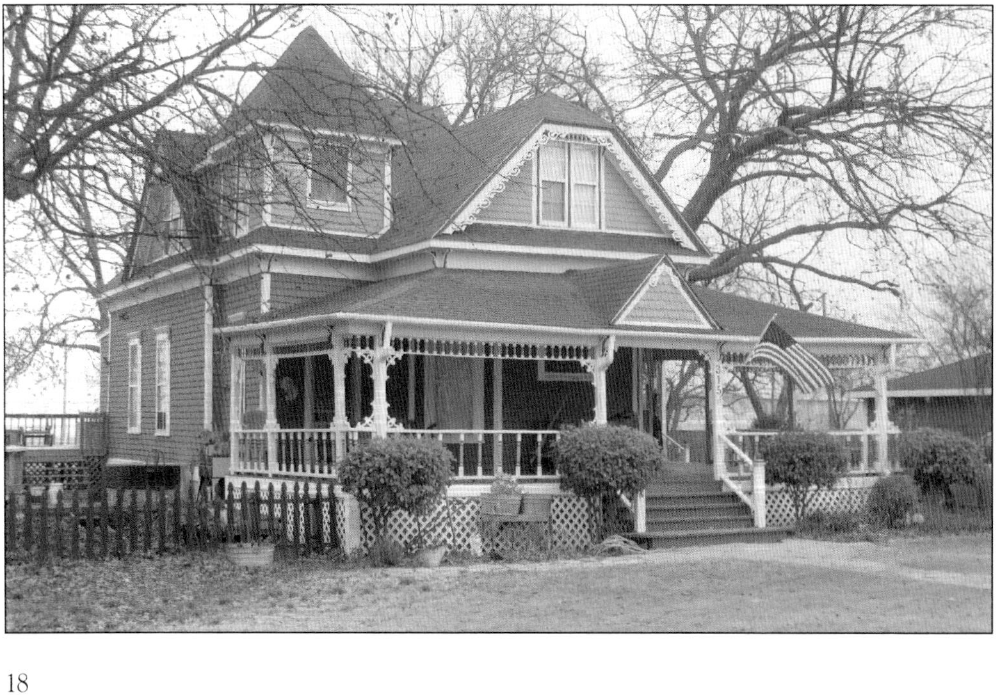

Two

Railroad Town

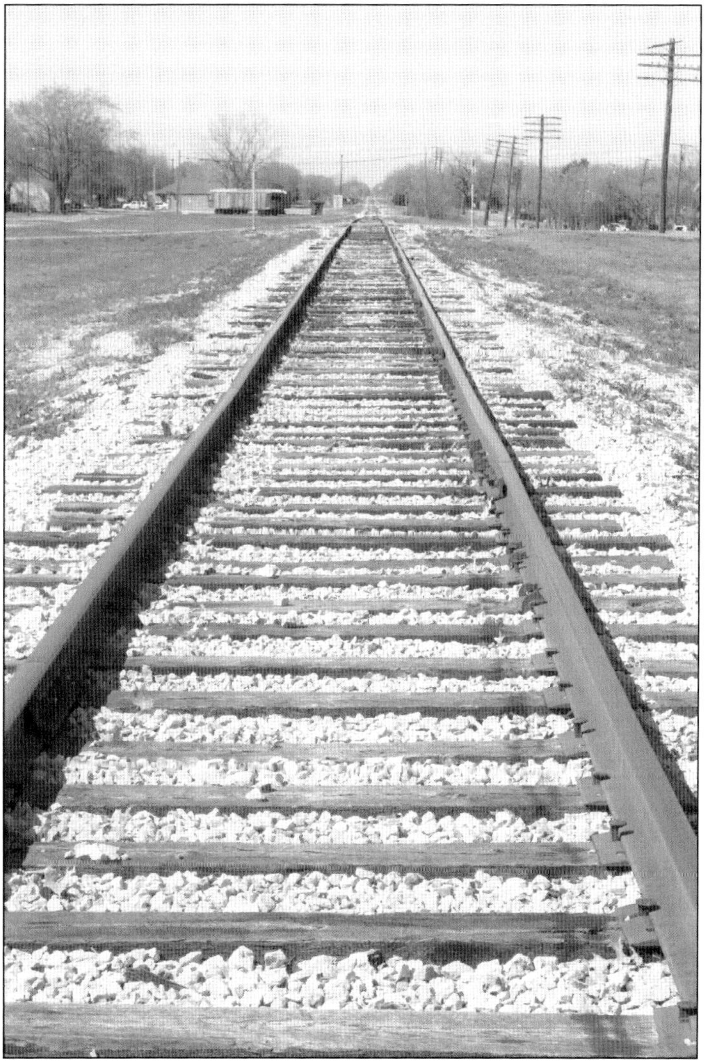

After the Civil War, railroad construction exploded across the United States, and more miles of track were laid in Texas than in any other state or territory. Railroads became America's greatest industry, dominating the economy and politics of the era. Tens of thousands of men were employed by railroad companies. Five transcontinental railroads were completed by 1893, and a network of branch lines tied into major trunk lines. Towns that were bypassed by railroads soon faded away, but a railway connection could assure a community's prosperity. Van Alstyne was one of the hundreds of towns that came into existence alongside a railroad. The H&TC tracks that entered Van Alstyne brought life to a new community. (Photograph by the author.)

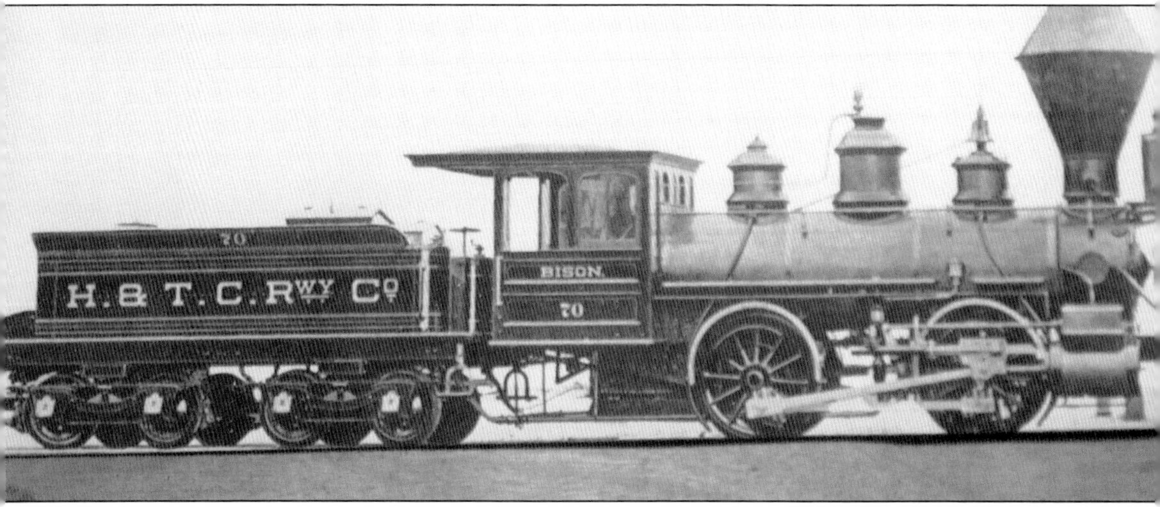

The Galveston & Red River Railway was chartered by the State of Texas in 1848. Four years passed before the company became active, and not until 1856 did track laying begin. Also in 1856, the company's name was changed to the Houston & Texas Central Railway—the H&TC. There were only 81 miles of H&TC track when the Civil War erupted, but construction resumed in 1867. By 1897, H&TC tracks reached Corsicana, then Dallas in 1872, and the Red River in 1873. The H&TC engine 70 was named *Bison*, had a 0-4-0 wheel arrangement, and was built in 1876 in Scranton, Pennsylvania. By 1892, the H&TC owned 115 locomotives and 2,271 cars, all the while enjoying passenger earnings of $1 million and freight earnings of $2.5 million. (Author's collection.)

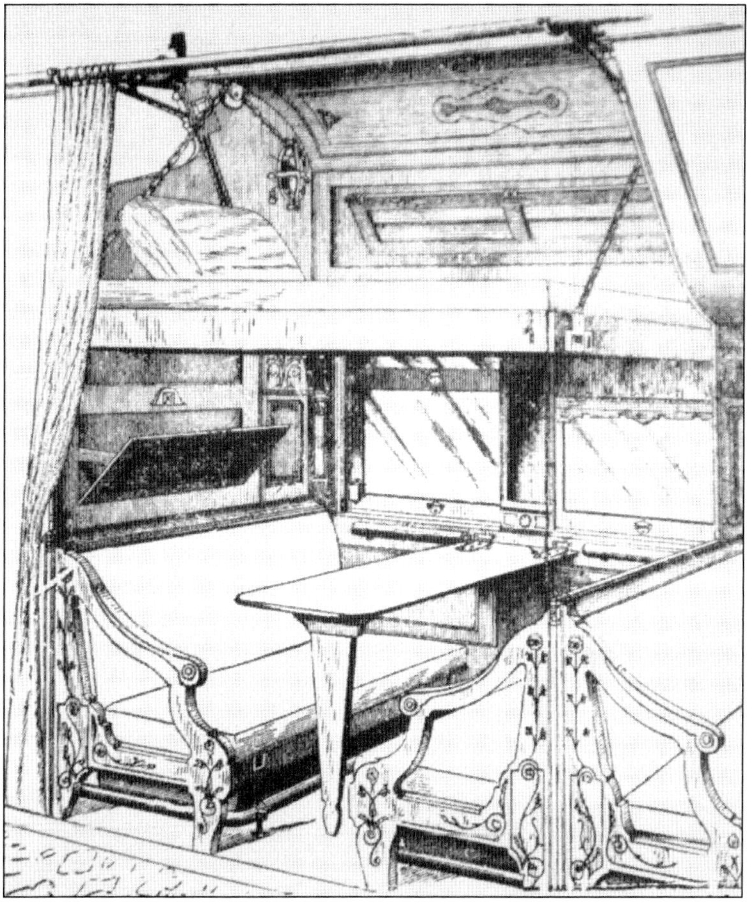

The H&TC was the first railroad in Texas to launch Pullman service in 1872, the year before Van Alstyne became a townsite. An 1870s manual for builders of railroad cars illustrated George Pullman's clever design; the upper berth, when opened, is suspended by chains, while the lower berth was fashioned by removing the table and rearranging the two facing seats. (Author's collection.)

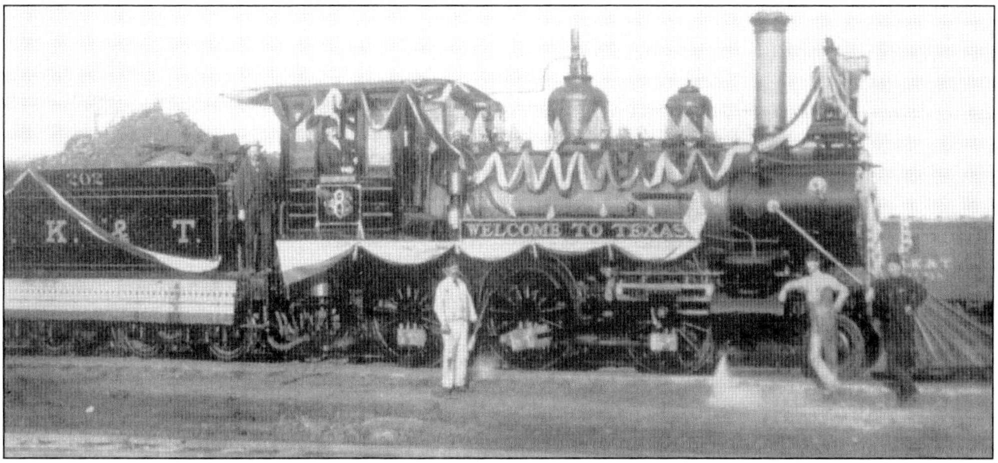

From Denison on the Red River, the H&TC connected with the Missouri, Kansas & Texas Railway (MK&T), which provided Texas with its first railroad connection to St. Louis and on to its cities of the East. This photograph of a decorated MK&T engine was taken in Denison in 1891. The excursion train (note the "Welcome to Texas" sign) was taking members of the Order of Railway Conductors on a tour of Texas and would pass through Van Alstyne en route to Dallas. (Author's collection.)

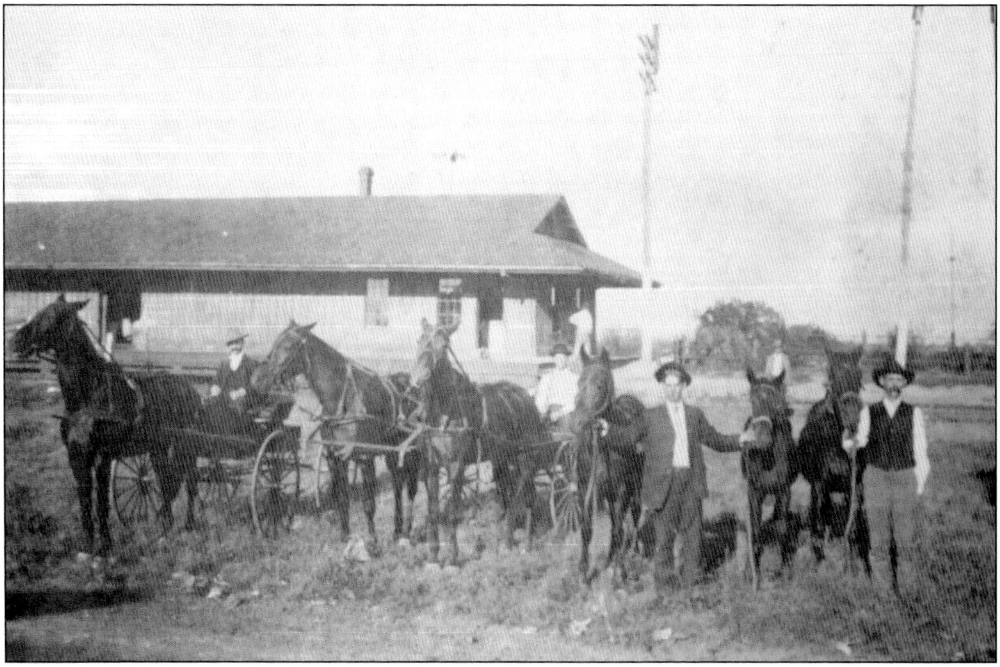

Shown from the west side, Van Alstyne's depot was especially busy when passenger trains arrived and departed. Citizens were present to meet relatives and friends. In the foreground of this 1912 view are, from left to right, career peace officer Will Echols, Vernie Neill, Walter Neill, and Andrew Neill. (Courtesy of Van Alstyne Historical Society.)

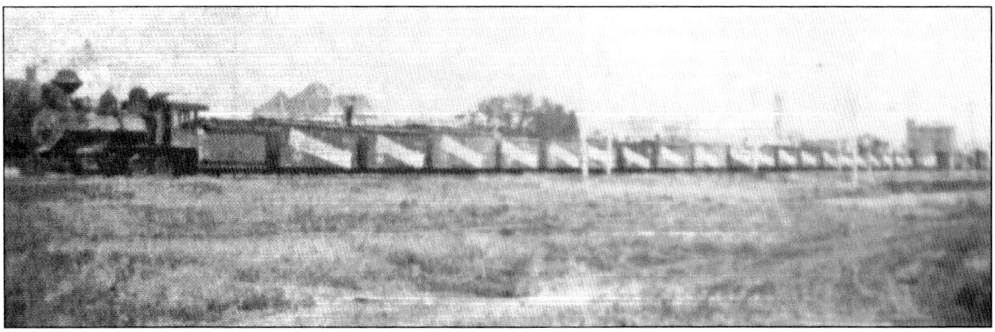

Van Alstyne enjoyed regular freight service, including this freight train. Two freight trains served Van Alstyne each morning, one heading north and the other south. Late in the day, there were two more freight trains, one northbound and one southbound. (Courtesy of Van Alstyne Historical Society.)

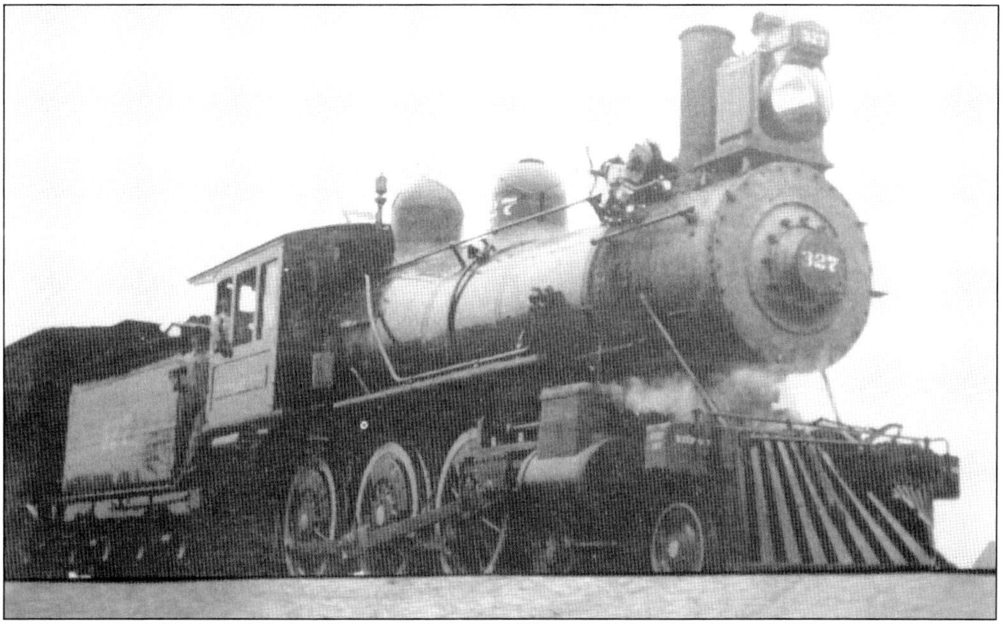

H&TC engine 327 was a 4-6-0 locomotive built in 1892 and not scrapped until 1937. In 1901, the H&TC became one of the first railroads in Texas to begin using oil as a locomotive fuel. (Author's collection.)

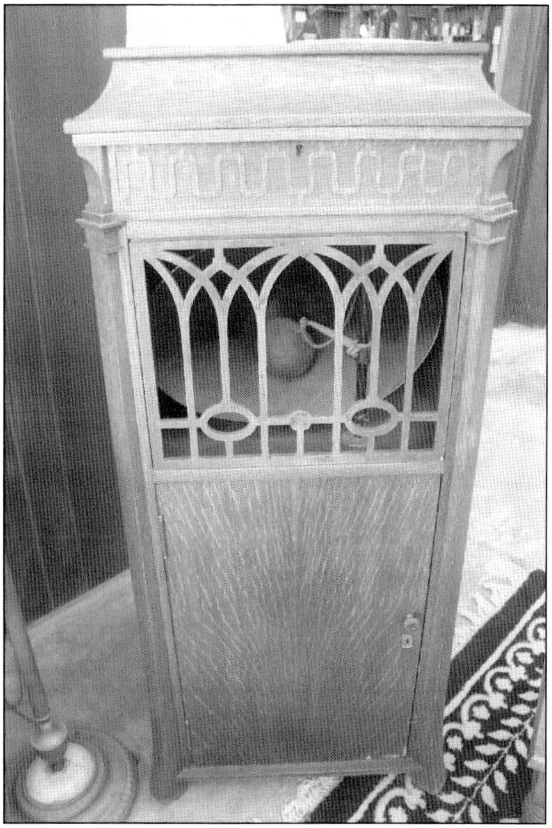

When residents of Van Alstyne gathered around a phonograph, they listened to recordings of railroad music ("The Midnight Flyer" or "Wreck of the Old 97," which was the first million-selling country song). Another musical reflection of Van Alstyne life was cotton ballads ("De Boll Weevil") and telephone songs ("Hello Central, Give Me My Baby" and "Can I Talk to My Mother in Heaven"). (Photograph by the author.)

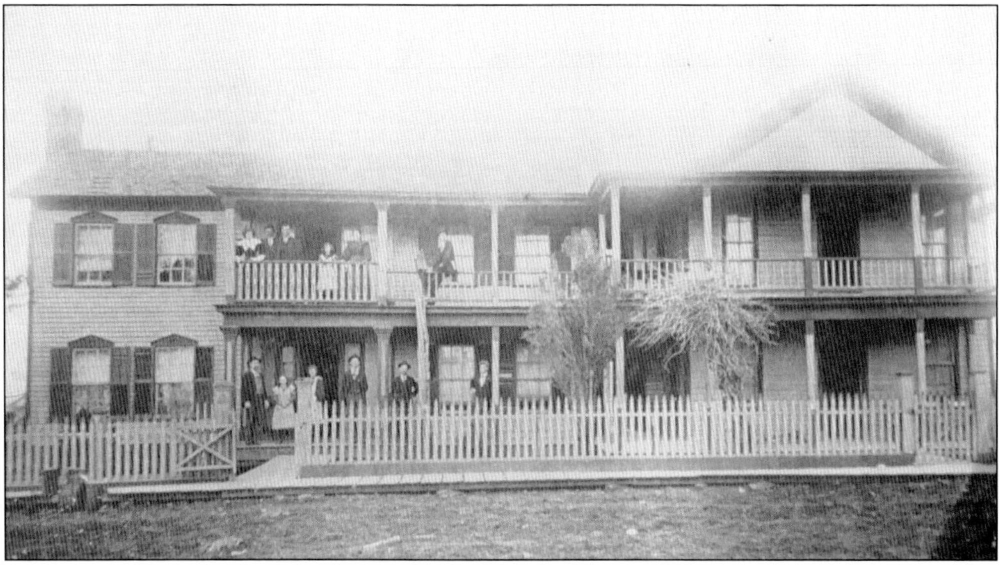

The two-story residence of Dr. James L. Leslie was moved from Mantua to Van Alstyne. The enterprising C.E. Carter (who also built a brick building to house his grocery store and an opera house), added the north wing, at right, and operated the Carter Hotel. Carter and his daughter, Sallie Mae, stand at left in the main entryway. After a change in ownership, the hotel was named the Commercial Hotel, which burned in 1922. (Courtesy of Van Alstyne Historical Society.)

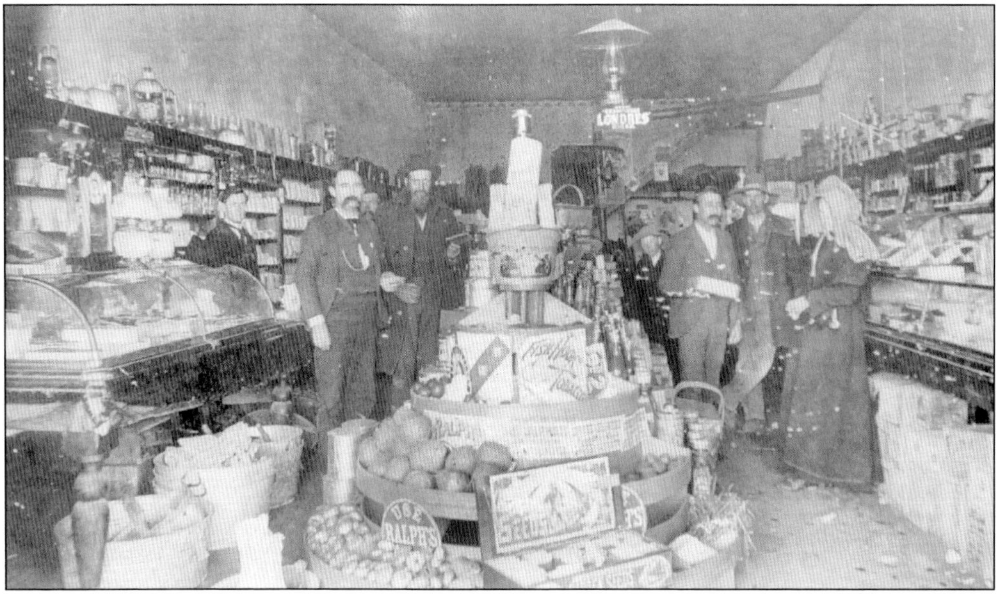

C.E. Carter, second from left, presides over his well-stocked grocery store. The two customers at right appear to have come in from an area farm. (Courtesy of Van Alstyne Historical Society.)

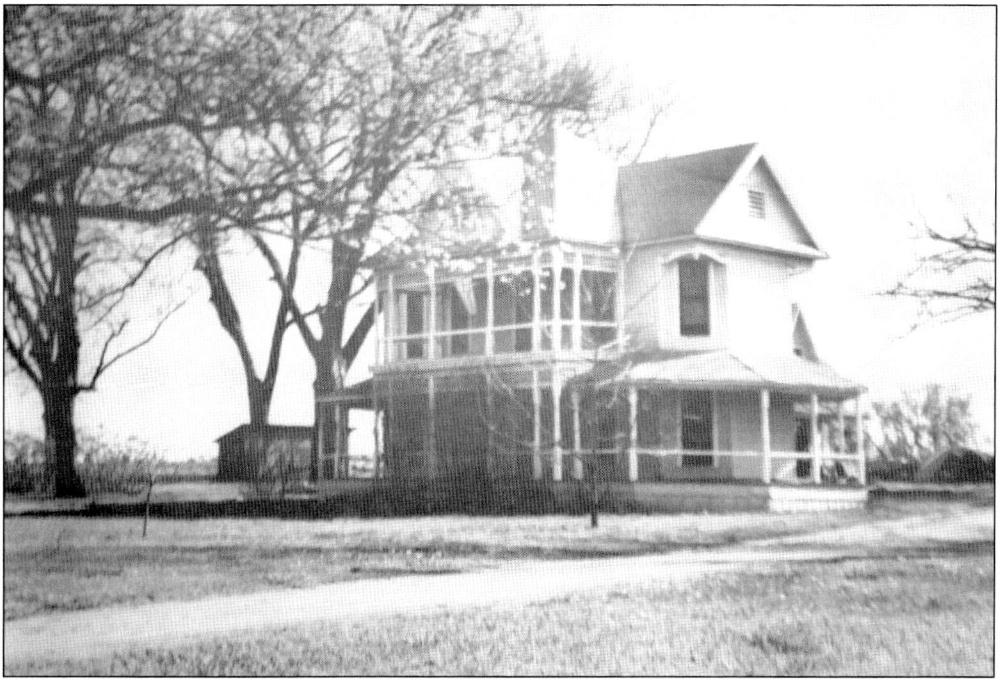

In the late 1890s, this substantial farmhouse was built by H.S. and Catherine Morris with lumber shipped by rail from Jefferson in east Texas. Such a sizeable home reflected the prosperity that was possible for farmers of the era. (Courtesy of Van Alstyne Historical Society.)

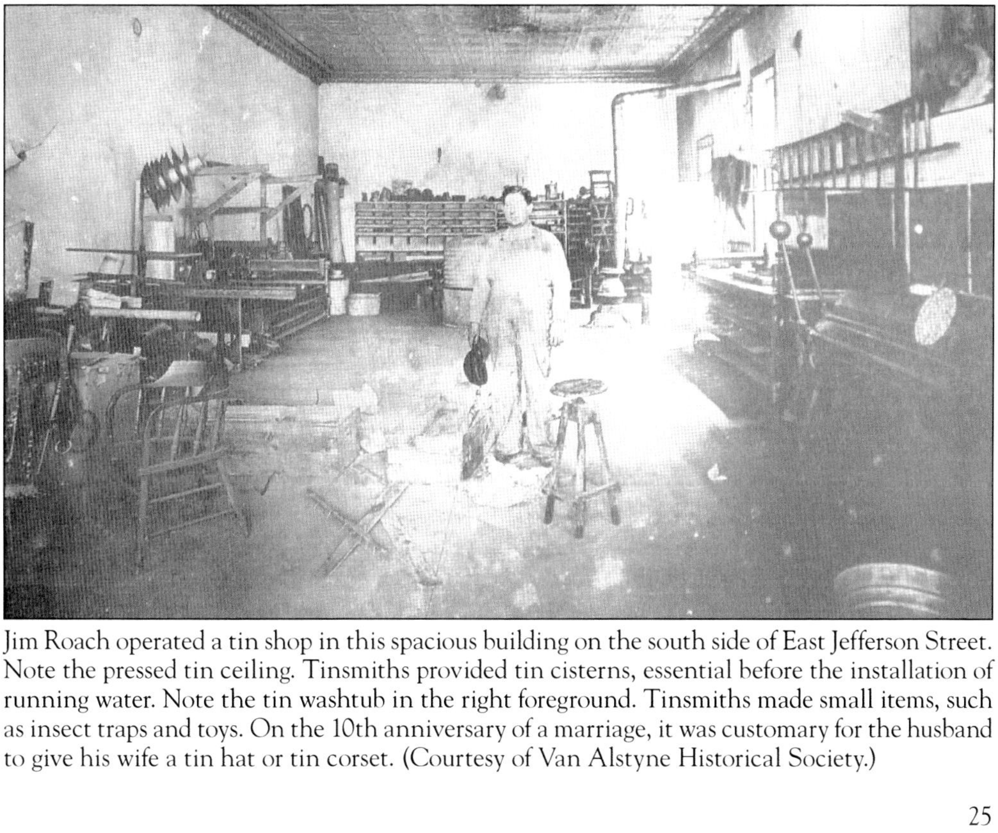

Jim Roach operated a tin shop in this spacious building on the south side of East Jefferson Street. Note the pressed tin ceiling. Tinsmiths provided tin cisterns, essential before the installation of running water. Note the tin washtub in the right foreground. Tinsmiths made small items, such as insect traps and toys. On the 10th anniversary of a marriage, it was customary for the husband to give his wife a tin hat or tin corset. (Courtesy of Van Alstyne Historical Society.)

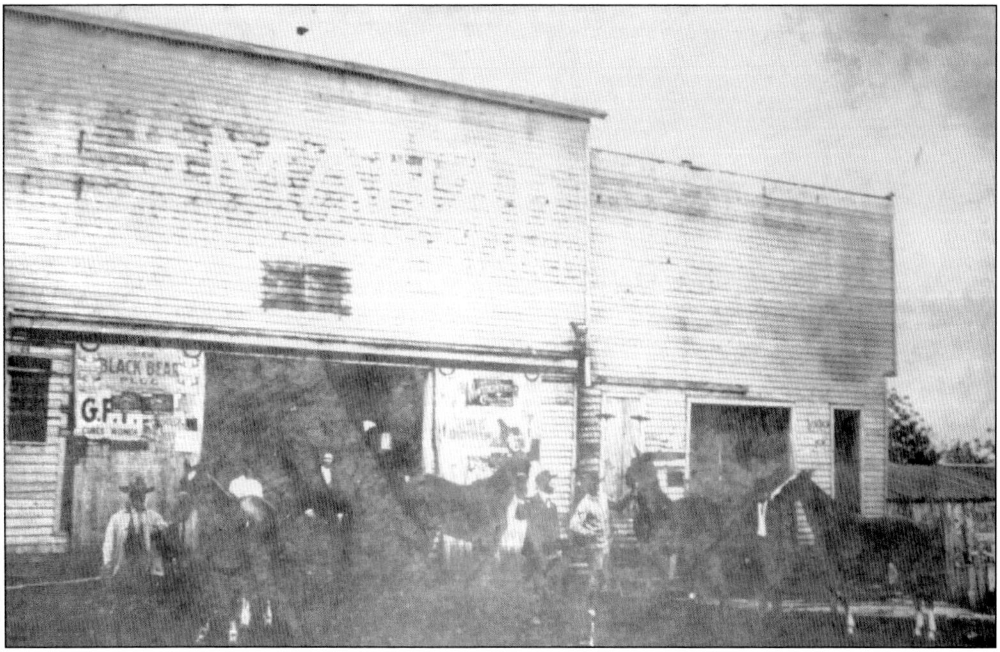

W.S. Mahar's Livery Barn was a typical establishment in early Van Alstyne. A traveler's horse could be stabled and fed, a saddle horse could be rented, or a horse-drawn buggy could be hired. In all horse-and-buggy towns, there were periodic wrecks when horses became spooked. Horse-drawn vehicles, whether wagon or buggy, would careen down the street, or mounts would unexpectedly break into a wild gallop. (Courtesy of Van Alstyne Historical Society.)

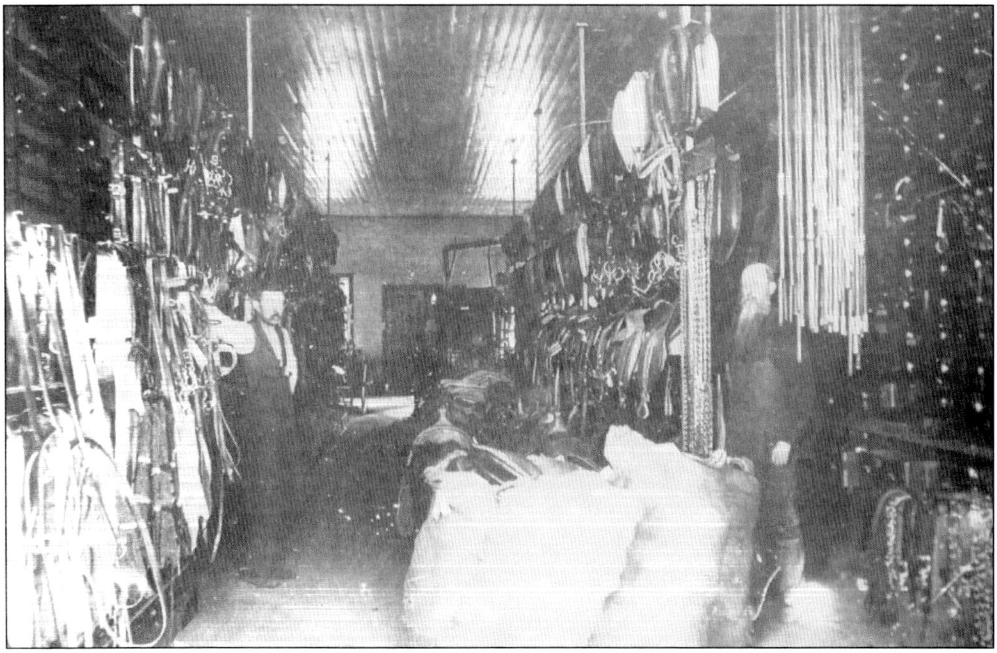

L.P. Walker's Harness and Buggy shop was located on the south side of East Jefferson Street. Walker, at left, stands amid harness, bridles, whips, horse collars, and saddles. Buggies were on display in an adjacent building. (Courtesy of Van Alstyne Historical Society.)

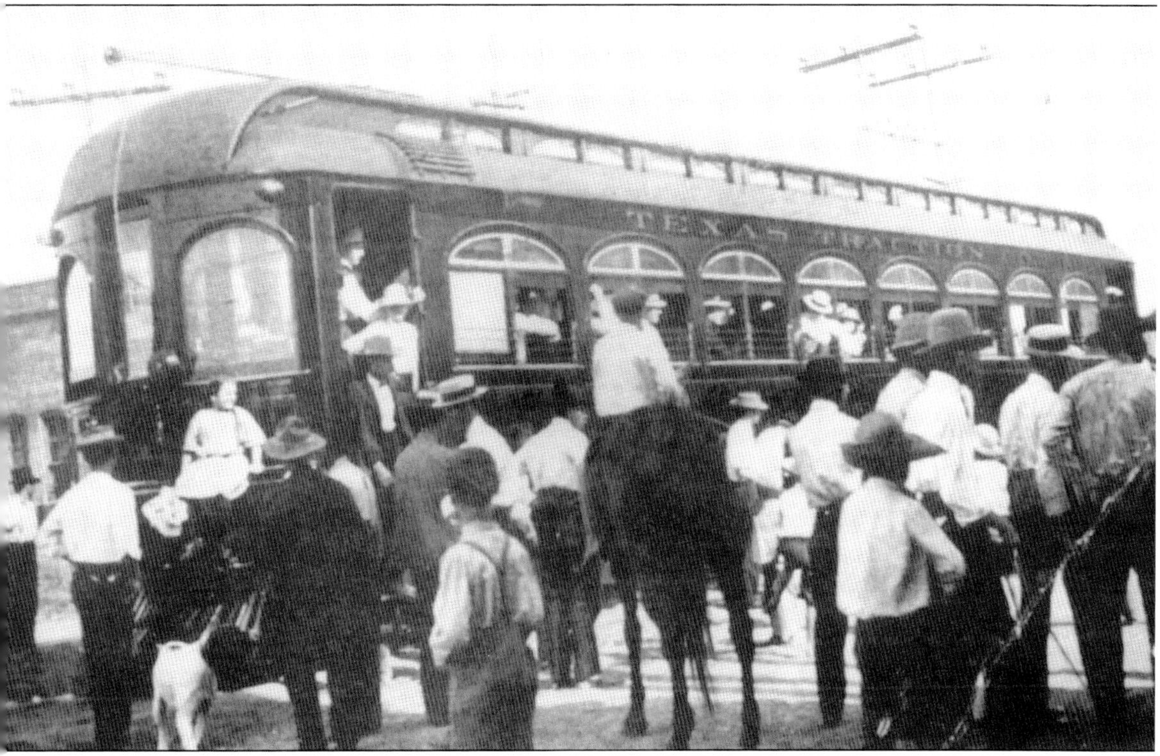

A new set of rails brought additional transportation to Van Alstyne. Van Alstyne was part of a region of Texas where 70 percent of the state's electric interurban system was built. There was nearly 500 miles of interurban railway in Texas, most of which was constructed by 1913. The state's first interurban line was laid out in 1901, ten miles between Sherman and Denison. A flurry of construction followed, including a 65-mile line from Sherman to Dallas erected by the Texas Traction Company in 1908. This company was organized in 1906, with shares offered to the public for $75 each. The City of Van Alstyne signed a contract with the Texas Traction Company in November 1906. Shown above is the first day of service in Van Alstyne on July 1, 1908. (Courtesy of Van Alstyne Historical Society.)

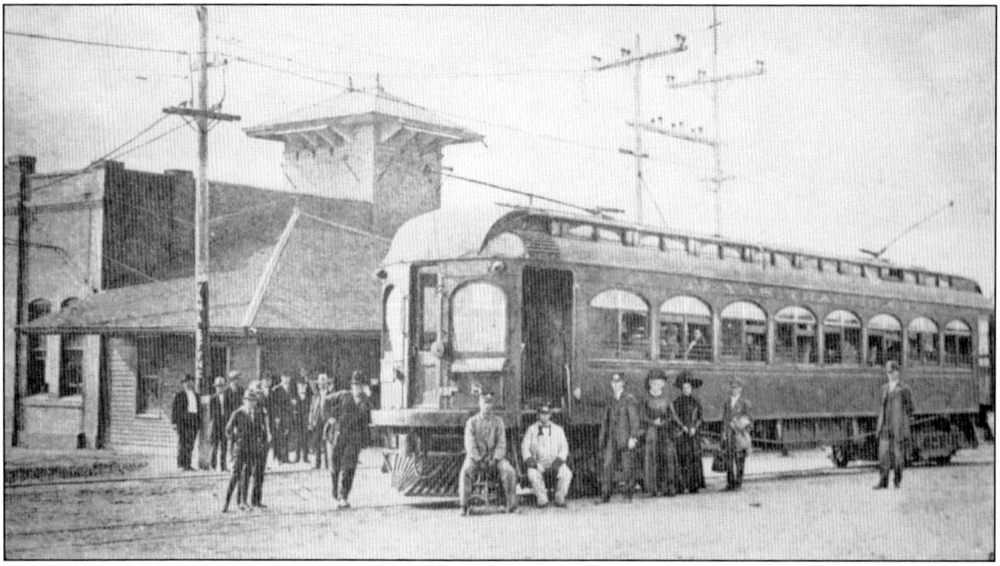

Two crewmen are seated in front of their interurban car, with the Van Alstyne station in the background. The conductor stands beside his colleagues, and on his left stand two stylish ladies, dressed for travel. (Courtesy of Van Alstyne Historical Society.)

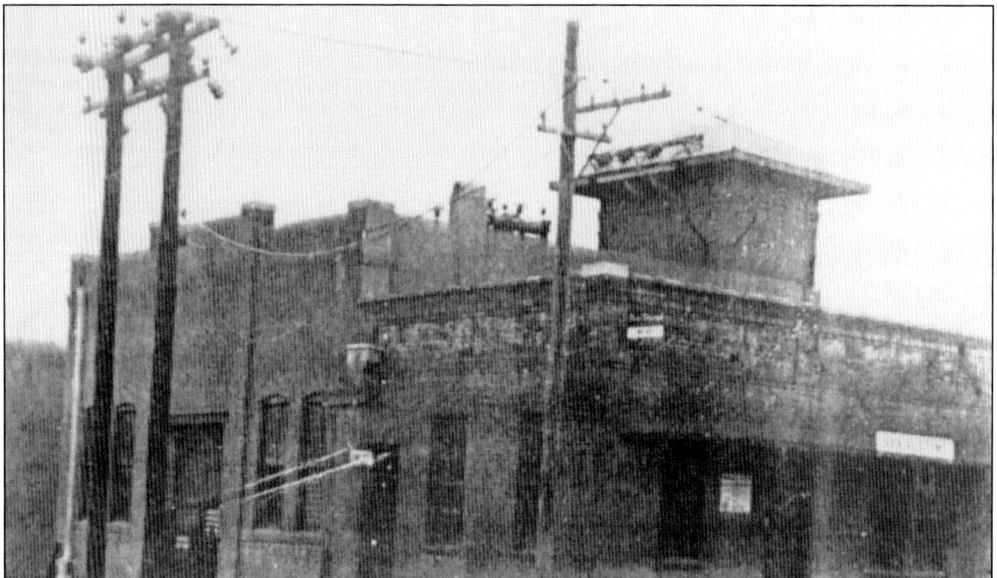

The Van Alstyne interurban station was built on the northwest corner of Preston and Marshall Streets. The building included an electric generator. The north-south rails ran along Preston Street, leading the city council to pass an ordinance requiring cars to limit their speed to eight miles per hour, while the driver sounded a bell at each intersection. (Courtesy of Van Alstyne Historical Society.)

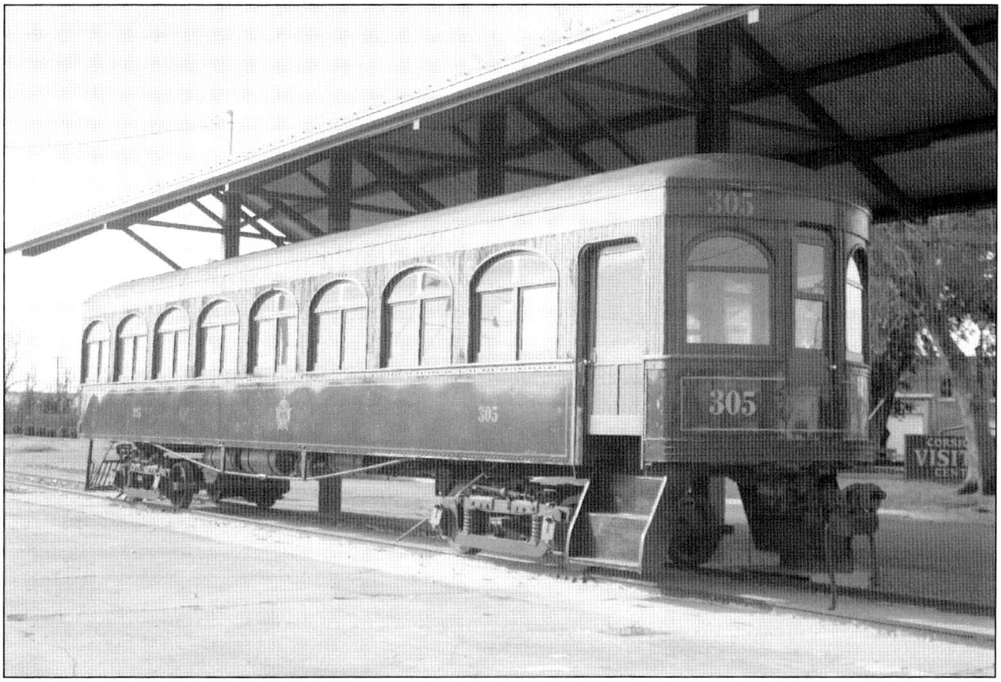

In 1913, a 56-mile interurban line was built from Dallas to Corsicana. A merger with the Texas Traction Company produced the Texas Railway Company, a 200-mile line from Denison to Corsicana, where the passenger car above is on exhibition. A connecting line westward could take a Van Alstyne passenger all the way to Waco, Texas. (Photograph by the author.)

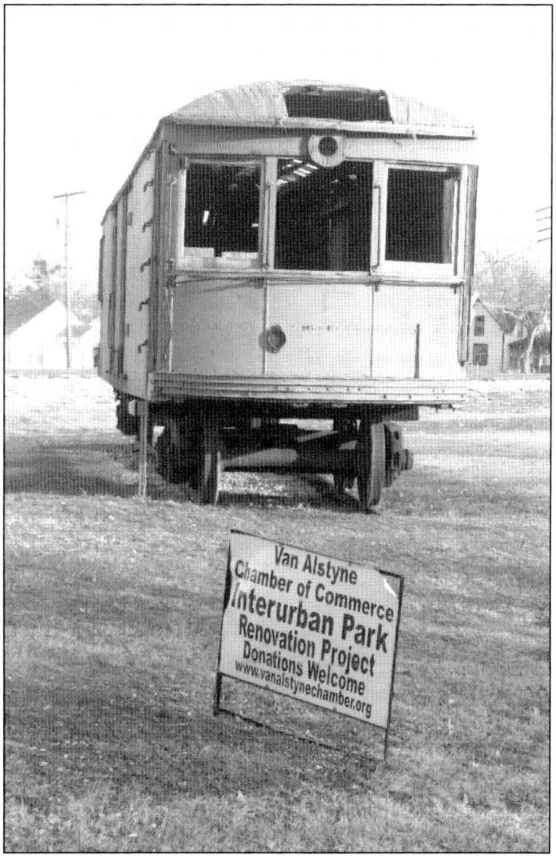

Interurban lines ran freight cars as well as passenger service. Each fall, freight car activity was heavy in Van Alstyne, as cotton bales were transported on the interurban. Two interurban freight cars are in Van Alstyne today; there are plans to restore these cars. (Photograph by the author.)

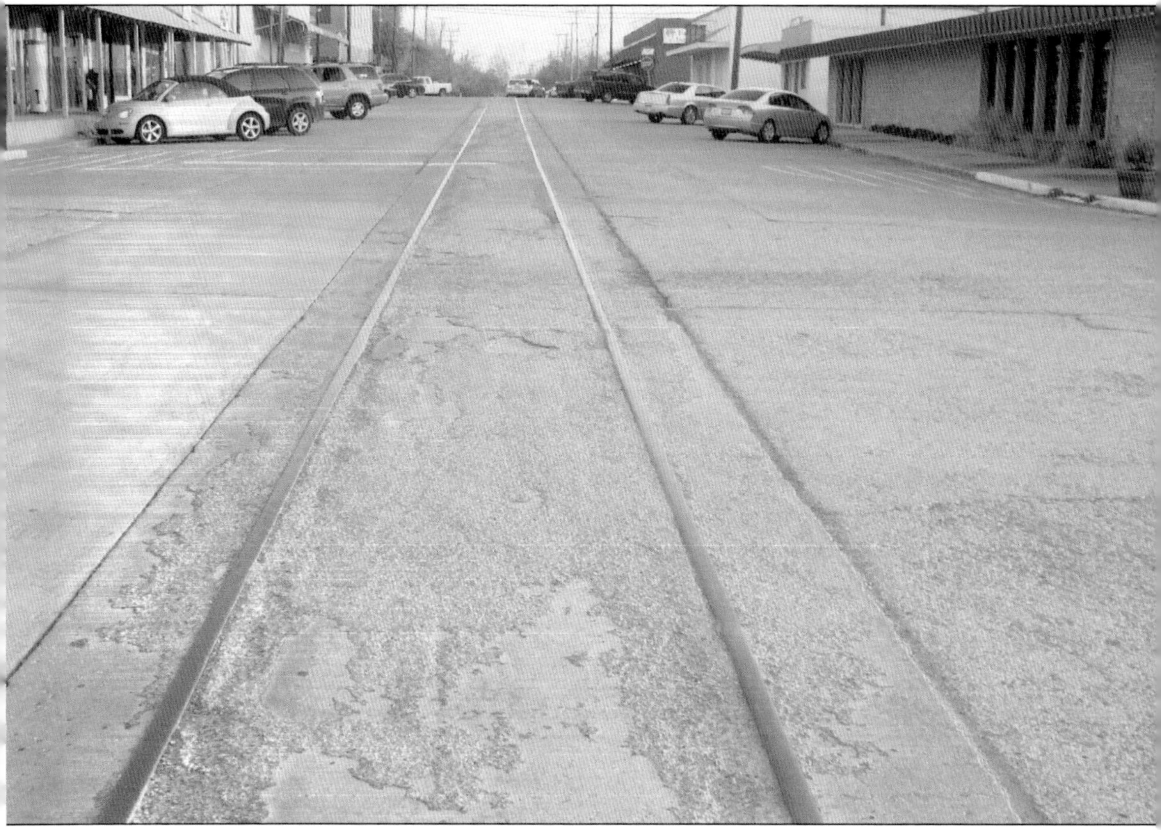

As paved roads spread across Texas, auto and truck traffic became common. Accordingly, interurban business declined, and most lines were discontinued during the 1930s. The Dallas–Corsicana line was closed in 1941, and in 1948, the Dallas–Denison line was discontinued after 40 years of service to Van Alstyne. Today, a section of interurban rails remains visible on Preston Street, looking uphill to the south. (Photograph by the author.)

Three

VICTORIAN HEYDAY

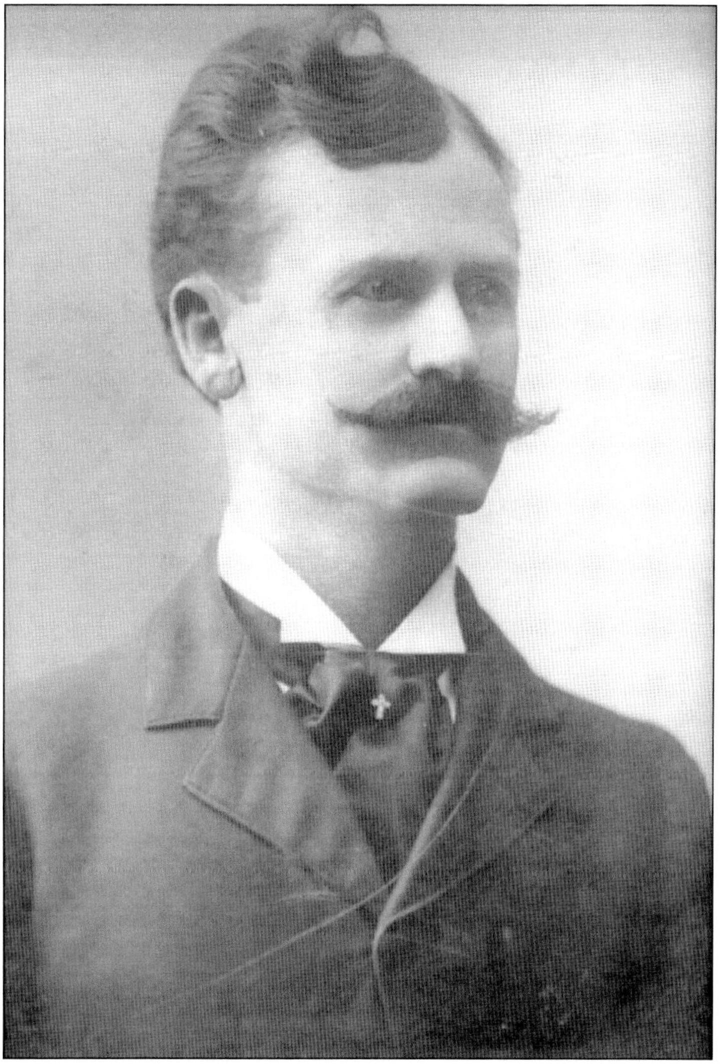

During the Victorian era, a handlebar moustache was the height of male fashion. In Van Alstyne, no man sported a finer handlebar than peace officer Will Echols, who also had a barber-styled wave atop his head. Always a dapper dresser, Echols added a badge to his ensemble as a constable, deputy sheriff, city marshal, and chief of police. (Courtesy of Van Alstyne Historical Society.)

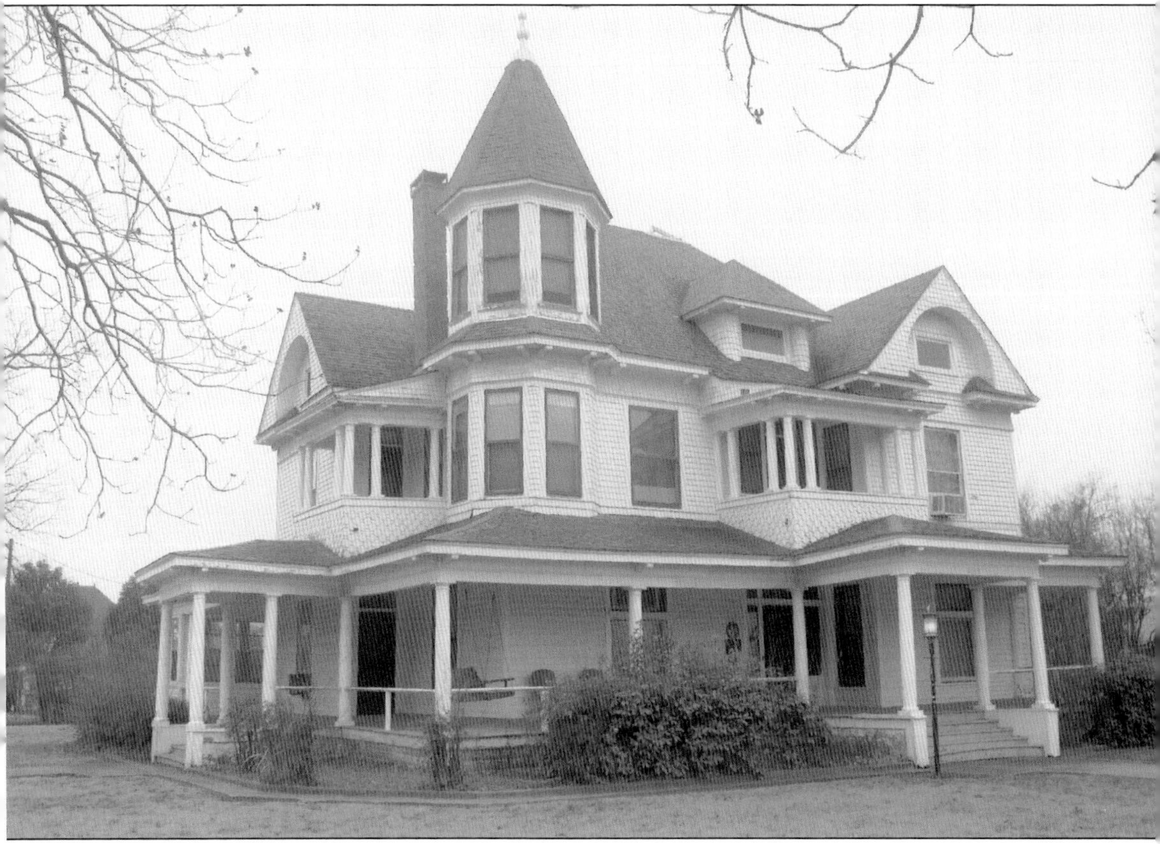

One of the most impressive Victorian homes in Van Alstyne was built in 1903 by banker, landowner, and community leader James C. Umphrees for his wife, Julia Veazy Umphrees. The dominant feature of Victorian architecture was a tower, also called a turret, and the Umphrees home boasted a superb third-floor tower. Following Julia's death in 1932, the house was inherited by daughter Maude Umphrees Taylor, a dedicated civic leader who lived there until 1974. Maude's husband was banker and grain dealer Spencer Taylor, who died in 1943. For the first several decades of the 20th century, this magnificent home was a center of Van Alstyne social life. (Photograph by the author.)

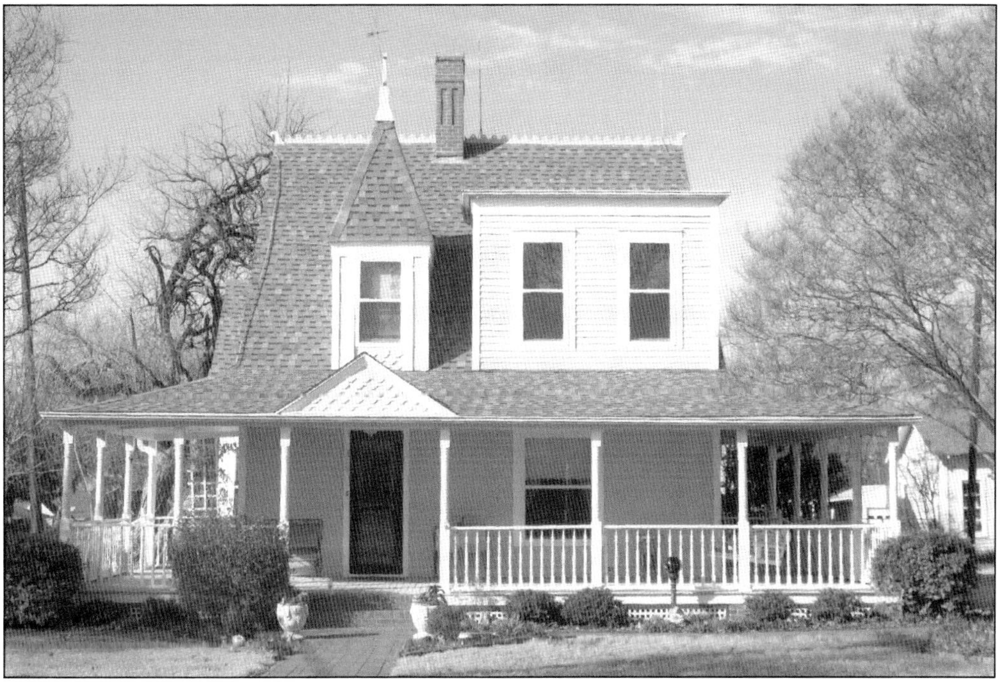

This two-and-a-half story Victorian residence on East South Main Street boasts a requisite, if small, tower, as well as lots of decorative gingerbread. Carpenters used the band saw to create the gingerbread features, which became an attractive feature of Victorian houses. (Photograph by the author.)

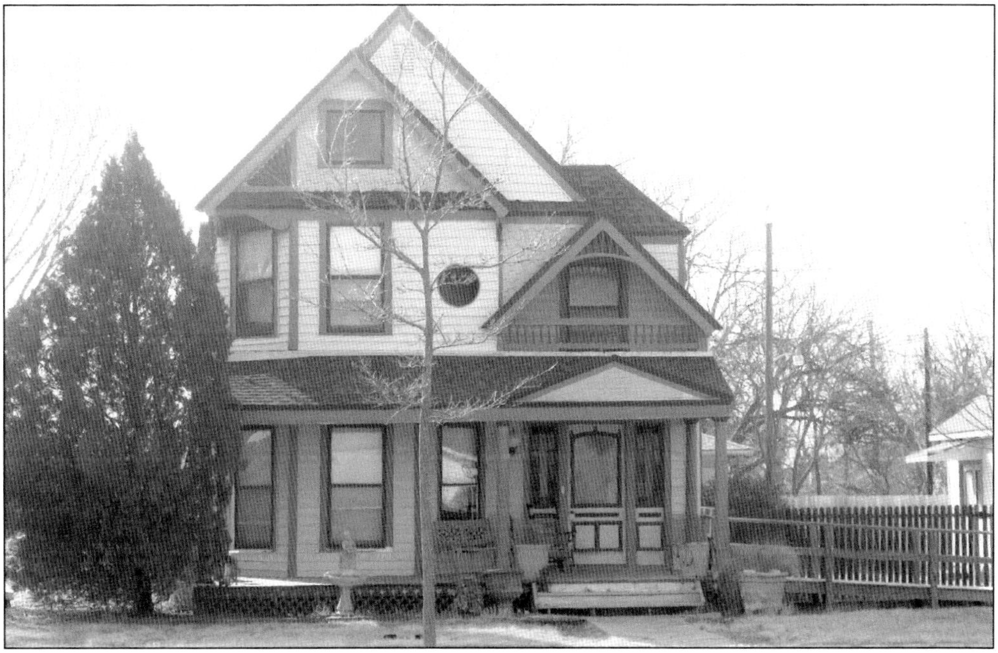

One of the individualistic features of this handsome Victorian residence is the tiny porch above the front entrance. This house still stands on East South Main Street, one of many venerable homes that are lovingly maintained around town. (Photograph by the author.)

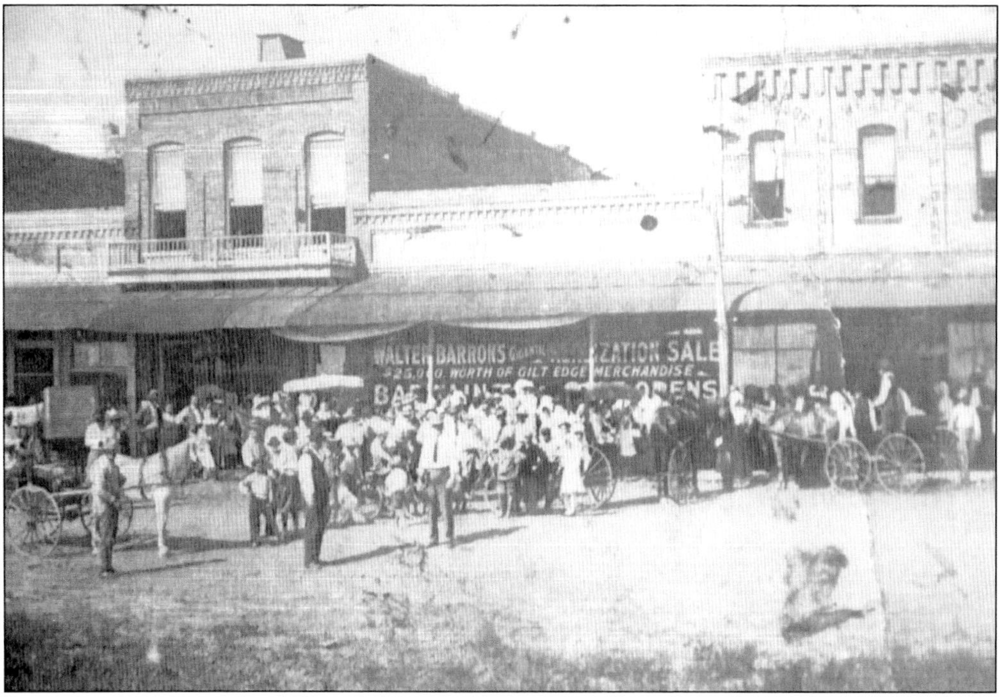

Main Street early in the 20th century teemed with what appears to be a Saturday crowd. Farmers and their families drove their wagons into Van Alstyne each Saturday. Men sold farm produce for ready cash and talked crops and weather with other farmers. Women shopped for the next week and enjoyed the company of other women. Stores and shops enjoyed their best day of the week and stayed open for business well into the night. (Courtesy of Van Alstyne Historical Society.)

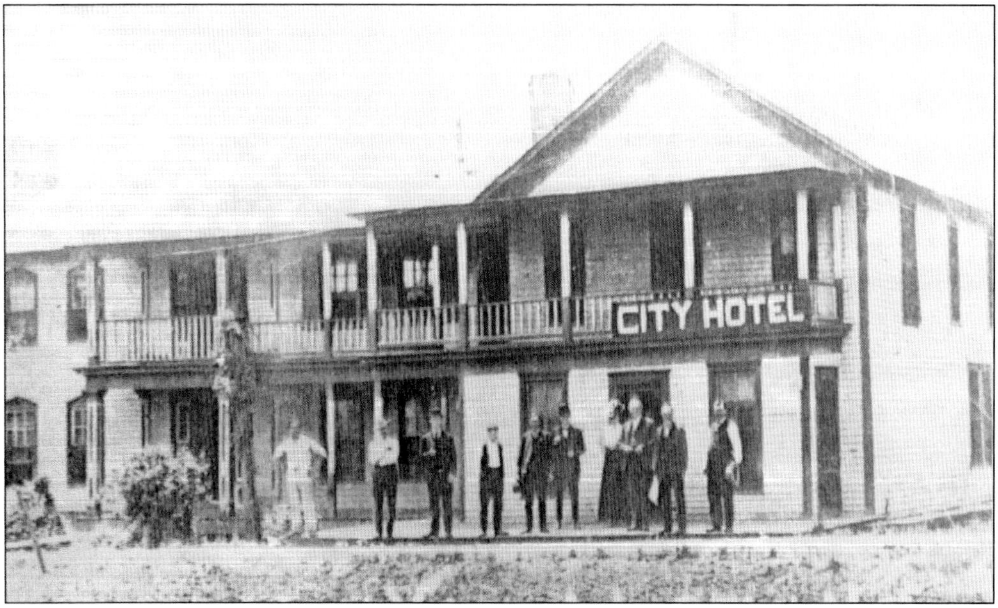

As Van Alstyne grew, there was a need for more hotels. The City Hotel was built on South Preston Street, on the site of the Diamond's Grocery parking lot. (Courtesy of Van Alstyne Historical Society.)

The First National Bank was established with the required capital of $50,000. In the 1890s, there were three classifications of national banks (as opposed to state and private banks): central reserve city banks, which existed in New York, Chicago, and St. Louis; reserve city banks; and country banks. In Texas, there were reserve city banks in Dallas, Fort Worth, San Antonio, Houston, Galveston, and Waco. All other national banks in Texas, including First National Bank of Van Alstyne, were classified as country banks. The offices of Dr. William Veazey were on the second floor. In the view of the bank lobby below, banker John Umphrees stands second from right, behind the teller cage. (Both, courtesy of Van Alstyne Historical Society.)

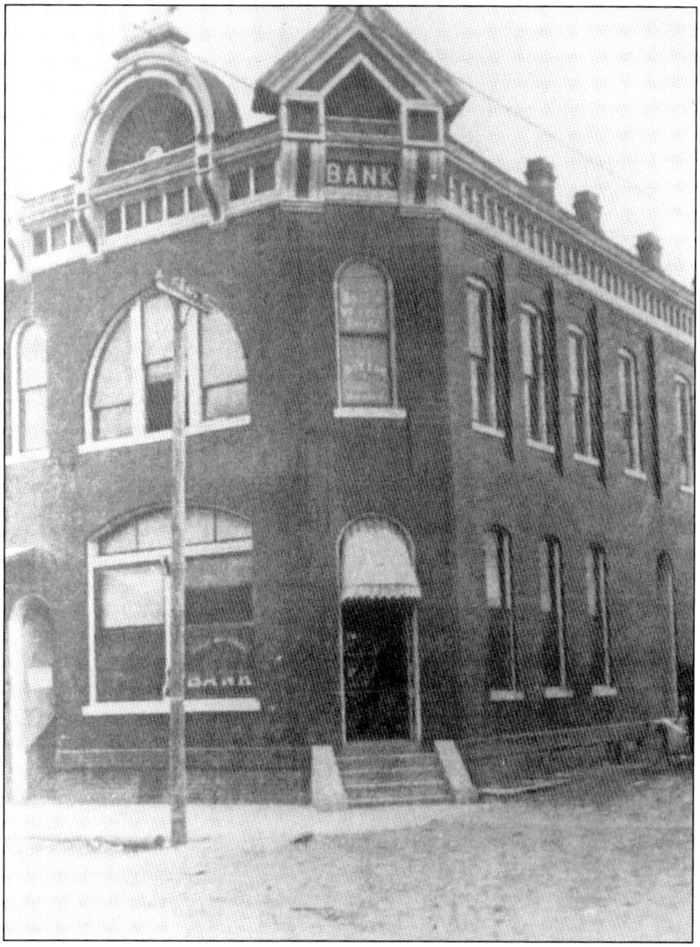

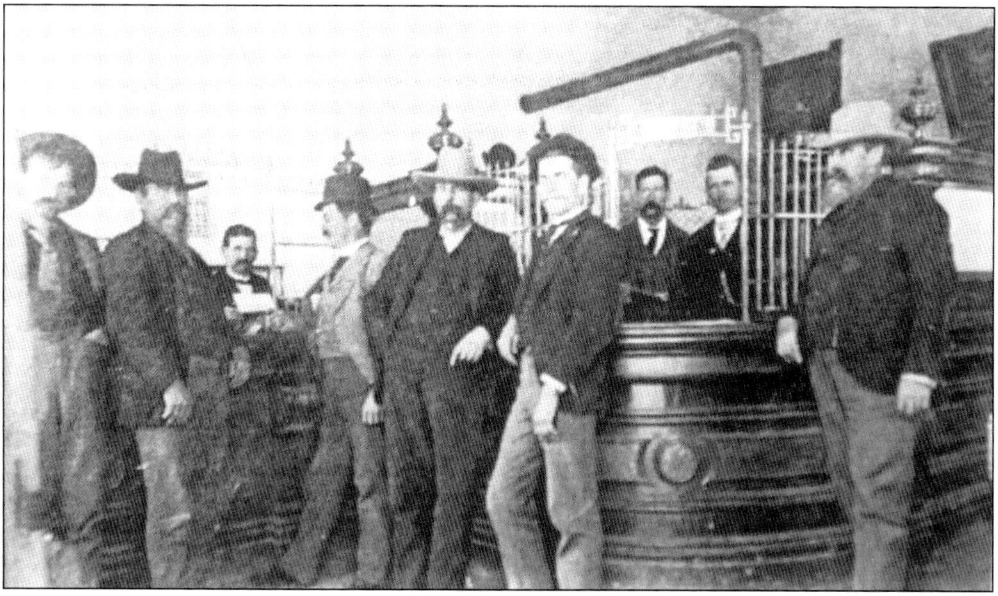

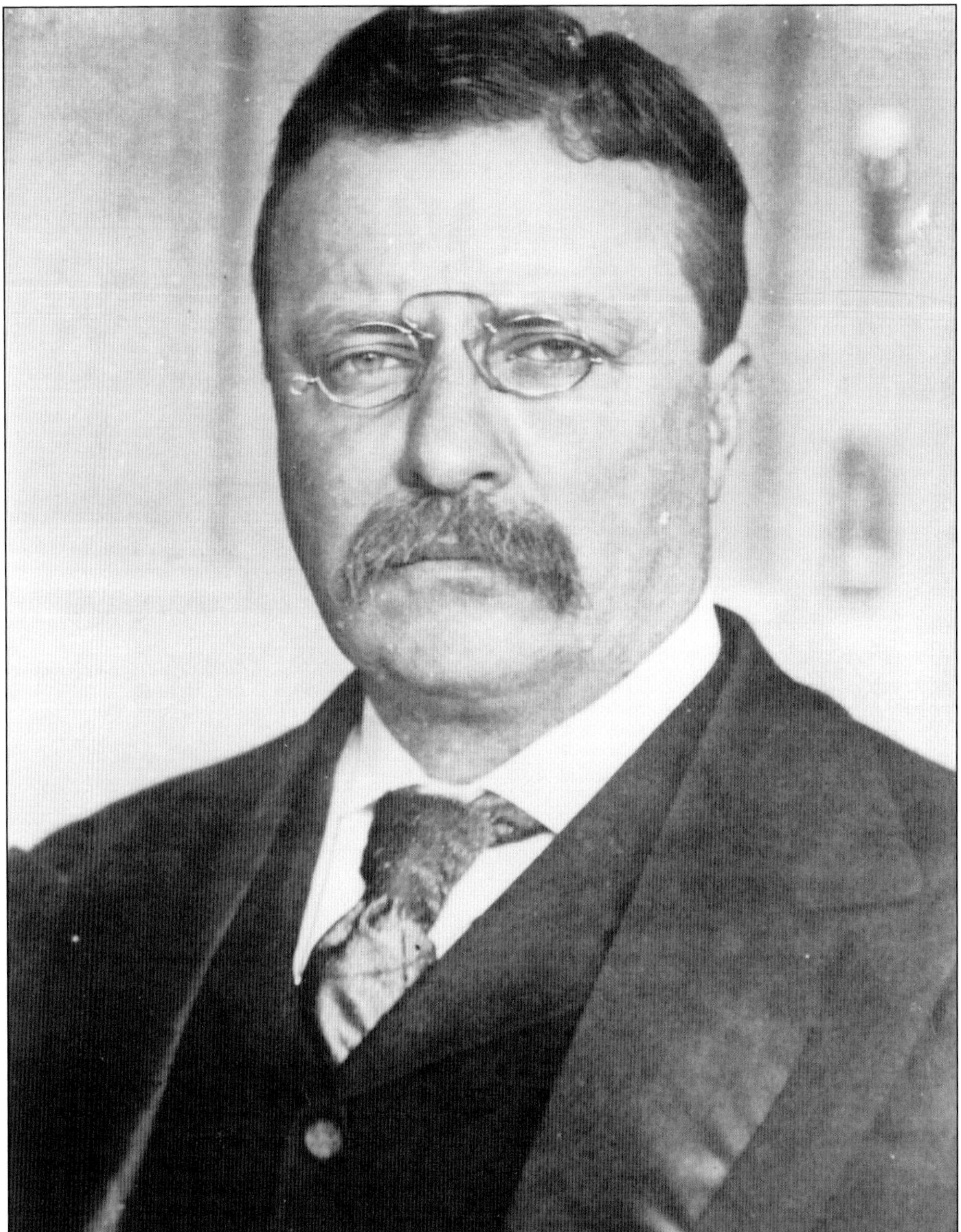

Pres. Theodore Roosevelt was in the second year of his second term when he traveled through Van Alstyne in 1906. Just eight years earlier, during America's war with Spain in 1898, Colonel Roosevelt led his regiment of Rough Riders in the charge up San Juan Hill, which made him a national hero. Within three years, Roosevelt was president of the United States. In 1906, he traveled to San Antonio for a Rough Rider reunion. Passing through Van Alstyne, he was greeted by a cheering, flag-waving populace, and he waved in response. In 1912, while campaigning vigorously for a return to the presidency, Roosevelt's train stopped long enough in Van Alstyne for him to deliver a quick campaign speech. (Courtesy of the National Archives.)

William Howard Taft was the 27th president of the United States (1909–1913). Before going to Washington, Taft had enjoyed a distinguished judicial career, and after leaving the White House, he returned to his alma mater, Yale University, as a professor of law. In 1921, he was appointed chief justice of the Supreme Court, the only man ever to serve as president and as chief justice. During his years as a Yale professor, Taft traveled widely on speaking tours. In 1920, the former president spoke to a Van Alstyne audience in the spacious auditorium of the First Methodist Church, below. (Left, courtesy of the National Archives; below, photograph by the author.)

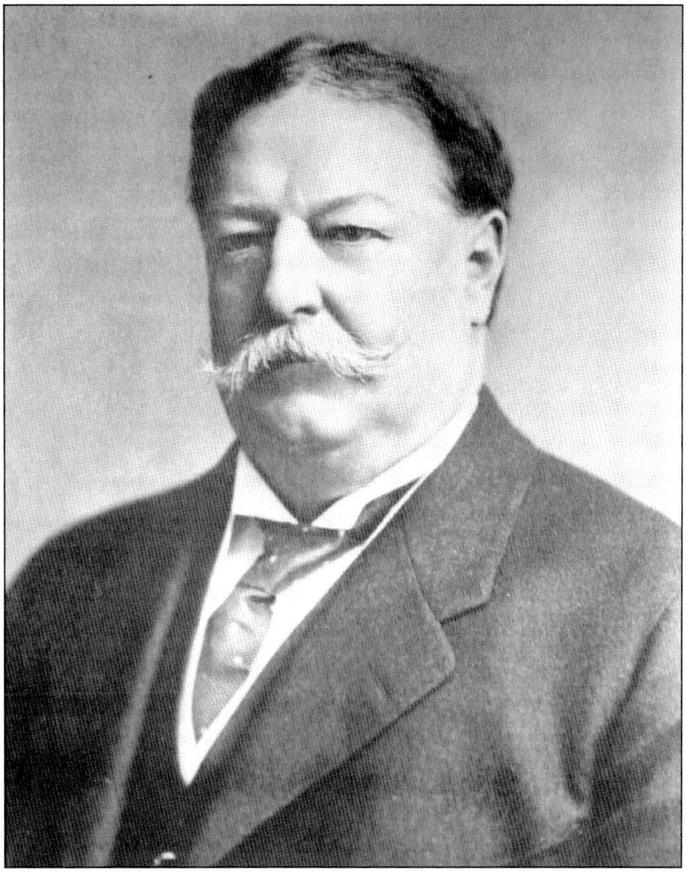

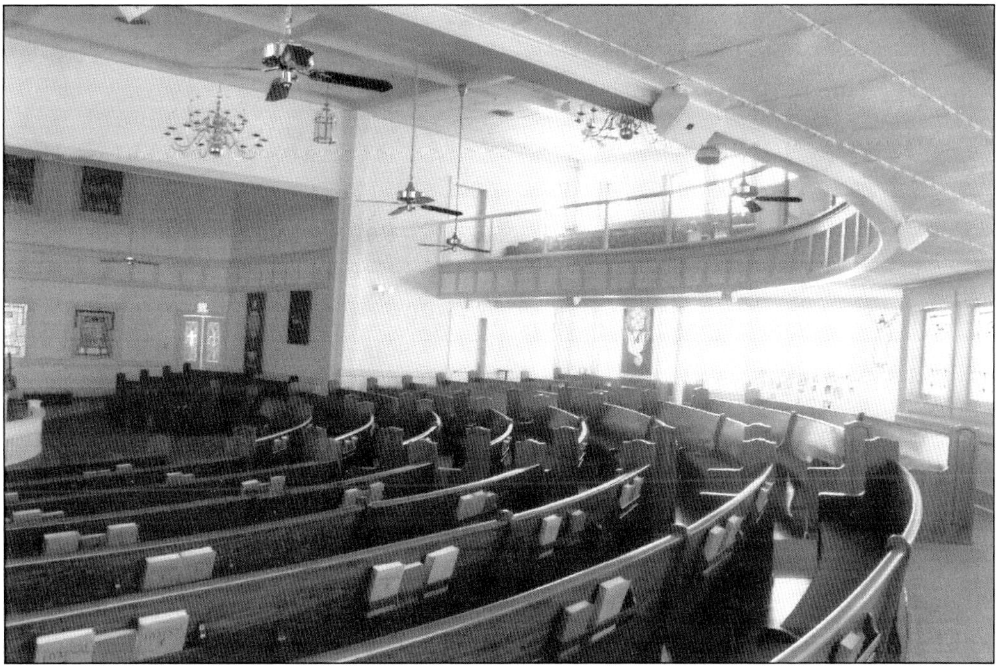

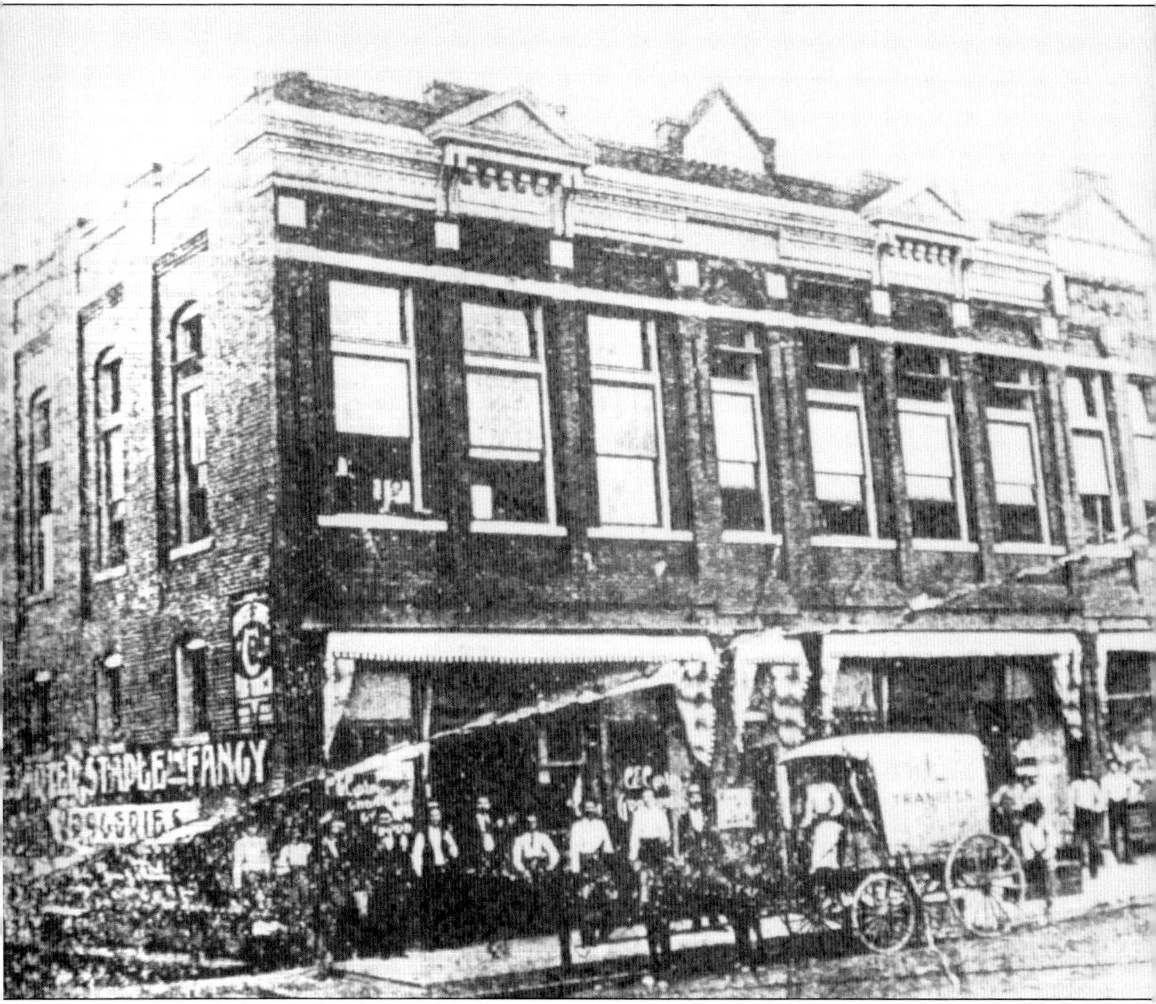

C.E. Carter erected a large brick building, installing his grocery business on the ground floor. Upstairs, he operated the Carter Opera House. The stairway entry to the auditorium was in between the two storefront recesses. Elevated grandstand seating was built along the inside of the front wall of the upstairs auditorium. The two upstairs windows at right marked a dormitory for performers. Front-rank singers, actors, comedians, and magicians did not perform in towns as small as Van Alstyne. But second-tier performers, such as Steen's American Mystifiers (whose "renowned specialities" included "Steenology versus Fakeology" and "Madame Steen's Rarealities") played the Carter Opera House. Political meetings and local performers also utilized the auditorium. (Courtesy of Van Alstyne Historical Society.)

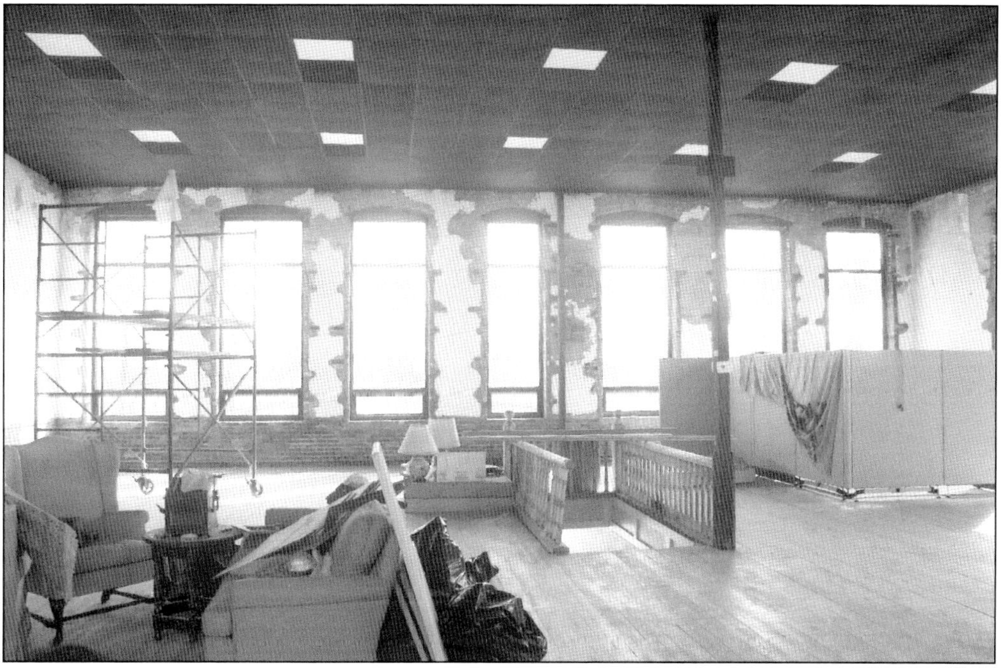

Today, the old opera house area is utilized for storage. But in its heyday, an elevated grandstand was erected in front of the windows. Rows of chairs were lined up on both sides of the stair railing. A raised stage with a curved front projected within a few feet of the stairs, and a backstage partition stretched from wall to wall, left to right. Behind the partition were dressing rooms and four sets of scenery. (Photograph by the author.)

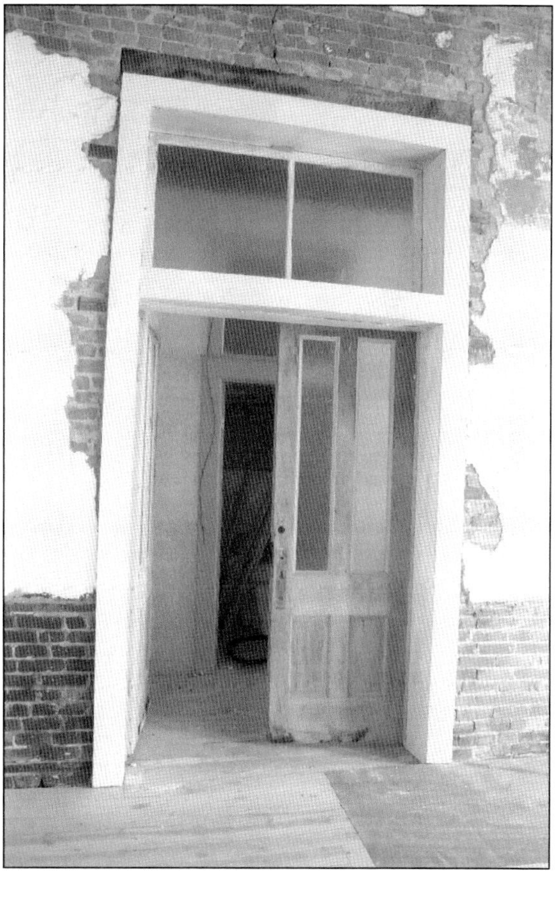

The backstage partition extended to the left side of this doorway. The double doors led to a dormitory area where members of a performing troupe could stay overnight. (Photograph by the author.)

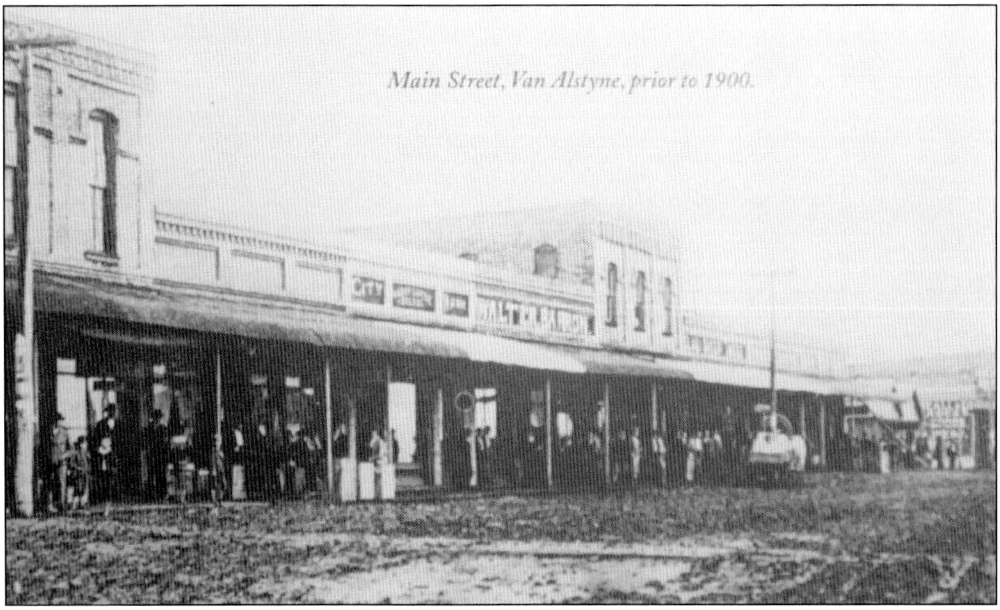

Signs in this view of Main Street indicate that the City Bank is at the center and that next door is the store of Walter Barron. Note the dirt street. On Saturday evenings, it was customary for everyone to stroll down Main Street, turn left on Jefferson Street, and walk all the way around the block, then continue to promenade for another round or two. This custom continued for decades. (Courtesy of Van Alstyne Historical Society.)

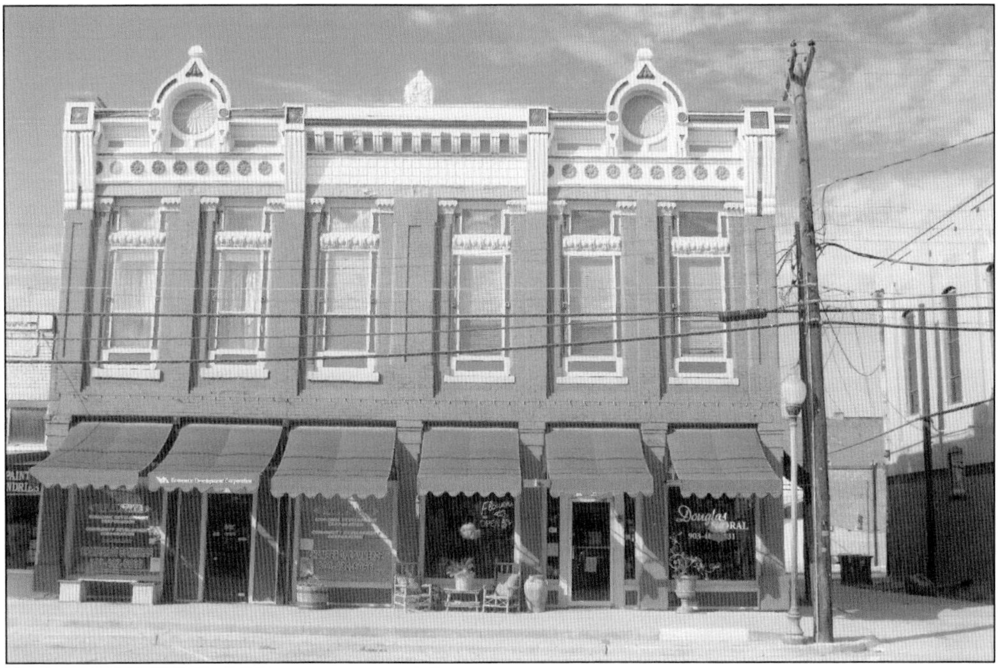

This brick commercial block on Marshall Street houses a bank at right, another business in the space at left, and second-floor offices. Saturday evening strollers passed by this Victorian structure, as well as Carter's Opera House across the alley at the right, or east. (Photograph by the author.)

The commercial space that first housed a bank in the brick block in the previous photograph is today home to Douglas Floral. The old bank vault can still be seen, and the vault door is decorated with a Douglas "D." (Photograph by the author.)

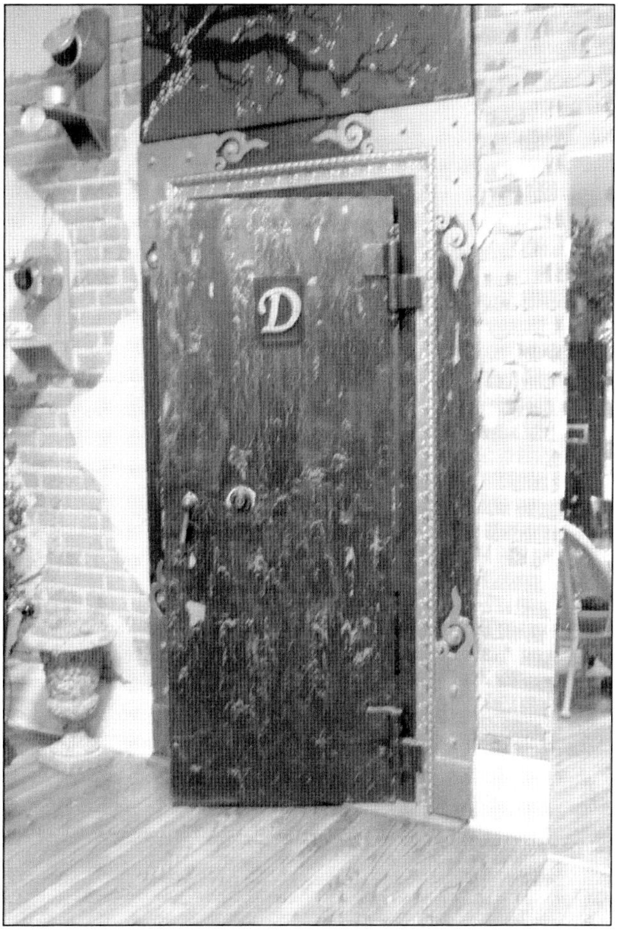

Locally owned by Jim Cannon and Lyman Umphrees, the Van Alstyne Telephone Company was launched in 1886 with a phone call to Sherman. By the early 20th century, Van Alstyne telephone services were operated by Jim McLemore under the Texas Telephone Company, with space rented in the old opera house auditorium. At the switchboard are Lula Biggs (left) and Betty Hendrick (right). (Courtesy of Van Alstyne Historical Society.)

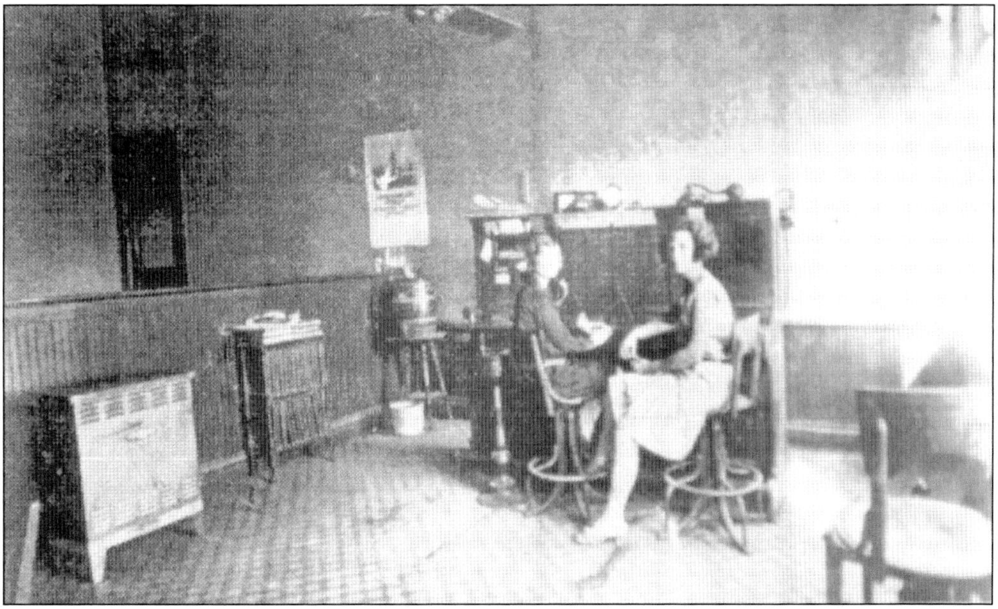

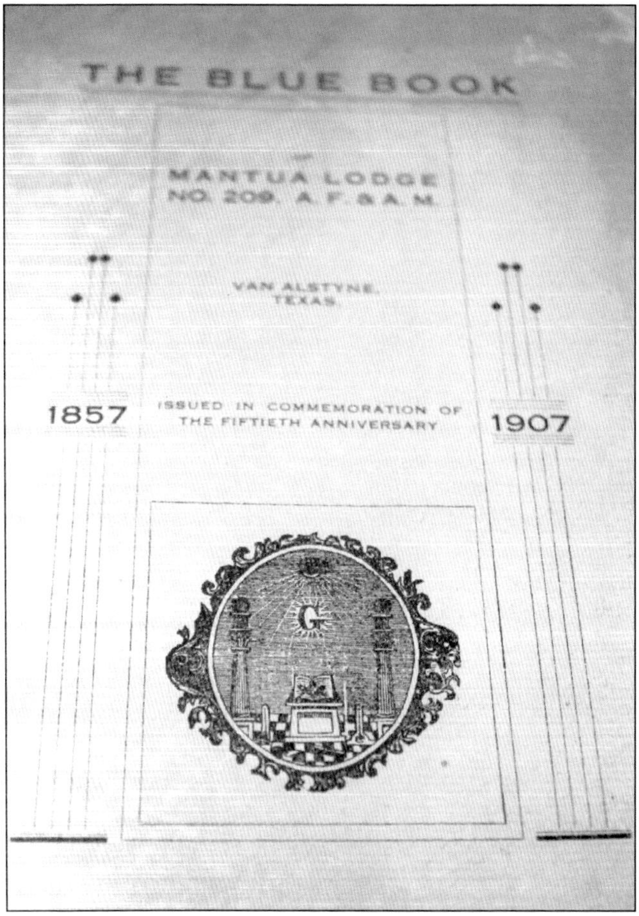

In 1907, Van Alstyne Masons celebrated the 50th anniversary of their lodge; the 1907 Blue Book, pictured left, in on display at the Van Alstyne Historical Museum. Mantua Masonic Lodge No. 209 was chartered in 1857, but after most of its members moved to Van Alstyne, the lodge relocated in 1880. The Masons met in several downtown locations, finally purchasing a two-story brick building in 1898. Still chartered as Mantua Masonic Lodge No. 209, the Masons built their current home in 1976, pictured below. Fraternal orders were highly popular when Van Alstyne was founded, and in 1882, the Van Alstyne Lodge of the Independent Order of Odd Fellows No. 268 was founded. IOOF members bought a two-story building the southeast corner of Marshall and Preston streets, using the second story as a lodge hall and renting the ground floor. (Both photographs by the author.)

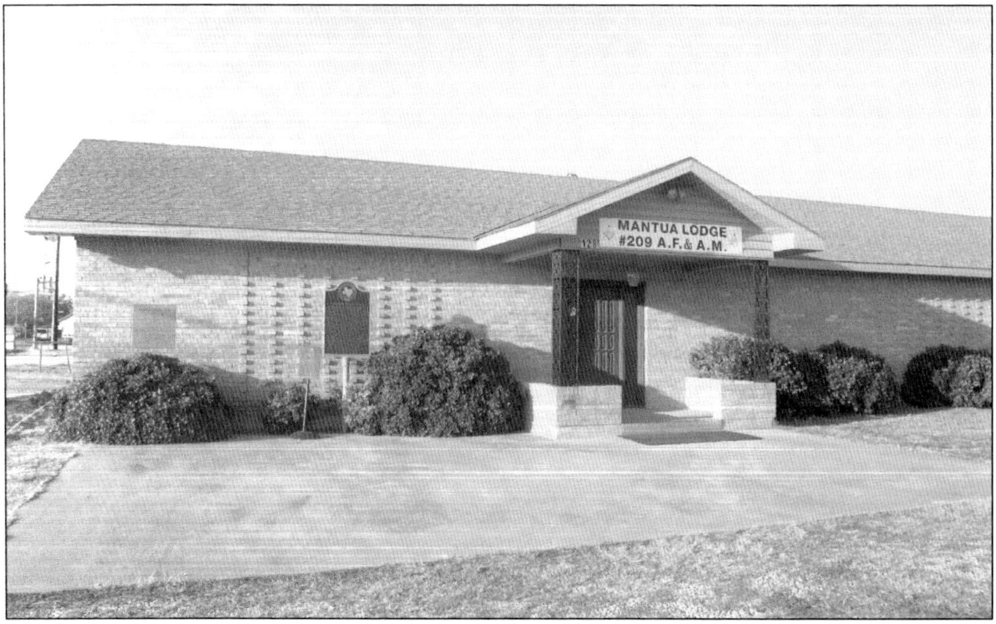

Pearl Fulton and nine other charter members formed the Tuesday Literary Club in 1896. The organization joined the Texas Federated Women's Clubs in 1898, and three years later, there was a name change to the Van Alstyne Culture Club. Mrs. Fulton served as president on four occasions through the years, including 1939 to 1941. Except for the Masonic lodge, the Culture Club is Van Alstyne's oldest civic organization. (Courtesy of Van Alstyne Historical Society.)

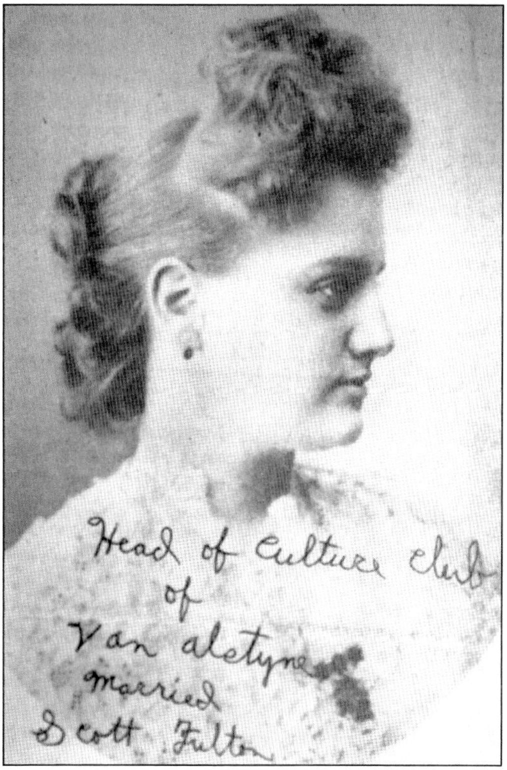

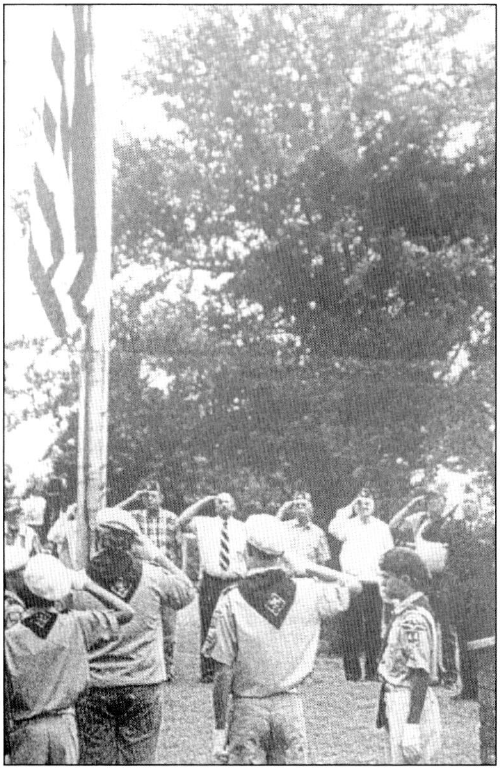

The Boy Scouts of America were founded in 1910, and just three years later, a troop was organized in Van Alstyne by school superintendent W.L. Barnett. Through the years, the troop has been on duty at numerous Memorial Day services. (Courtesy of Van Alstyne Public Library.)

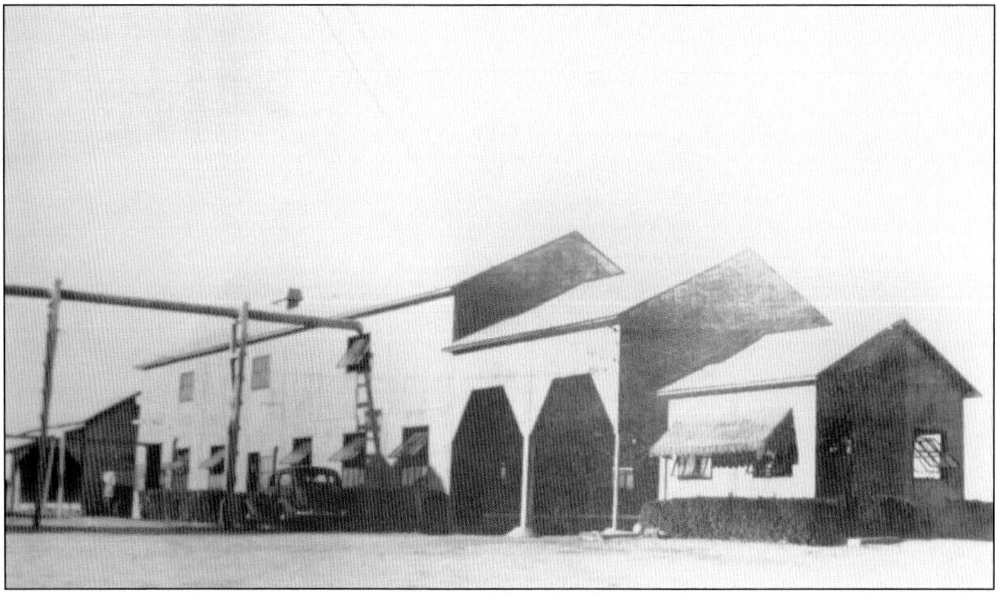

Cotton was Texas's first cash crop. By 1880, Texas was the leading cotton-producing state in America, a distinction it maintains today. During the late 1800s, there were 30,000 cotton-ginning operations in Texas, including three, four, or even five in Van Alstyne. The largest operations were the Van Alstyne Cotton Oil Company, pictured above, and the Van Alstyne Roller Mills and Cotton Gin, both located on the south edge of town east of the tracks. (Courtesy of Van Alstyne Historical Society.)

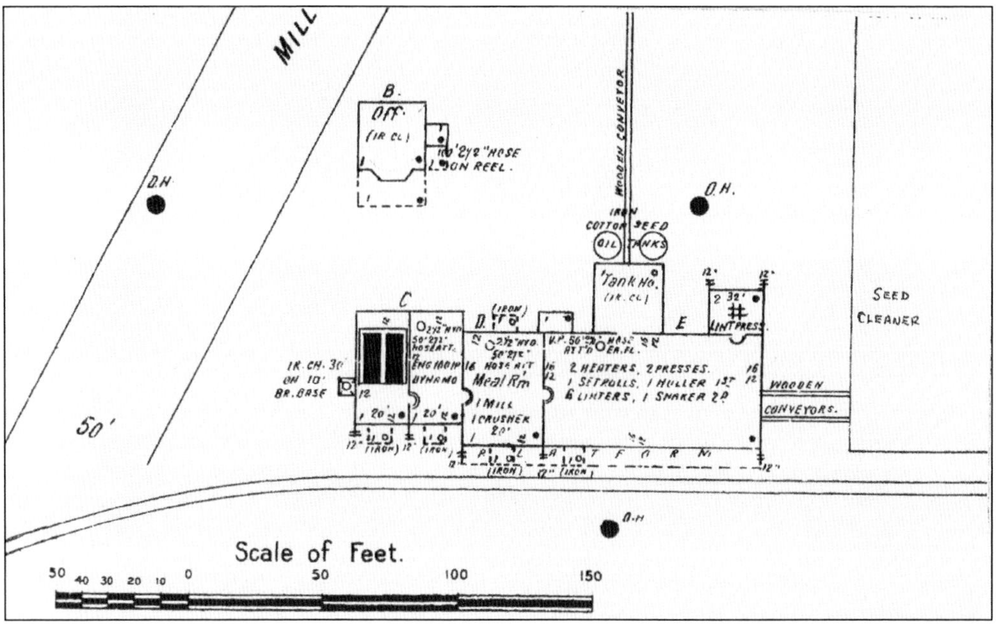

This diagram of the Van Alstyne Cotton Oil Company came from a Sanborn Fire Insurance map of the city compiled in 1907. The Van Alstyne Roller Mills and Cotton Gin buildings stood across the road at left, or north. There were detailed Sanborn maps of Van Alstyne for 1896, 1901, 1907, and 1914, yielding a wealth of information about the town. (Courtesy of Sherman Public Library.)

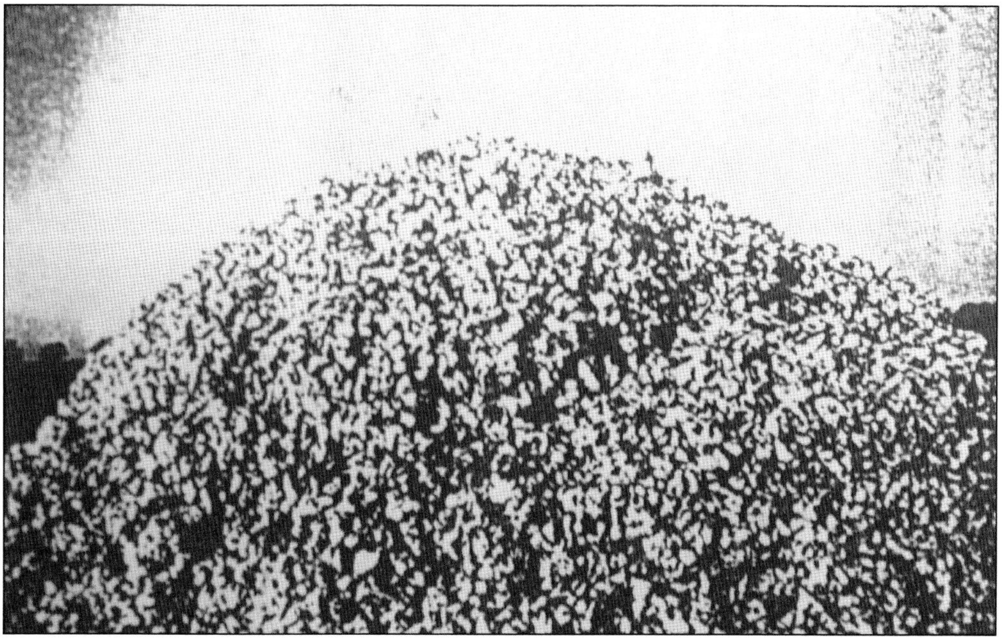

During the ginning process, waste cotton periodically was placed in piles. At the height of the cotton season each fall, Van Alstyne gins operated around the clock. From nearby farms, long lines of cotton wagons moved slowly toward each gin. (Courtesy of Van Alstyne Historical Society.)

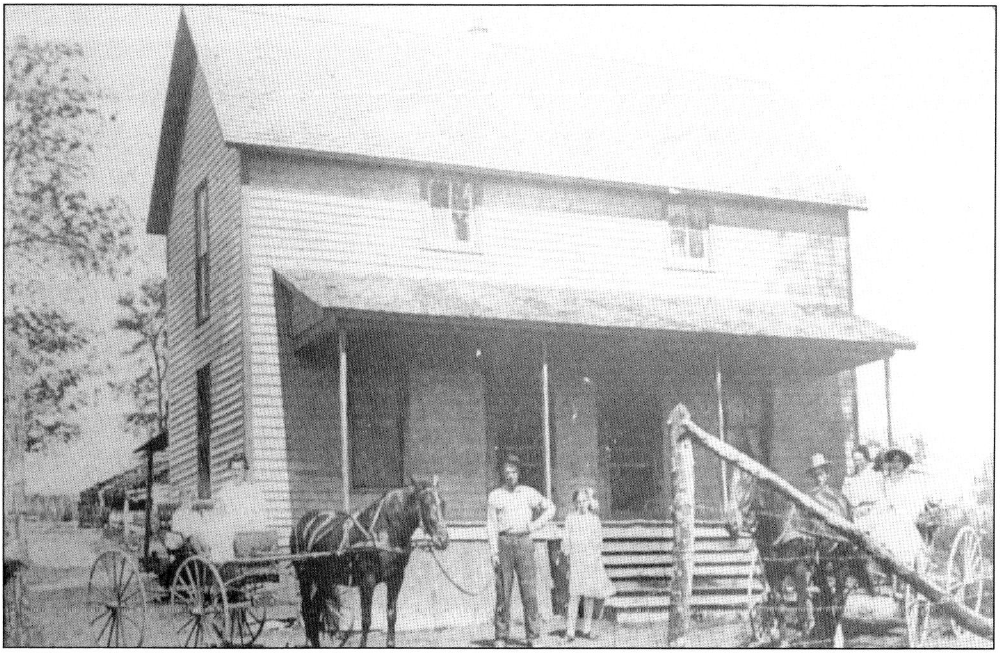

The farm home of Albert and Alma Spain was located 1.5 miles east of Van Alstyne. During the second decade of the 20th century, a photograph was taken in the front yard of the Spain home. Alma sits in the buggy at left with her little daughter, Ruby. Albert stands beside Alma's younger sister, Birdie. Arch Williams stands beside the buggy at right, but the two ladies in the buggy seat are unidentified. (Courtesy of Van Alstyne Historical Society.)

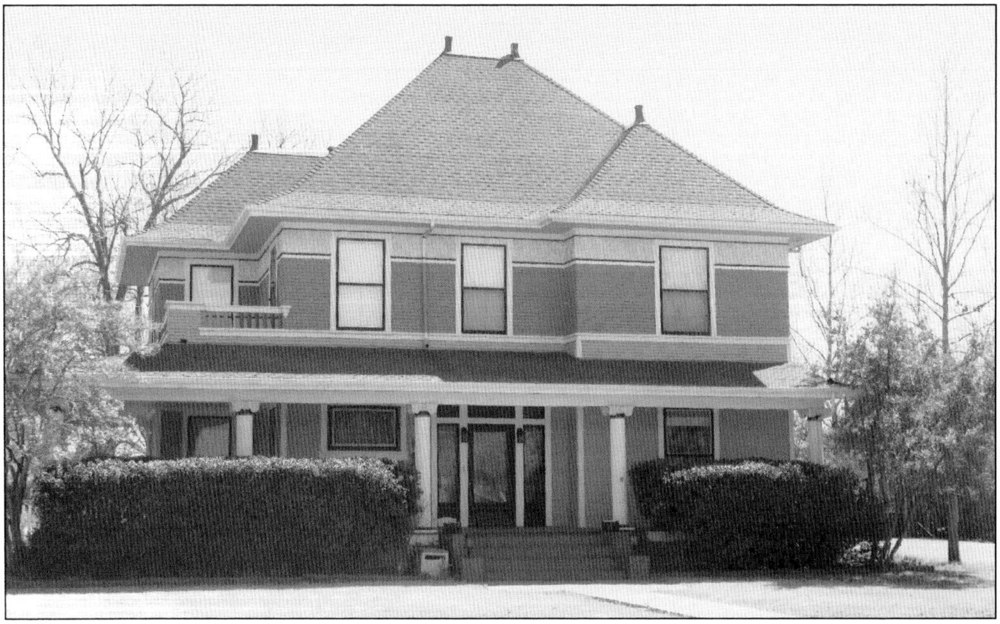

Victorian residential architecture was giving way to the Prairie style of Frank Lloyd Wright when successful Van Alstyne merchant Walter Barron and his wife, Pearl Cannon Barron, built this home for $4,000 in 1905. Another leading citizen, William Veazey, later bought this spacious house. (Photograph by the author.)

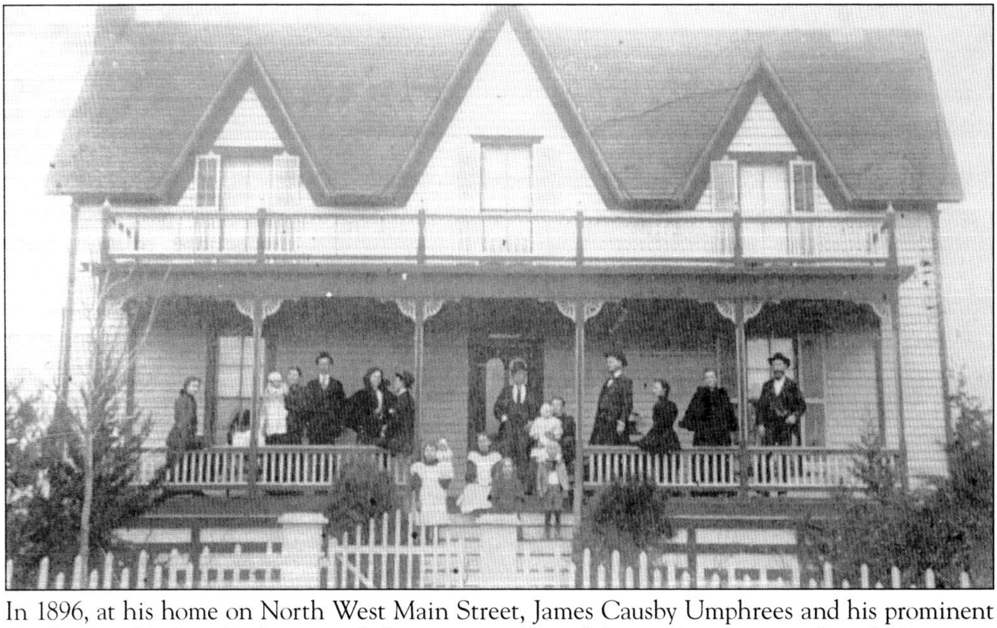

In 1896, at his home on North West Main Street, James Causby Umphrees and his prominent family assembled on the front porch for a portrait. From left to right are an unidentified servant; Eula Cannon Umphrees with baby Carl Cannon Umphrees, John Umphrees, Pearl Cannon, Lyman Umphrees, Paul Bean, Mary Umphrees Bean with baby Harry Bean, Judge Harvey L. Davis, Emma Umphrees Davis, Julia Caroline Veazey Umphrees, and James Causby Umphrees. The children on steps are, from left to right, Maude Umphrees, Dixie Umphrees, Nannie Cave, and Don O. Davis. (Courtesy of Van Alstyne Historical Society.)

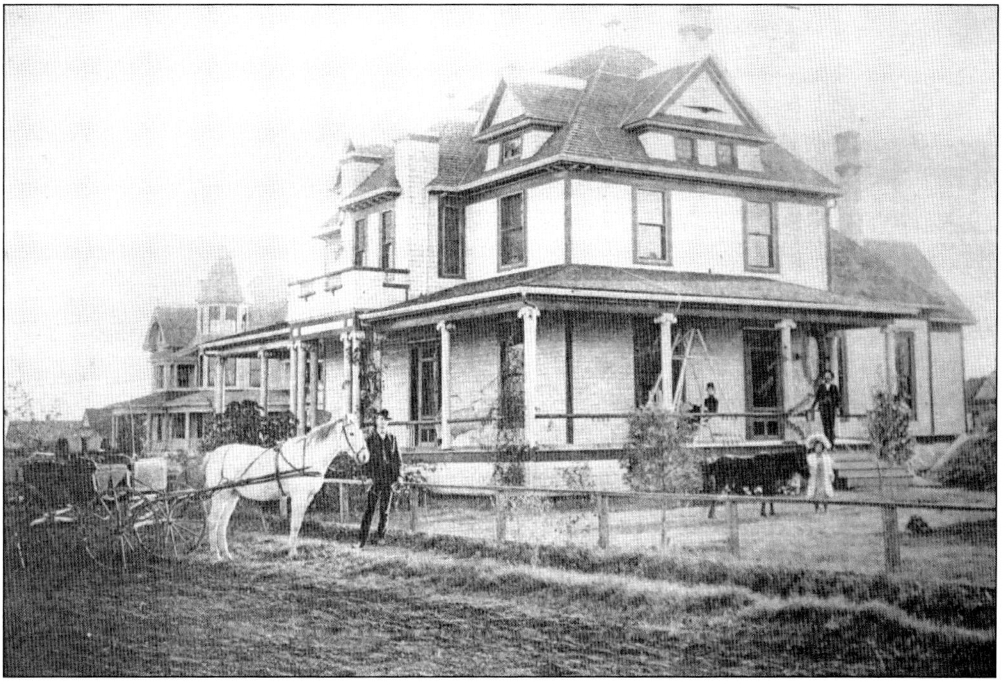

Joe A. McKinney built his home on the west side of Preston Street, facing east. The little girl in the yard stands with her pony. In the background is the stately home of James and Julia Umphrees. (Courtesy of Van Alstyne Historical Society.)

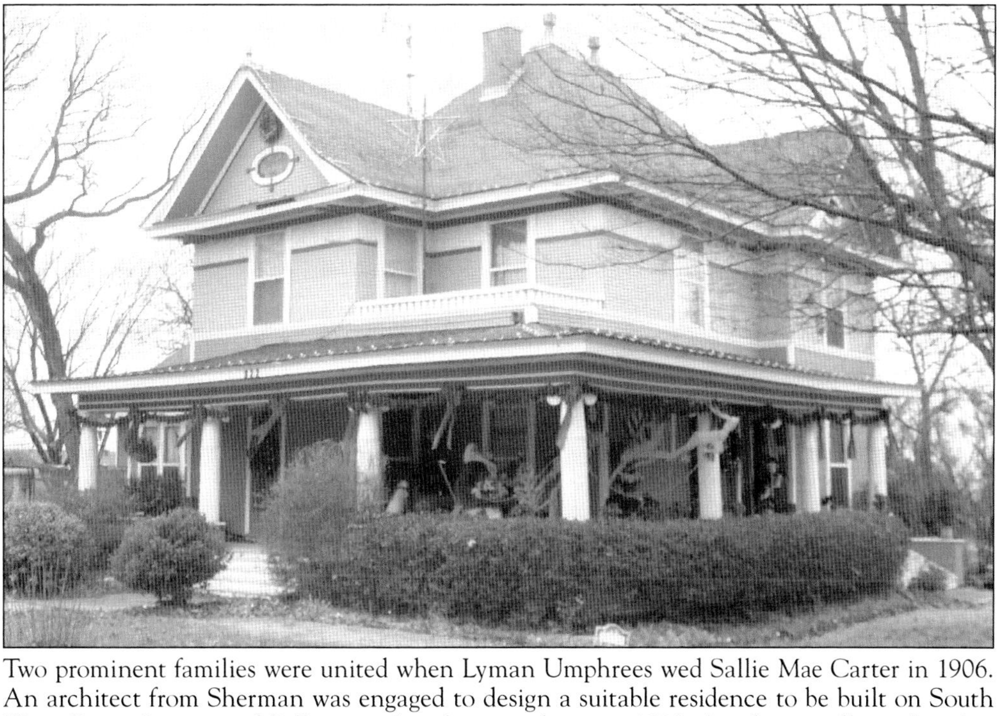

Two prominent families were united when Lyman Umphrees wed Sallie Mae Carter in 1906. An architect from Sherman was engaged to design a suitable residence to be built on South Waco Street. Lyman and Sallie moved to their new home in 1908; their home still stands today. (Photograph by the author.)

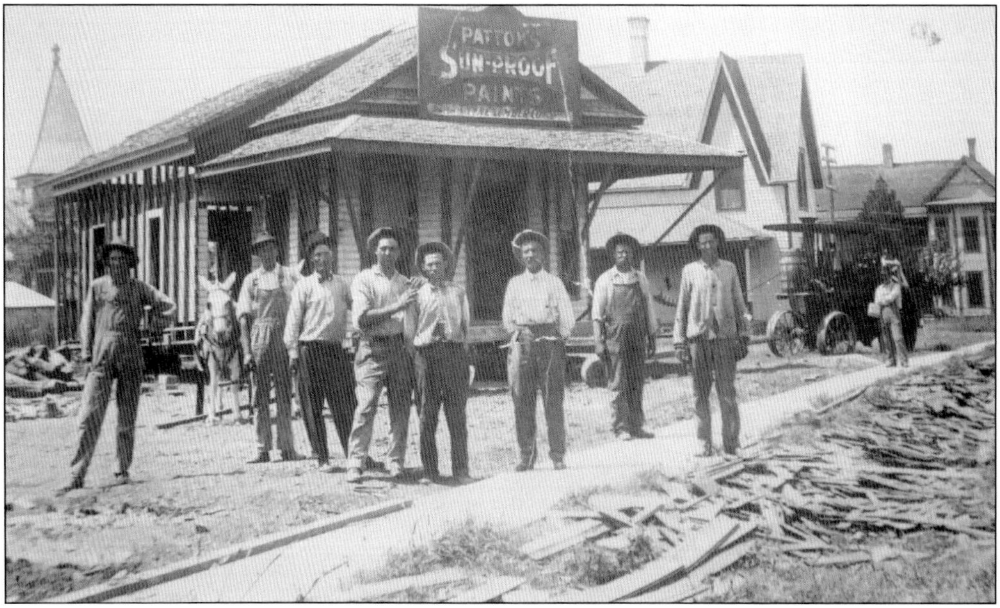

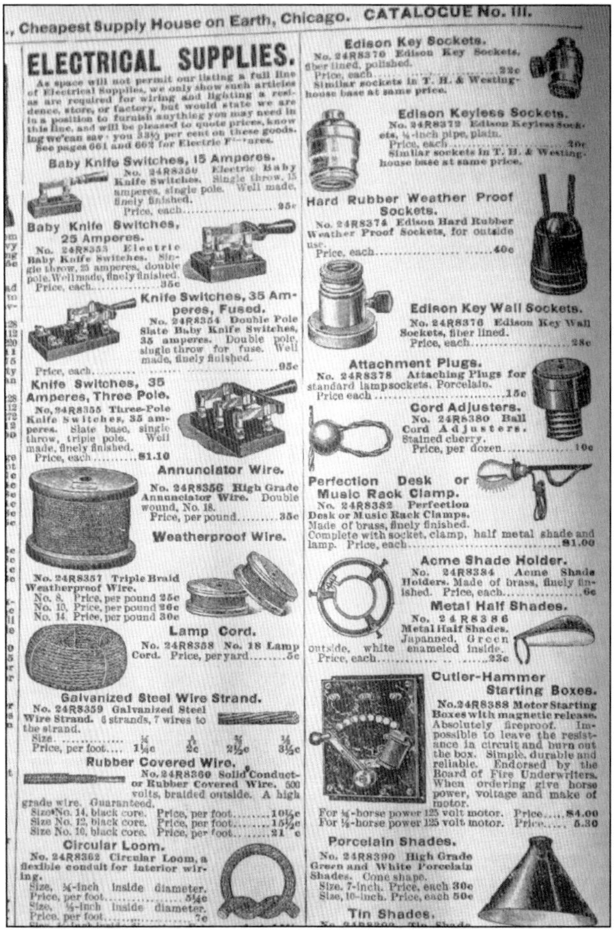

., Cheapest Supply House on Earth, Chicago. CATALOGUE No. III.

ELECTRICAL SUPPLIES.

As space will not permit our listing a full line of Electrical Supplies, we only show such articles as are required for wiring and lighting a residence, store, or factory, but would state we are in a position to furnish anything you may need in this line, and will be pleased to quote prices, knowing we can save you 33⅓ per cent on these goods. See pages 661 and 662 for Electric Fixtures.

Baby Knife Switches, 15 Amperes.
No. 24R8350 Electric Baby Knife Switches. Single throw, 15 amperes, single pole. Well made, finely finished.
Price, each........95c

Baby Knife Switches, 25 Amperes.
No. 24R8353 Electric Baby Knife Switches. Single throw, 25 amperes, double pole. Well made, finely finished.
Price, each........35c

Knife Switches, 35 Amperes, Fused.
No. 24R8354 Double Pole Slate Baby Knife Switches, 35 amperes. Double pole, single throw for fuse. Well made, finely finished.
Price, each........95c

Knife Switches, 35 Amperes, Three Pole.
No. 24R8355 Three-Pole Knife Switches, 35 amperes. Slate base, single throw, triple pole. Well made, finely finished.
Price, each........$1.10

Annunciator Wire.
No. 24R8356 High Grade Annunciator Wire. Double wound, No. 18.
Price, per pound........35c

Weatherproof Wire.
No. 24R8357 Triple Braid Weatherproof Wire.
No. 8. Price, per pound 25c
No. 10. Price, per pound 26c
No. 14. Price, per pound 30c

Lamp Cord.
No. 24R8358 No. 18 Lamp Cord. Price, per yard........5c

Galvanized Steel Wire Strand.
No. 24R8359 Galvanized Steel Wire Strand. 6 strands, 7 wires to the strand.
Size........
Price, per foot.... 1¼c 2c 2½c 3½c

Rubber Covered Wire.
No. 24R8360 Solid Conductor Rubber Covered Wire. 500 volts, braided outside. A high grade wire. Guaranteed.
Size No. 14, black core. Price, per foot........10¼c
Size No. 12, black core. Price, per foot........15½c
Size No. 10, black core. Price, per foot........21 c

Circular Loom.
No. 24R8362 Circular Loom, a flexible conduit for interior wiring.
Size, ⅜-inch inside diameter. Price, per foot........5¼c
Size, ½-inch inside diameter. Price, per foot........7c

Edison Key Sockets.
No. 24R8370 Edison Key Sockets, fiber lined, polished.
Price, each........22c
Similar sockets in T. H. & Westinghouse base at same price.

Edison Keyless Sockets.
No. 24R8372 Edison Keyless Sockets, ⅛-inch pipe, plain.
Price, each........20c
Similar sockets in T. H. & Westinghouse base at same price.

Hard Rubber Weather Proof Sockets.
No. 24R8374 Edison Hard Rubber Weather Proof Sockets, for outside use.
Price, each........40c

Edison Key Wall Sockets.
No. 24R8376 Edison Key Wall Sockets, fiber lined.
Price, each........28c

Attachment Plugs.
No. 24R8378 Attaching Plugs for standard lampsockets. Porcelain.
Price each........15c

Cord Adjusters.
No. 24R8380 Ball Cord Adjusters. Stained cherry.
Price, per dozen........10c

Perfection Desk or Music Rack Clamp.
No. 24R8382 Perfection Desk or Music Rack Clamps. Made of brass, finely finished. Complete with socket, clamp, half metal shade and lamp. Price, each........$1.00

Acme Shade Holder.
No. 24R8384 Acme Shade Holders. Made of brass, finely finished. Price, each........6c

Metal Half Shades.
No. 24R8386 Metal Half Shades. Japanned. Green outside, white enameled inside.
Price, each........23c

Cutler-Hammer Starting Boxes.
No. 24R8388 Motor Starting Boxes with magnetic release. Absolutely fireproof. Impossible to leave the resistance in circuit and burn out the box. Simple, durable and reliable. Endorsed by the Board of Fire Underwriters. When ordering give horse power, voltage and make of motor.
For ¼-horse power 125 volt motor. Price.....$4.00
For ½-horse power 125 volt motor. Price..... 5.30

Porcelain Shades.
No. 24R8390 High Grade Green and White Porcelain Shades. Cone shape.
Size, 7-inch. Price, each 30c
Size, 10-inch. Price, each 50c

Tin Shades.

The main building of the Van Alstyne Lumber Company was partially dismantled so that it could be moved to the north part of town, onto a lot beside the frame First Baptist Church. The frame church in the background is the First Christian Church, standing on the site where a new brick sanctuary would be built within a few years. (Courtesy of Van Alstyne Historical Society.)

As the 20th century dawned, electrical illumination began to spread throughout the homes of Van Alstyne. The McKinney and Marr Gin utilized its big dynamos to generate electricity for homes daily from 6:30 a.m. to 9:30 p.m. The Yoder Ice Plant also began supplying electricity before Texas Power and Light extended its operations to Van Alstyne. The town's mercantile stores stocked sockets, plugs, and an assortment of other electrical devices. (From the *Sears, Roebuck Catalogue, 1902 Edition*.)

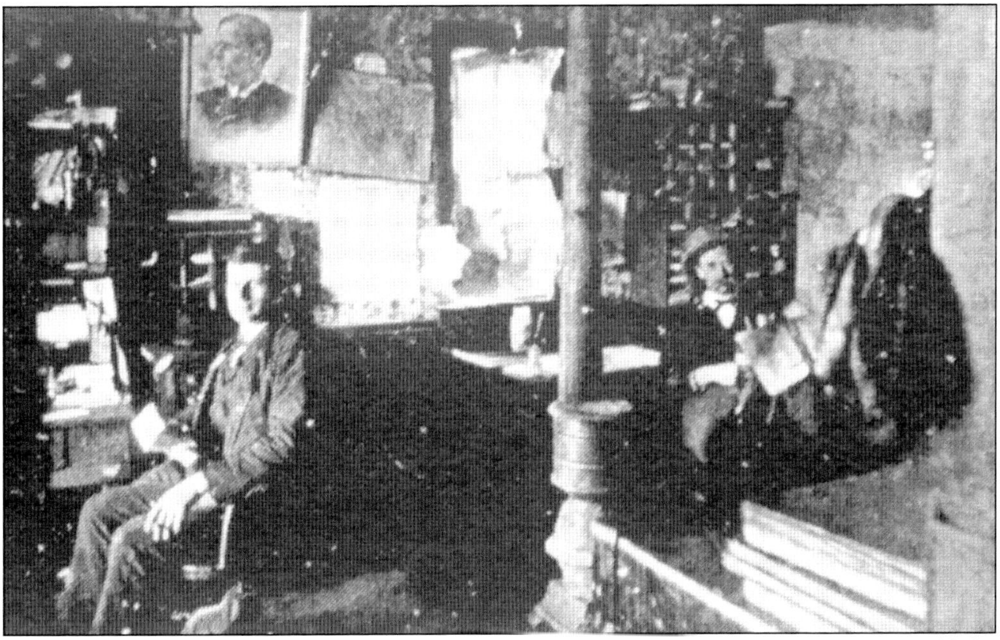

Van Alstyne's first newspaper was the *Enterprise*, founded in 1882 by J. Perry Leslie. Leslie sold the *Enterprise* in 1890 to S.P. Evans, who changed the name to the Van Alstyne *News*. Owner-editor Evans is shown at his desk (left), while Dr. B.F. Hines visits the *News* office. Evans died in 1899, and the *News* was sold to J.E. McComb. (Courtesy of Van Alstyne Historical Society.)

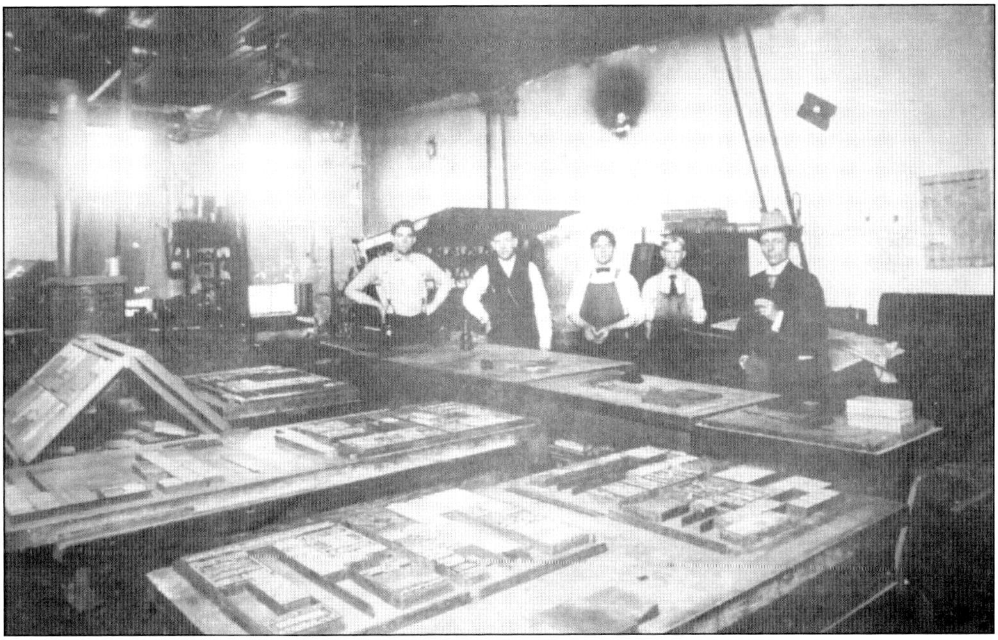

The Van Alstyne *Leader* was founded in 1892 by W.B. Duncan and L.J. Reynolds, who sold it to R.S. Fulton four years later. Fulton bought the Van Alstyne *News* from J.E. McCombs in 1905, forming the Leader Publishing Company. Today, the *Leader* still provides newspaper service to Van Alstyne, as well as to Anna and Melissa. (Courtesy Van Alstyne Historical Society.)

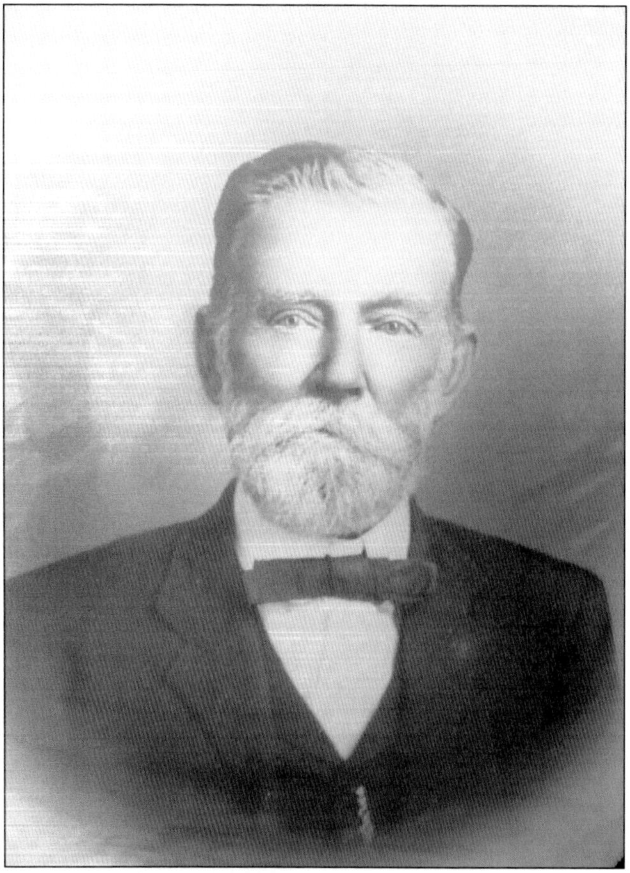

Dr. T.M. West was Van Alstyne's first dentist, establishing his practice about 1890. (Courtesy of Van Alstyne Historical Society.)

Around the turn of the century, Dr. Z.D. Emerson moved into this home, which faces south on Jefferson Street, looking down Preston Avenue. Doctor Emerson practiced medicine on the ground floor, with the family living upstairs. (Photograph by the author.)

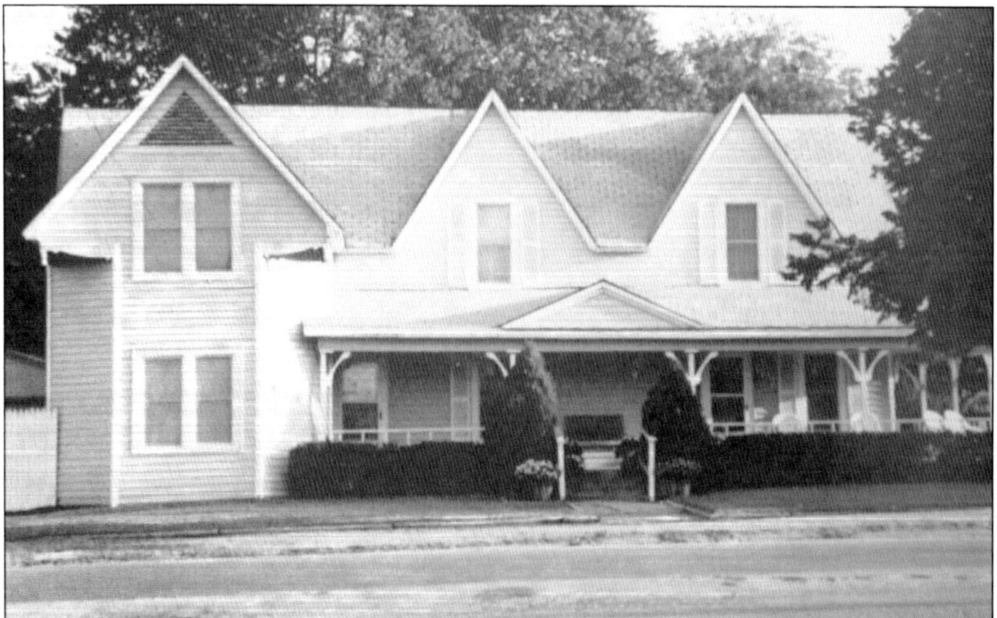

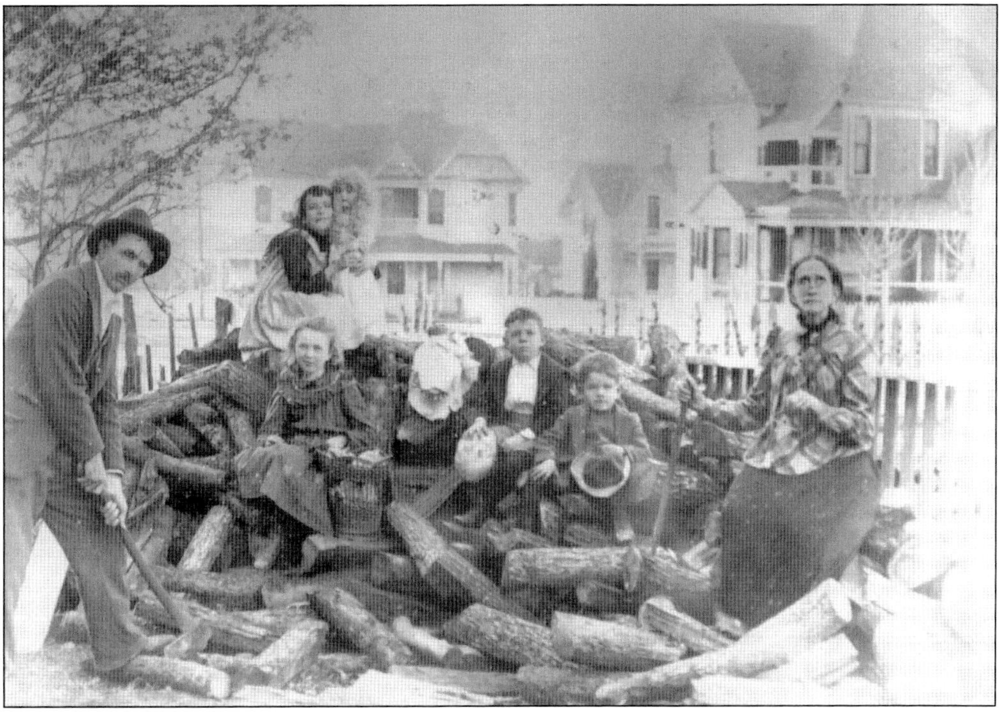

This family poses beside and atop the woodpile in the backyard of their two-story house, built in 1884. (Courtesy of the Quilt Shoppe, Van Alstyne.)

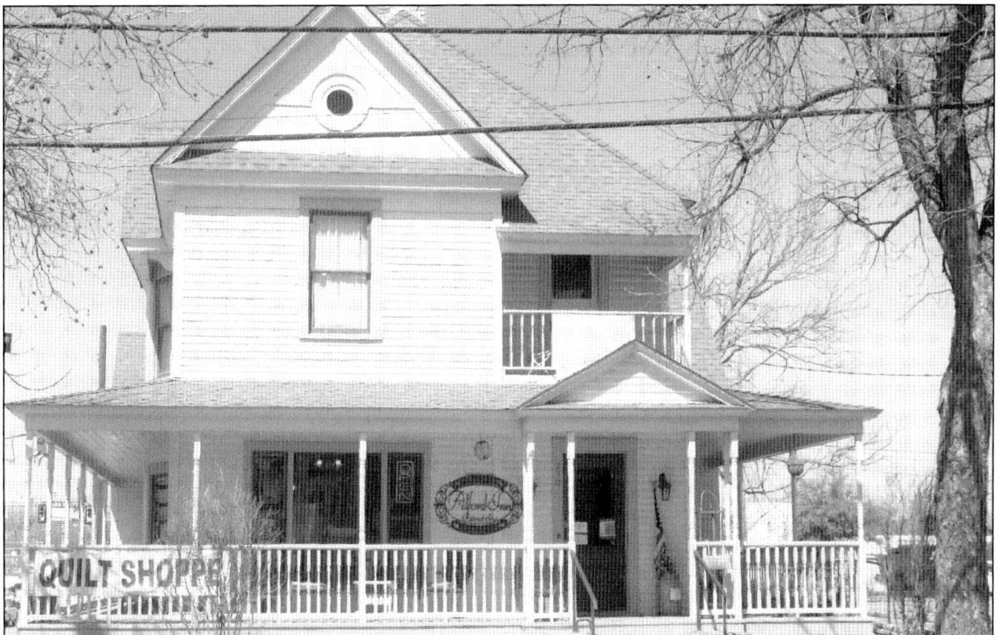

One of the many Victorian houses that still serves the community is this fine 1884 structure. It is now home to the Quilt Shoppe, which stands across the street from the First Baptist Church. (Photograph by the author.)

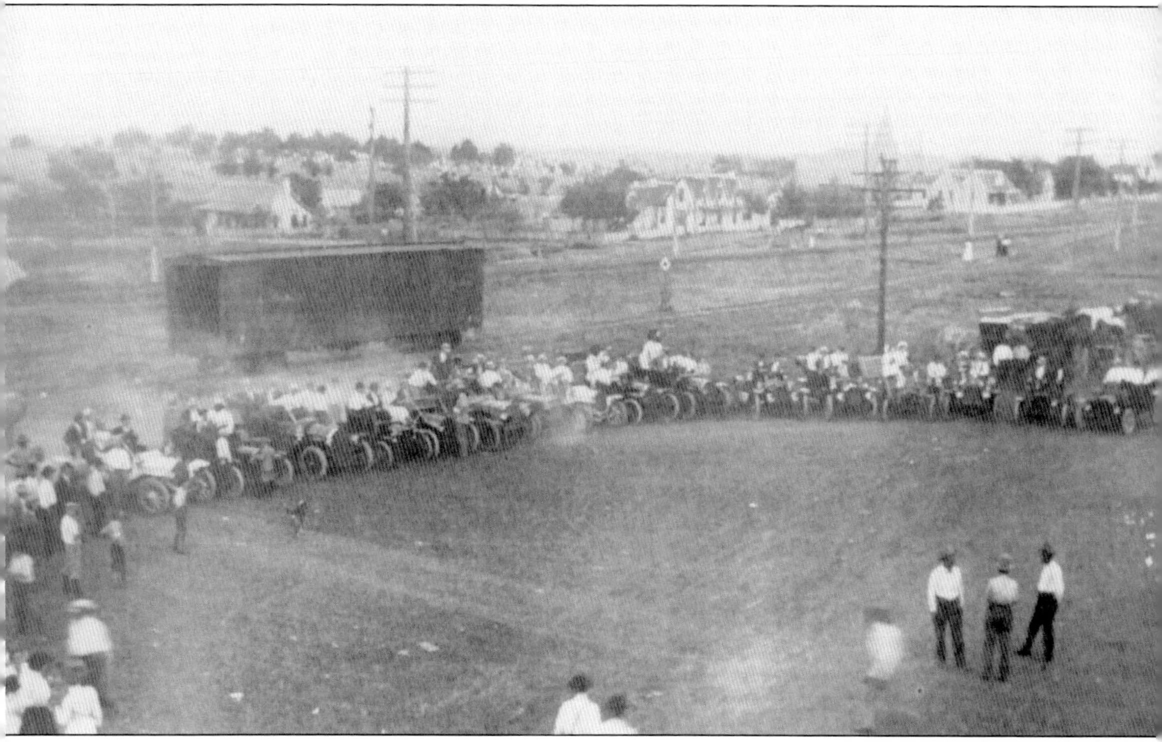

The population of Van Alstyne was close to 3,000 in 1910, when the community's automobile owners drove to an open area just east of downtown at the corner of Marshall and West Main Streets. These 16 automobiles were carefully parked beside each other. This view is toward the southeast, with the cemetery visible to the left of center and the Presbyterian church to the right of center. In the previous year, Henry Ford began producing his inexpensive Model T, and soon there would be far more than 16 automobiles in Van Alstyne. The Victorian era was ending, and a more modern America lay ahead. (Courtesy of Van Alstyne Historical Society.)

Four

THAT OLD TIME RELIGION

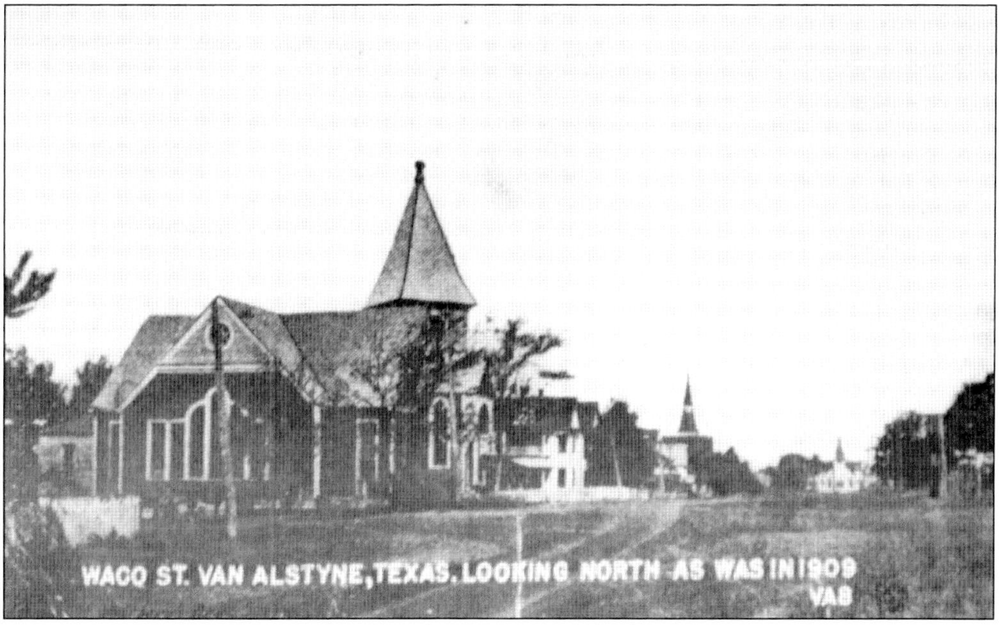

Waco Street boasted three frame churches in 1909, all built within a few years of each other during the 1890s. The First Christian Church is prominent in the foreground on the west side of Waco Street. A block to the north is the steeple of First Methodist Church. The Baptists erected a building at the north end of Waco Street facing south, and the steeple can be seen in the distance. (Courtesy of Griff Servati.)

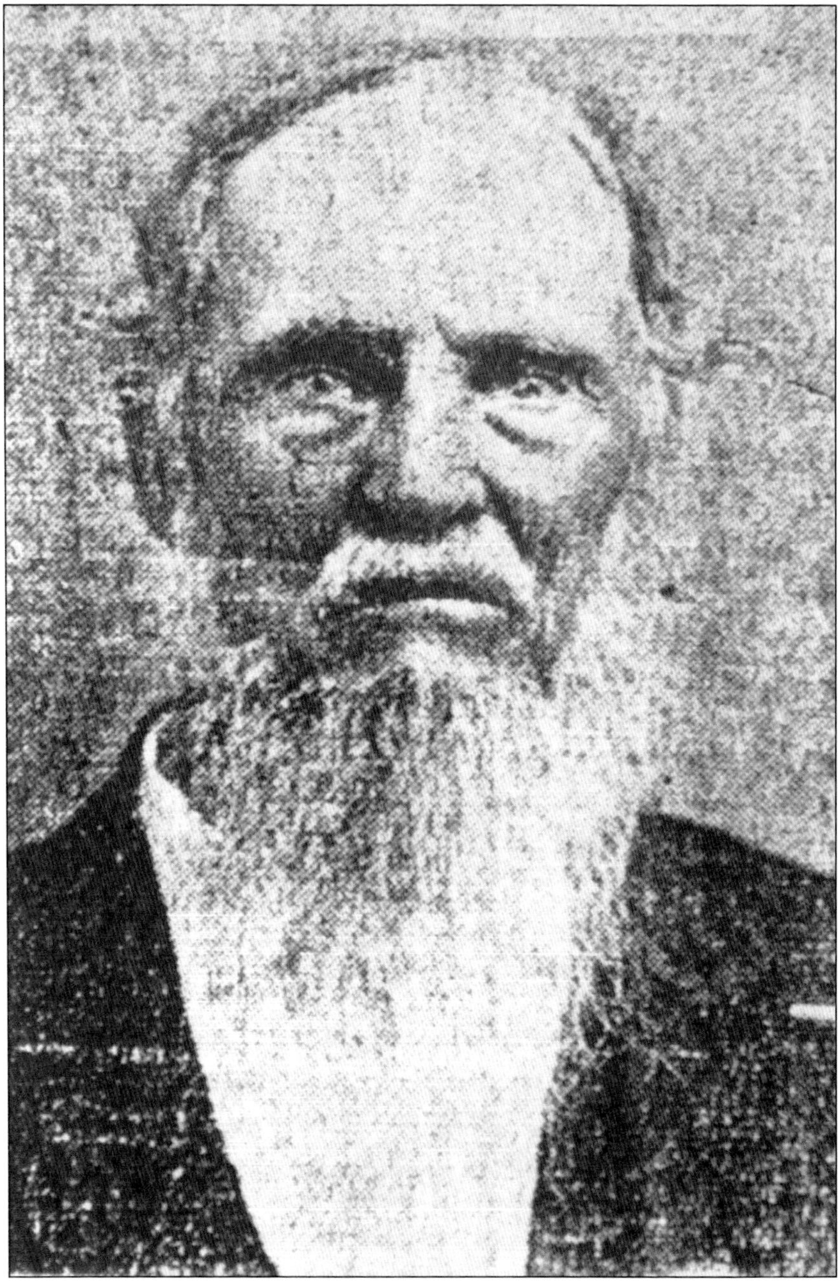

Methodist missionaries came to Texas immediately after independence from Mexico was achieved. Methodists founded churches, organized circuits, and formed Sunday schools. Soon there were more than 200 circuit riders, including Joab Biggs, who was in charge of the Dallas Methodist circuit. Biggs founded the Old Liberty Class in 1847 in a log cabin less than two miles south of the future townsite of Van Alstyne. In 1855, Rev. Y.S. McKinney conducted a "protracted meeting" for three weeks, resulting in 60 conversions. Two years later, the growing band of Methodists relocated to Mantua, a couple of miles to the west, erecting a frame building and changing their name to the Mount Zion Class. Rev. Y.S. McKinney, pictured above, was assigned a four-county circuit, which included his class in Mantua. (Courtesy of First Methodist Church.)

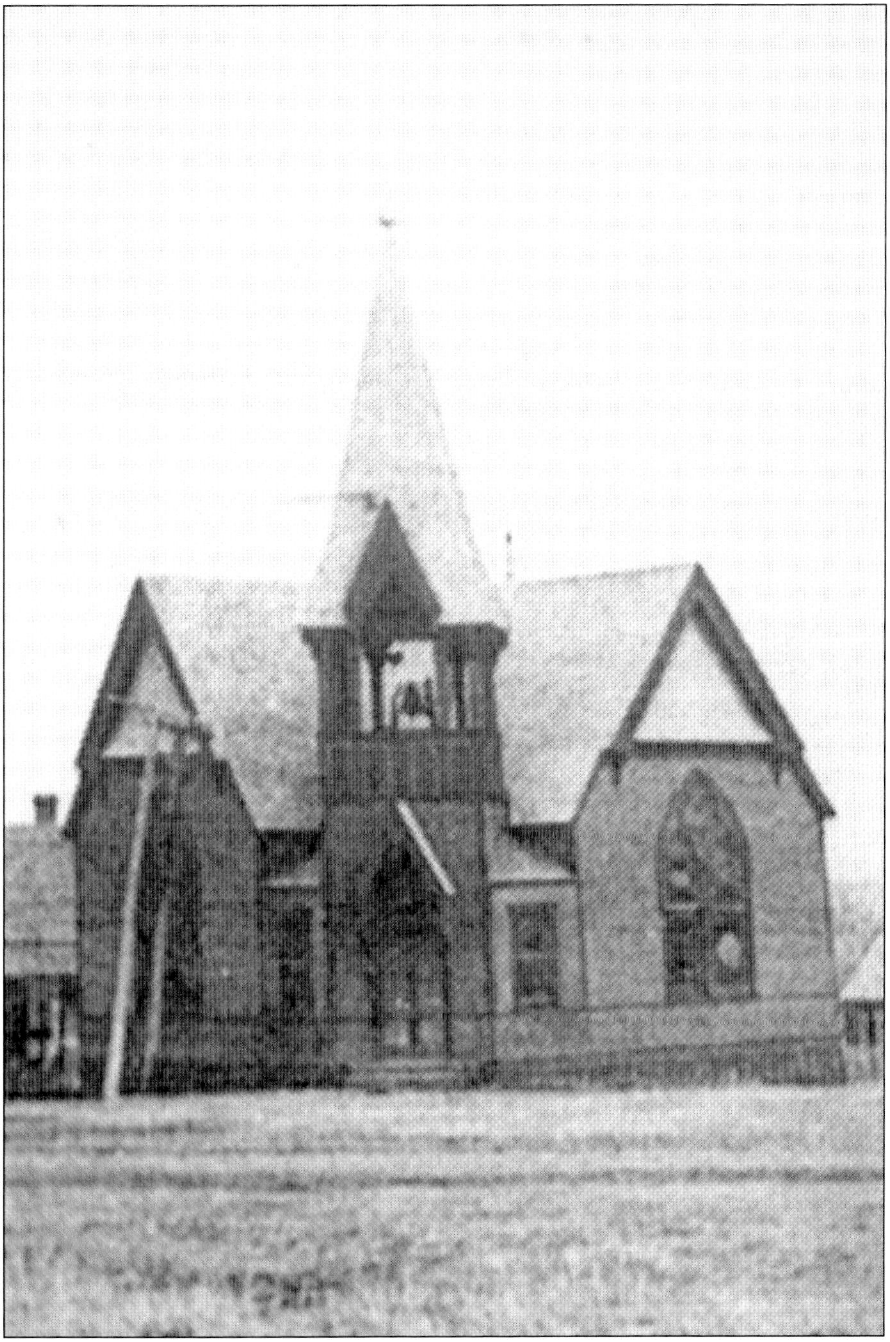

The Methodist congregation became part of the exodus from Mantua to Van Alstyne. The frame church was dismantled and materials were used in the new building in the east part of Van Alstyne, where the cemetery would grow on what had been McKinney property. The steepled frame church shown above became the home of a growing congregation, which numbered 400 by 1890. The congregation decided to move west of the railroad, to property at the corner of Waco and Jefferson Streets. Another steepled building was erected there in 1893, and the congregation was granted status as the Van Alstyne Methodist Church. (Courtesy of Van Alstyne Historical Society.)

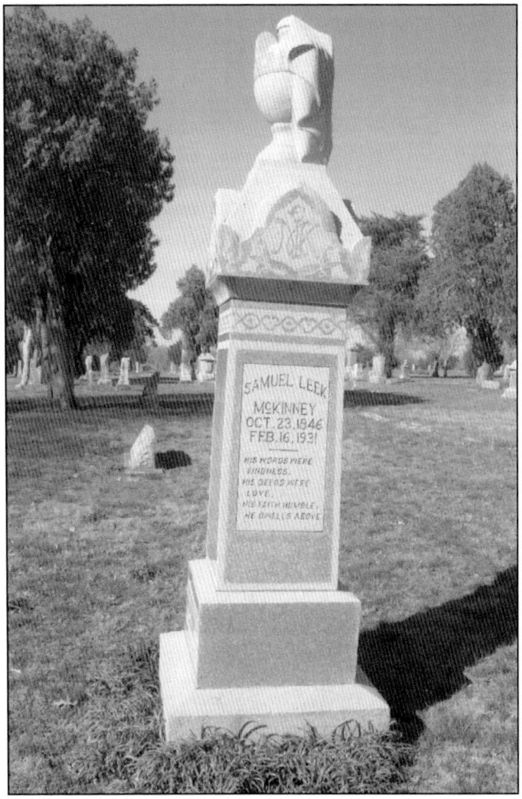

By 1880, S.L. McKinney was church treasurer, a position he held for more than half a century until his death in 1931. (Courtesy of First Methodist Church.)

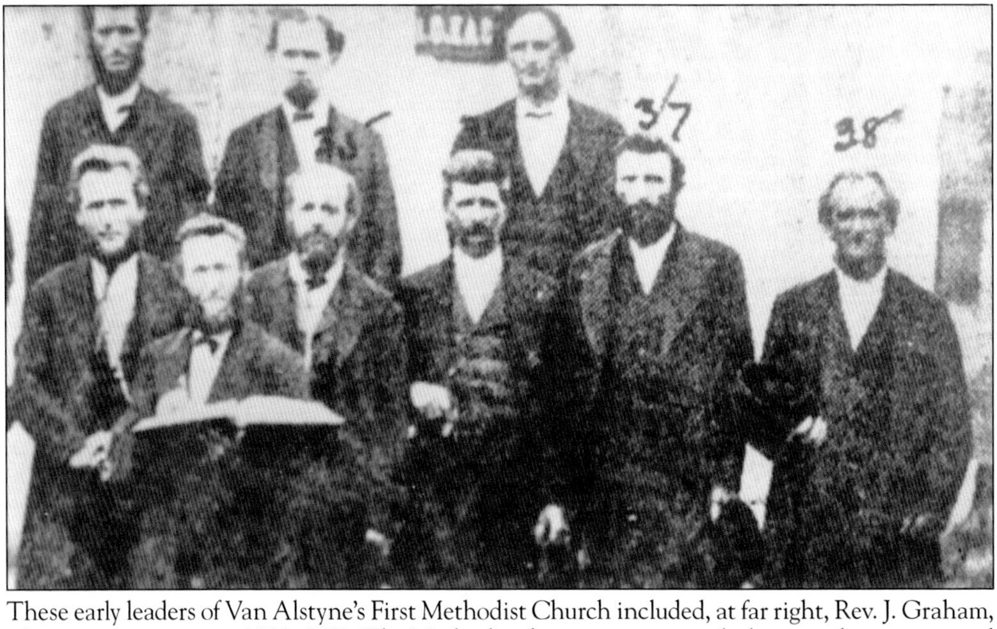

These early leaders of Van Alstyne's First Methodist Church included, at far right, Rev. J. Graham, who served as pastor in 1880–1881. The Methodist denomination regularly rotated ministers, and for the first several decades of its existence, First Methodist Church experienced pastoral changes every year or two. The church had little continuity of leadership but enjoyed considerable variety. (Courtesy of First Methodist Church.)

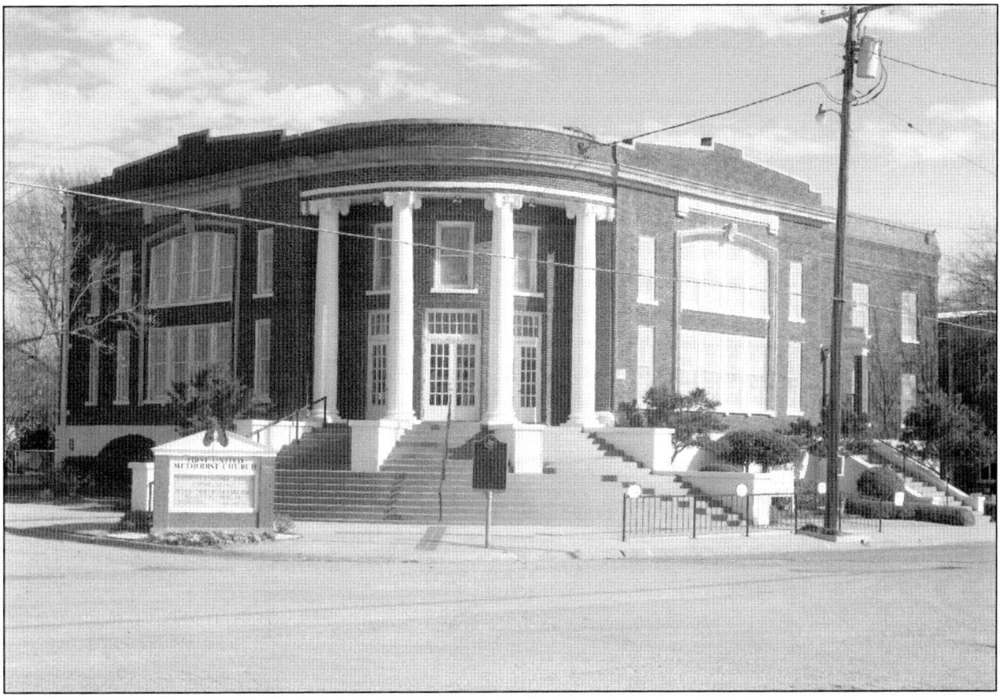

As Van Alstyne's first church continued to thrive, the congregation decided to erect a brick house of worship. Lots were acquired at the corner of Preston and Fulton Streets in 1914, and by 1917, a handsome redbrick edifice was completed at the cost of $50,000. The entrance featured striking white columns and steps. (Photograph by the author.)

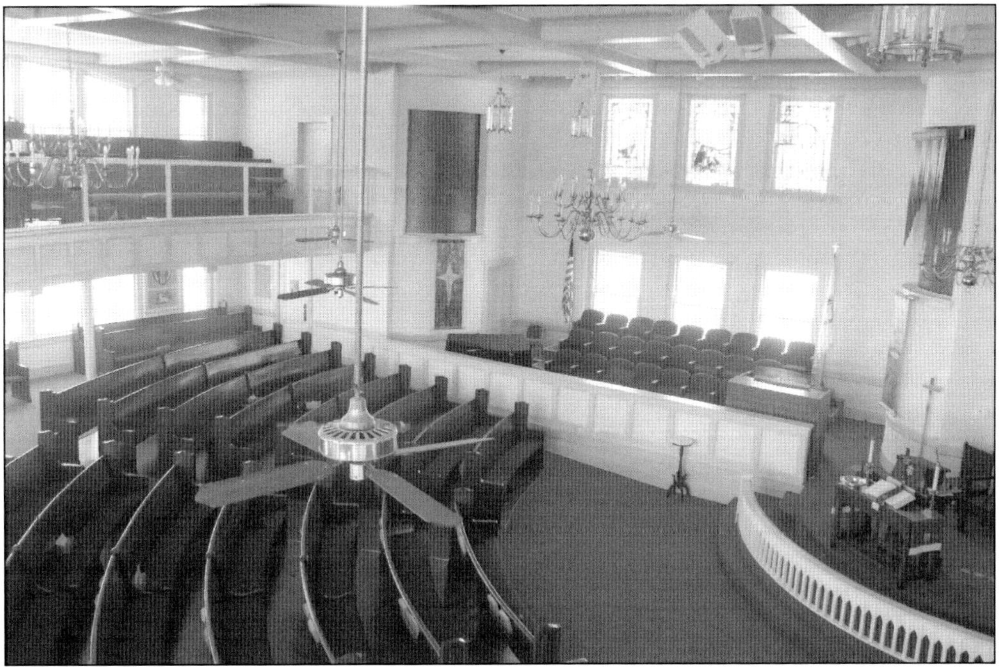

The auditorium offered a fan-shaped seating arrangement, along with a balcony. Van Alstyne High School often conducted traditional baccalaureate services here. (Photograph by the author.)

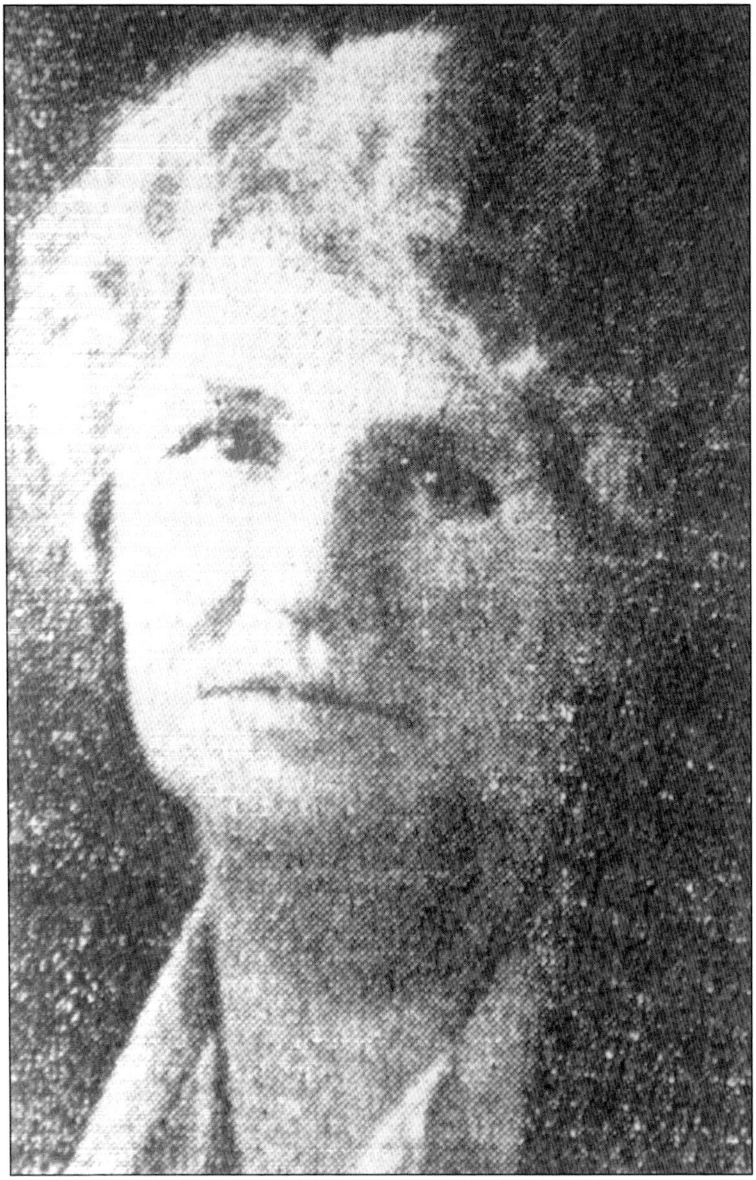

In 1894, Mrs. J.D.L. McKinney became the first president of the newly organized Women's Parsonage and Home Mission Society. Her husband served as chairman of the board of stewards for 42 years. (Courtesy of First Methodist Church.)

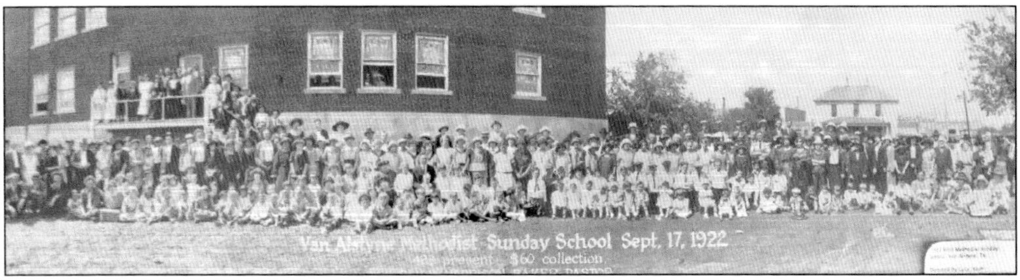

On September 17, 1922, Sunday School attendance totaled 423, with a collection of $60 (most children in the 1920s could only contribute pennies, a nickel, or a dime). This vast crowd assembled at the rear of the church for a panoramic photograph. (Courtesy of First Methodist Church.)

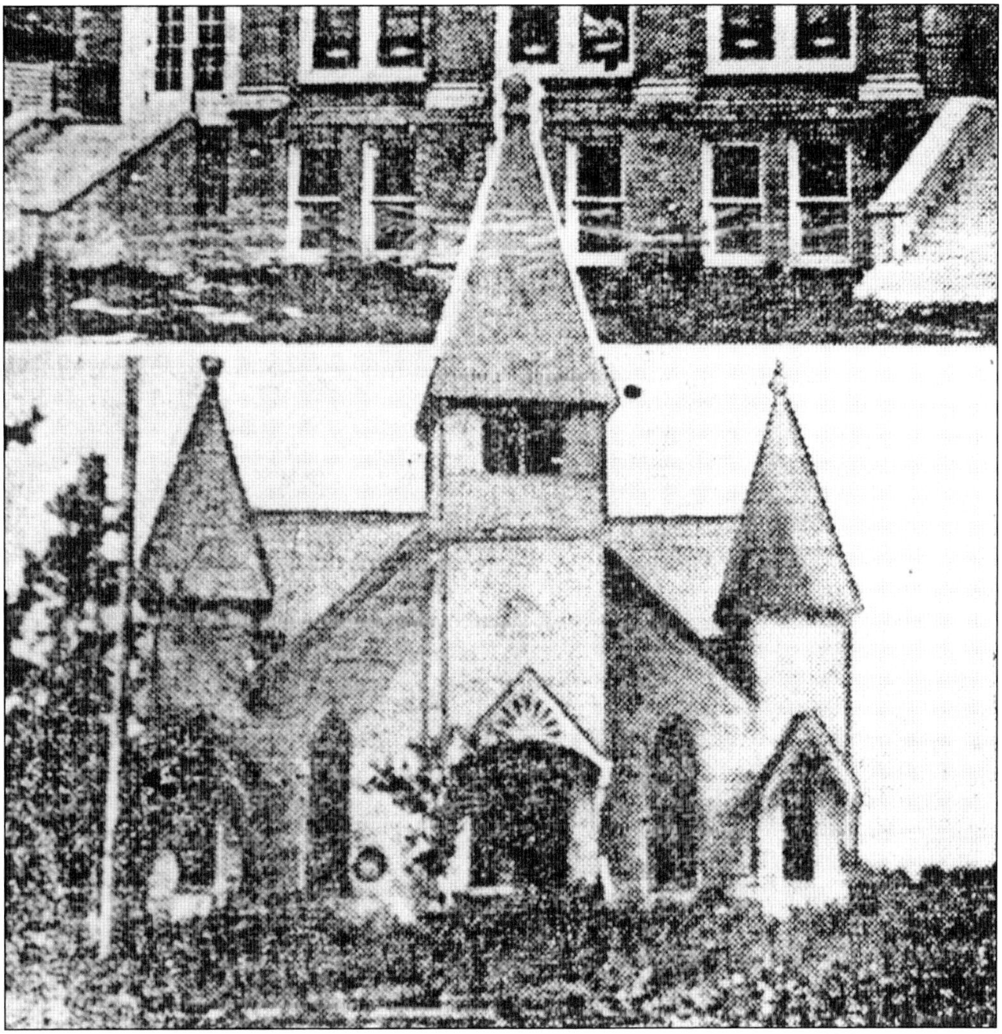

By 1870, shortly before the founding of Van Alstyne, there were 843 churches of all denominations in Texas, with a total of 200,000 members. While Methodists had the largest denomination, Baptists were growing rapidly and by the turn of the century would total more than one-third of all Texas churchgoers. In early Van Alstyne, Baptists met in private homes and even under a tent. In 1882, eight charter members organized the First Baptist Church. A one-room frame house of worship was erected in 1884 on donated land one block east of the railroad. In 1896, a greatly expanded congregation moved to the head of Waco Street, using materials from the original building to erect a frame Victorian church with an impressive steeple flanked by two spires. (Courtesy of Griff Servati.)

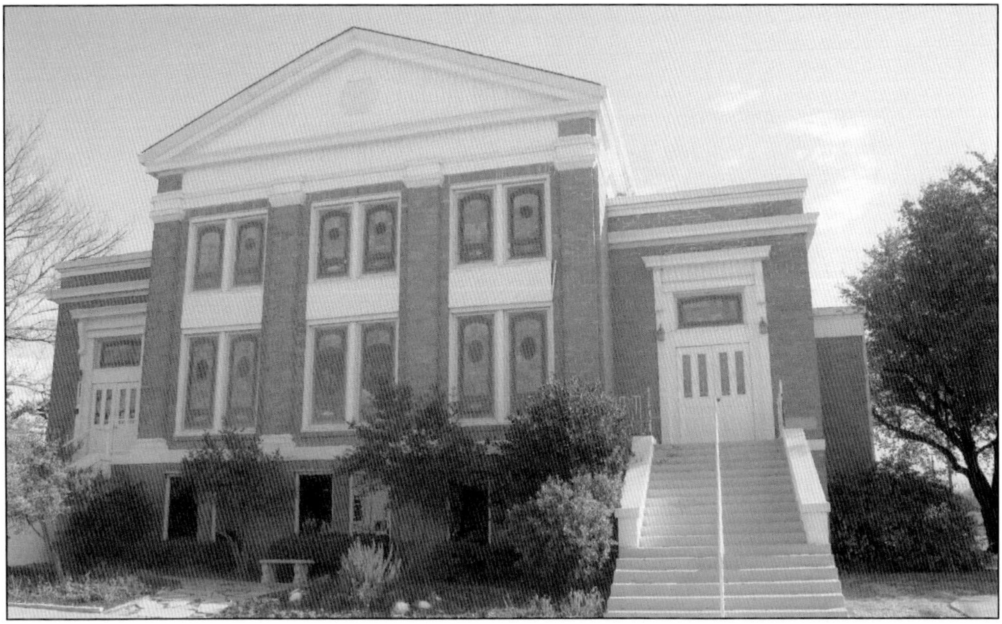

During the second decade of the 20th century, handsome new brick churches were built by the Disciples of Christ (1914) and the Methodists (1917). Baptists soon erected their own brick house of worship. Local grocer C.E. Carter donated property at the corner of Waco and Marshall Streets, a few blocks south of the 1896 church. Construction began in 1919 and was completed at a cost of $35,000. (Courtesy of Griff Servati.)

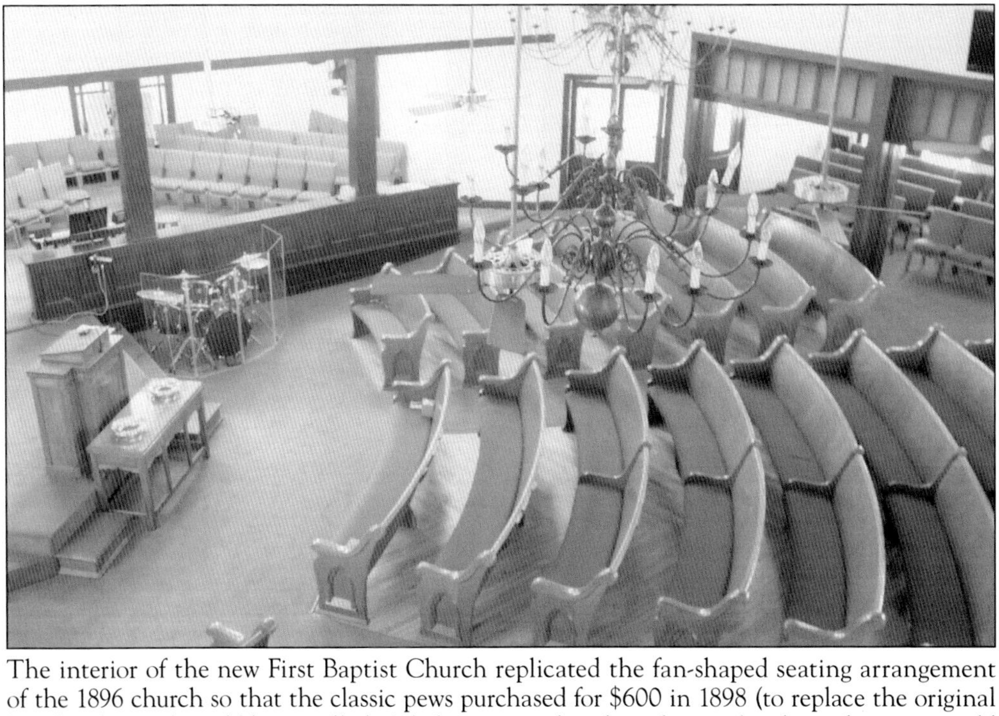

The interior of the new First Baptist Church replicated the fan-shaped seating arrangement of the 1896 church so that the classic pews purchased for $600 in 1898 (to replace the original handmade pews) could be installed. A balcony was placed on the north side, and seating could comfortably accommodate 350 worshippers. (Photograph by the author.)

The First Baptist Church was dedicated by Dr. Frank S. Groner, a towering figure among Texas Baptists. Born on a Collin County farm, Groner gave up a career as an attorney and politician to answer a call to preach. A highly successful pastor, Dr. Groner was appointed executive head of the Baptist General Convention of Texas in 1918. It was in this capacity that Dr. Groner shared a day of dedication in Van Alstyne. (Courtesy of East Texas Baptist University.)

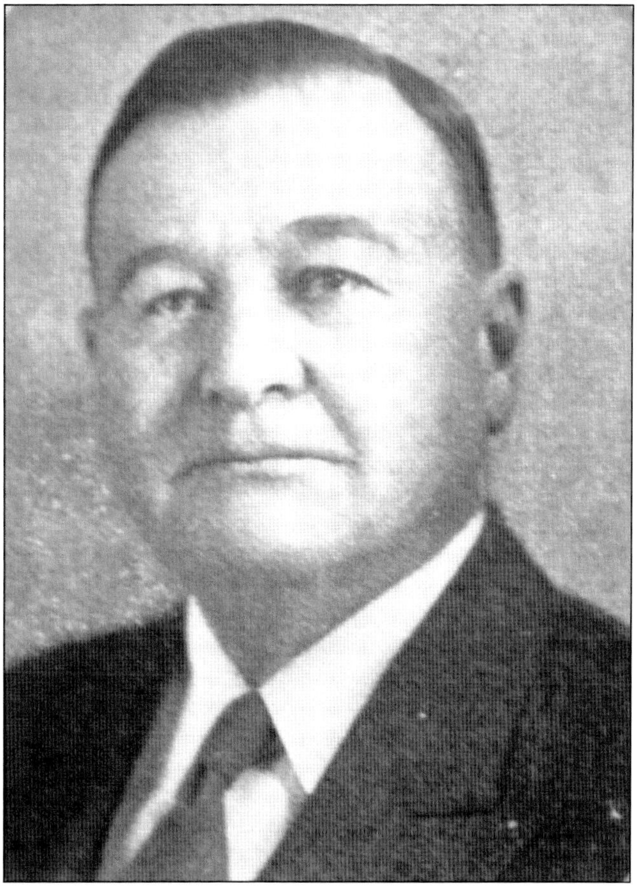

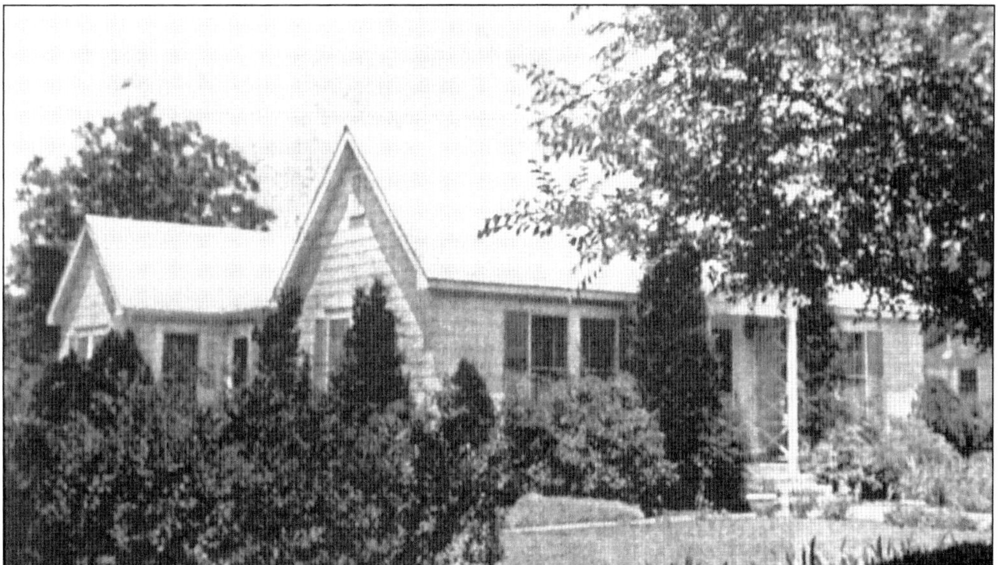

For a number of years, First Baptist Church pastors lived in this parsonage. (Courtesy of First Baptist Church.)

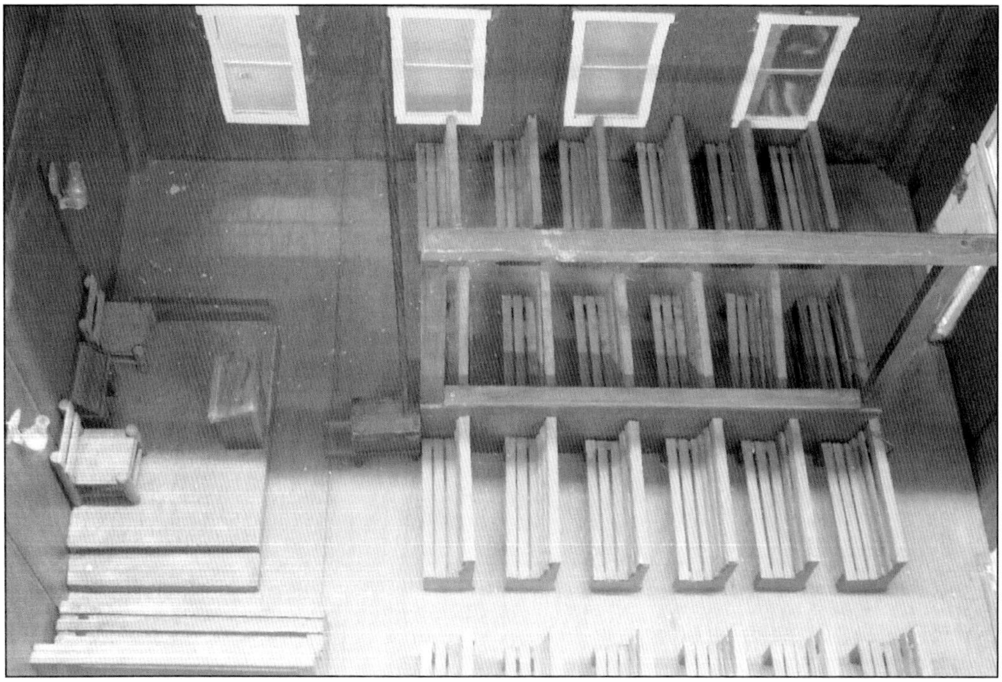

Collin McKinney was instrumental in organizing the oldest Disciples of Christ congregation in Texas. In 1841, worshippers began meeting at McKinney's Landing on the Texas-Arkansas border. Five years later, McKinney reorganized 18 believers at his new home (at the future townsite of Van Alstyne). Within a few years, there were nearly 70 members, and in 1850, the Liberty Church began meeting in the log structure that doubled as the Liberty (Mantua) School. In 1854, a building was erected to house the renamed Mantua Christian Church. Russell Haun's detailed model is on display at the Van Alstyne Historical Museum. A larger frame church, shown below, was built in 1871 for the thriving congregation. But Mantua soon began to dry up, and in 1887, the congregation voted to move to Van Alstyne. (Above, photograph by the author; below, courtesy of First Christian Church.)

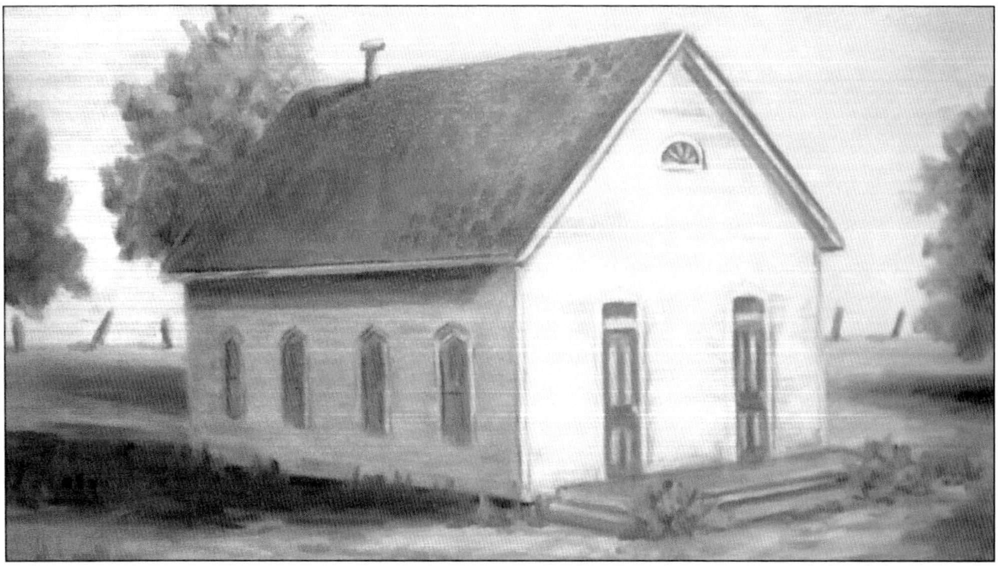

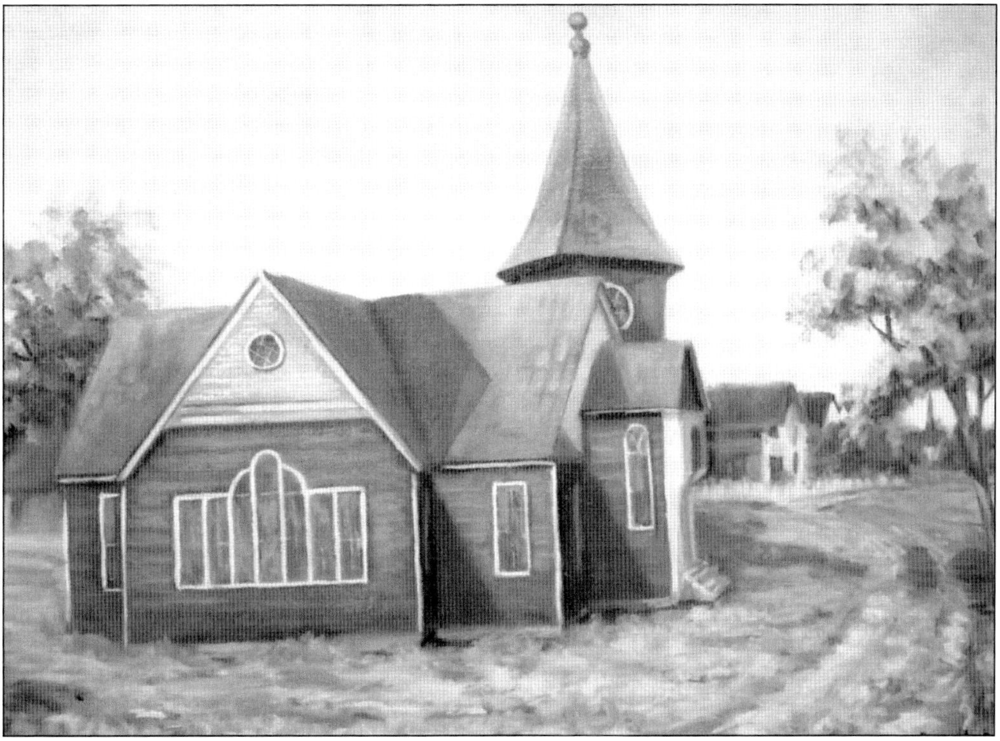

The Disciples of Christ purchased lots in 1887, and late the following year, the Van Alstyne Christian Church occupied a new steepled building. The lots cost $100, and $1,400 was spent on the building. Within a decade, the church faced debt problems, but a resourceful set of deaconesses rapidly raised the needed funds. (Courtesy of Van Alstyne Historical Society.)

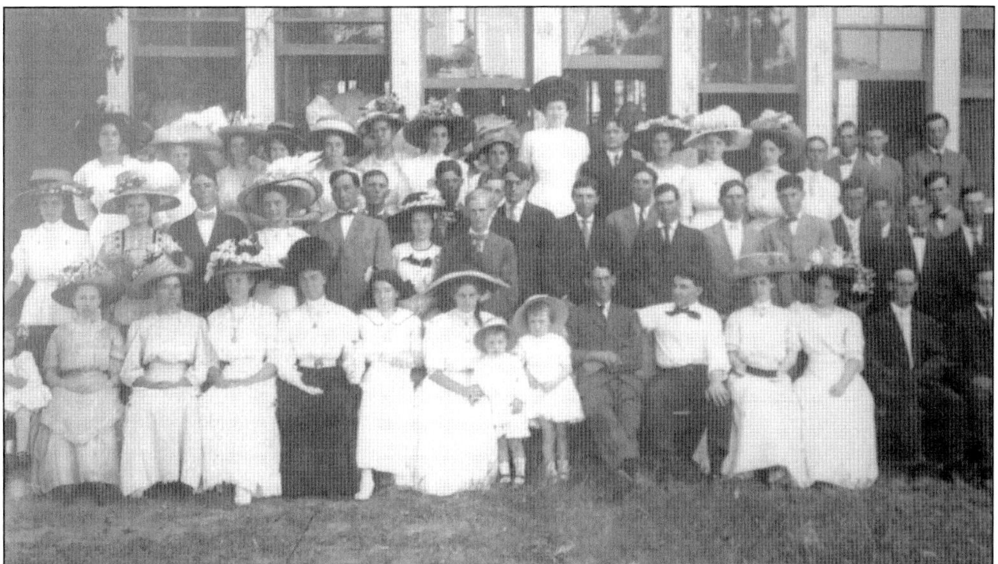

This image was labeled "Mrs. Fay Moore's Sunday School Class, September 1910." (Courtesy of First Christian Church.)

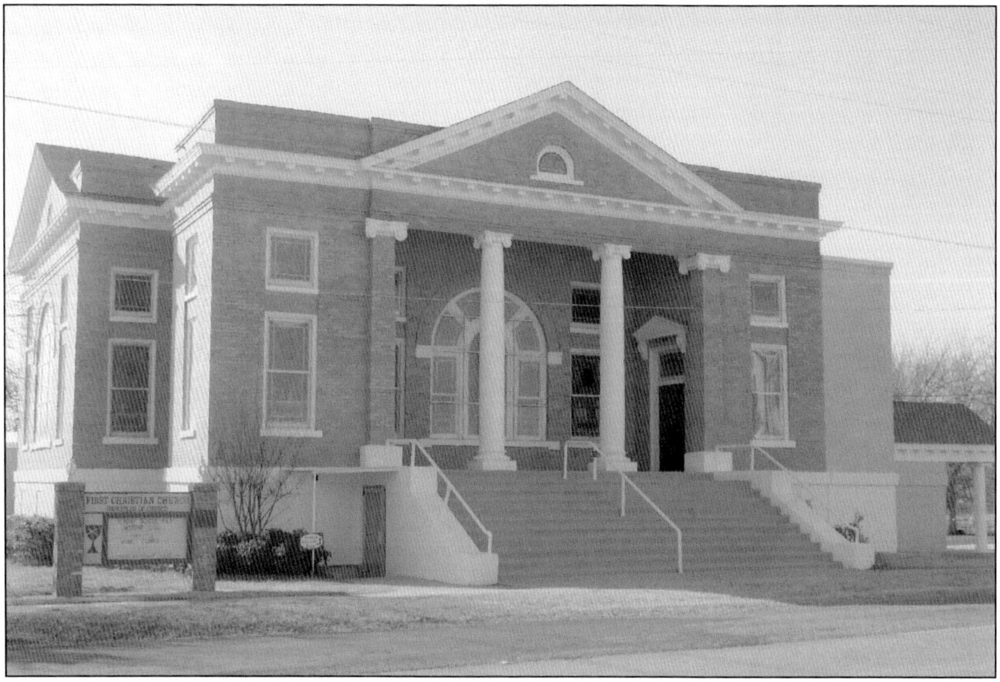

Rev. E.H. Holmes led the movement for a new brick house of worship, which was begun in 1914. This classic church building was completely paid off within five years and has now housed the oldest Disciples of Christ congregation in Texas for nearly a century. (Photograph by the author.)

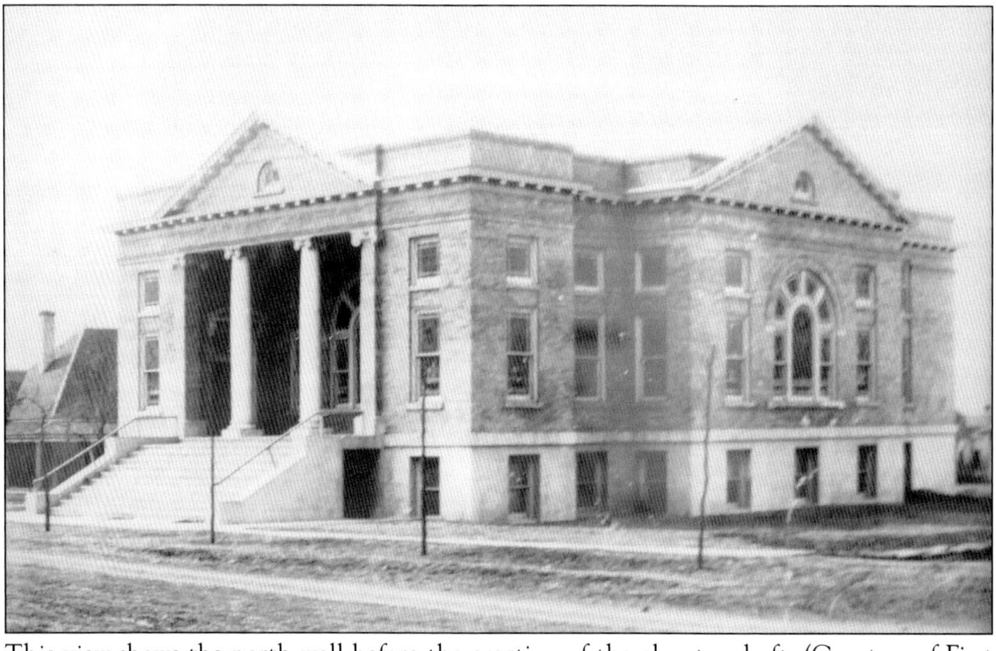

This view shows the north wall before the erection of the elevator shaft. (Courtesy of First Christian Church.)

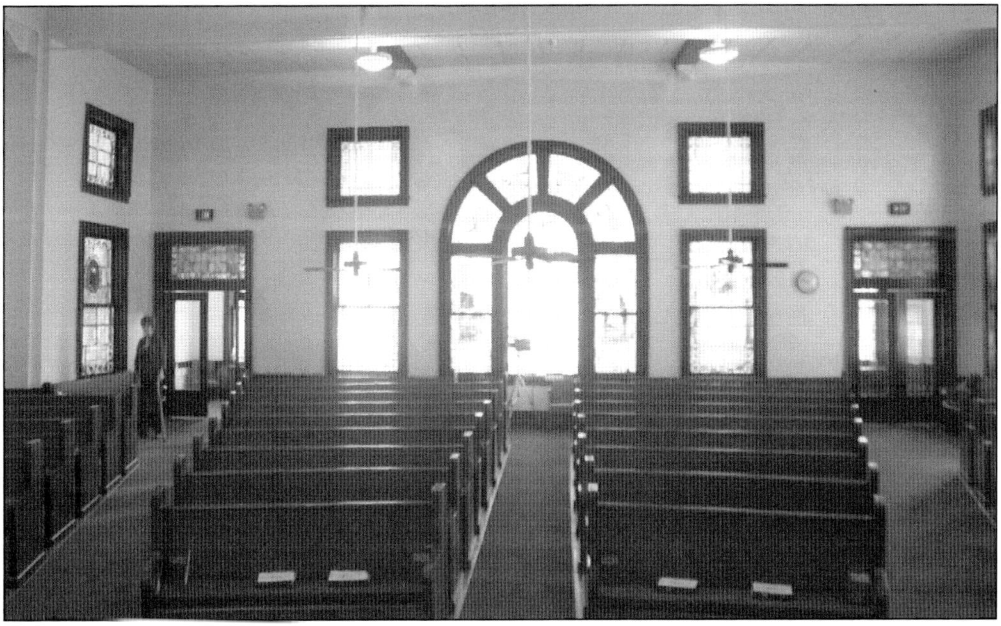

This auditorium was packed to overflowing on Sunday, November 2, 1923, during a grand reunion that was perhaps the most memorable day in the history of the Van Alstyne Christian Church. Sunday school attendance was a record 449, and during the worship hour, the crowd could not all fit into the auditorium. Following a barbeque dinner on the church lawn, the crowd returned inside for a "Reminiscence Meeting." (Photograph by the author.)

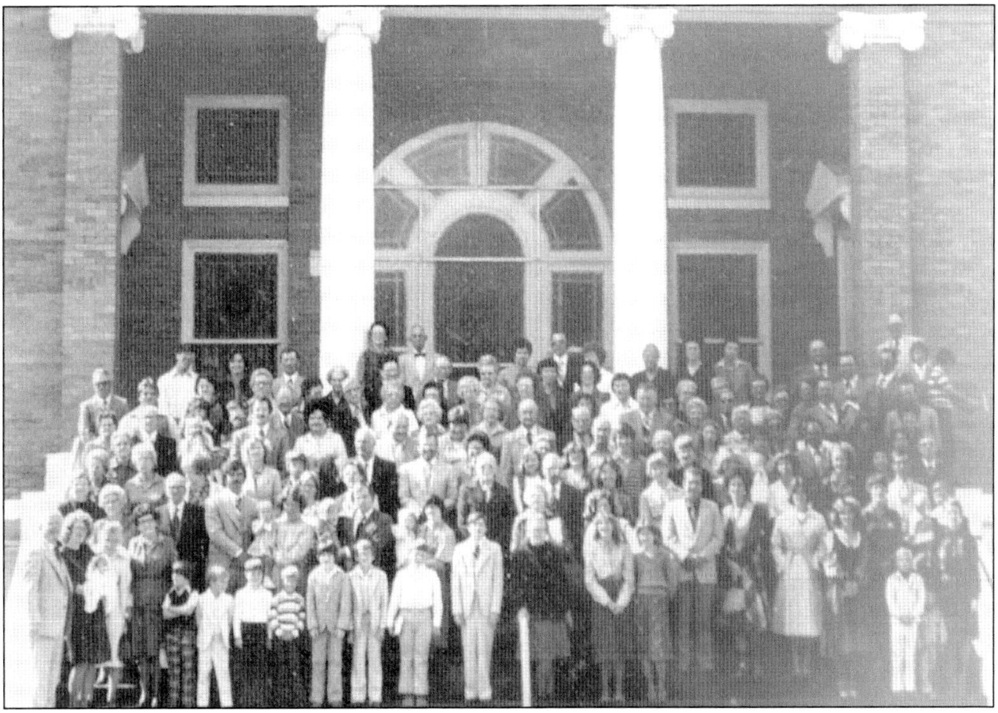

On other banner Sundays through the years, the congregation briefly posed on the front steps. (Courtesy of First Christian Church.)

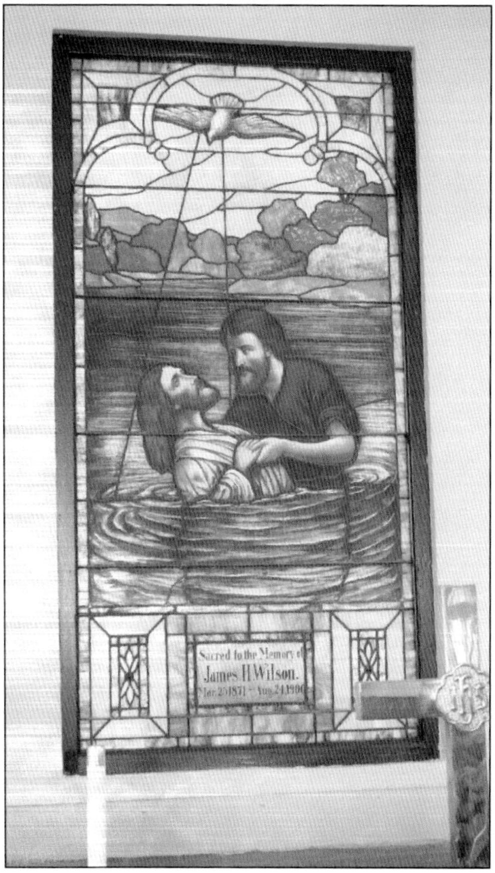

The stained glass windows of the church are numerous and beautiful. At left, the baptistry features the baptism of Jesus by John the Baptist. The focus of the window below is Elder R.C. Horn, a stalwart of the early church. (Both photographs by the author.)

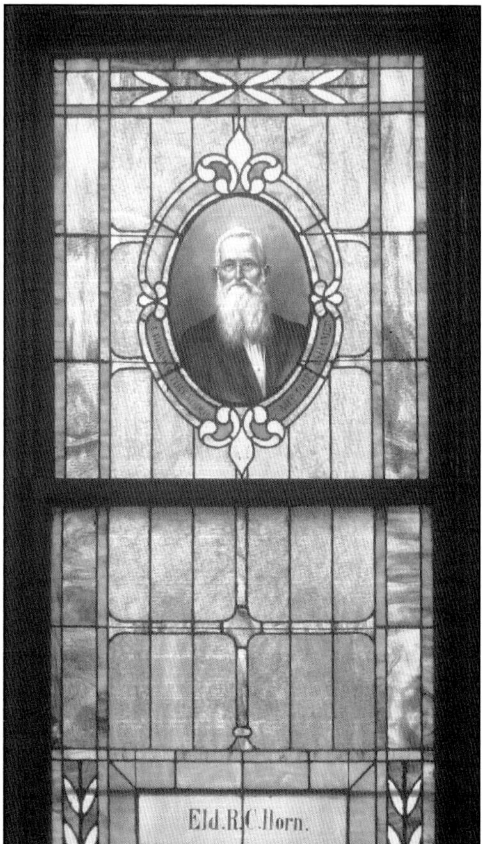

Van Alstyne native Rev. Lloyd Motley was a beloved pastor who led the church for several years before World War II, served as a chaplain during the war, then returned to his Van Alstyne pastorate after the war. (Courtesy of First Christian Church.)

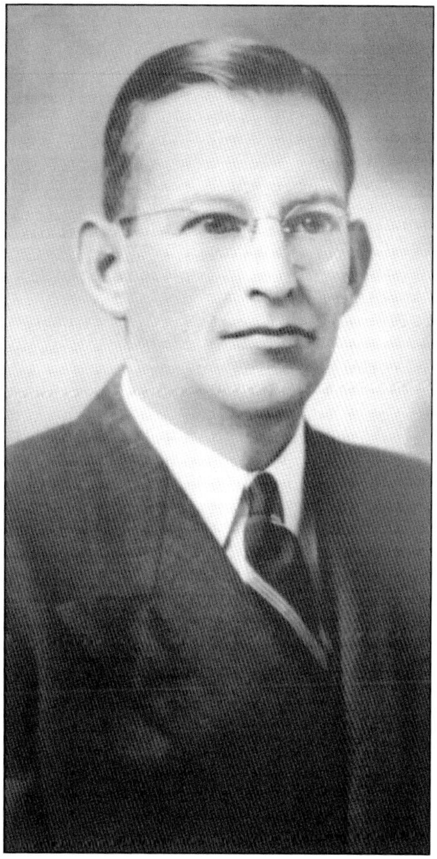

For many years, the First Christian parsonage stood west of the church, until replaced by a new residence. The old parsonage was sold and moved a few blocks to the west. (Photograph by the author.)

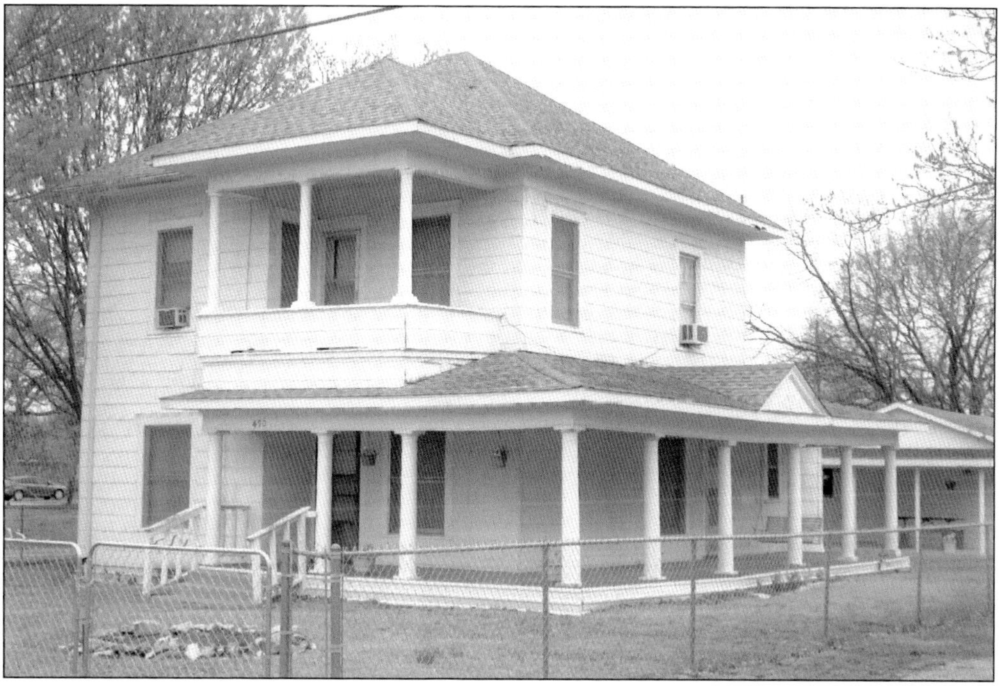

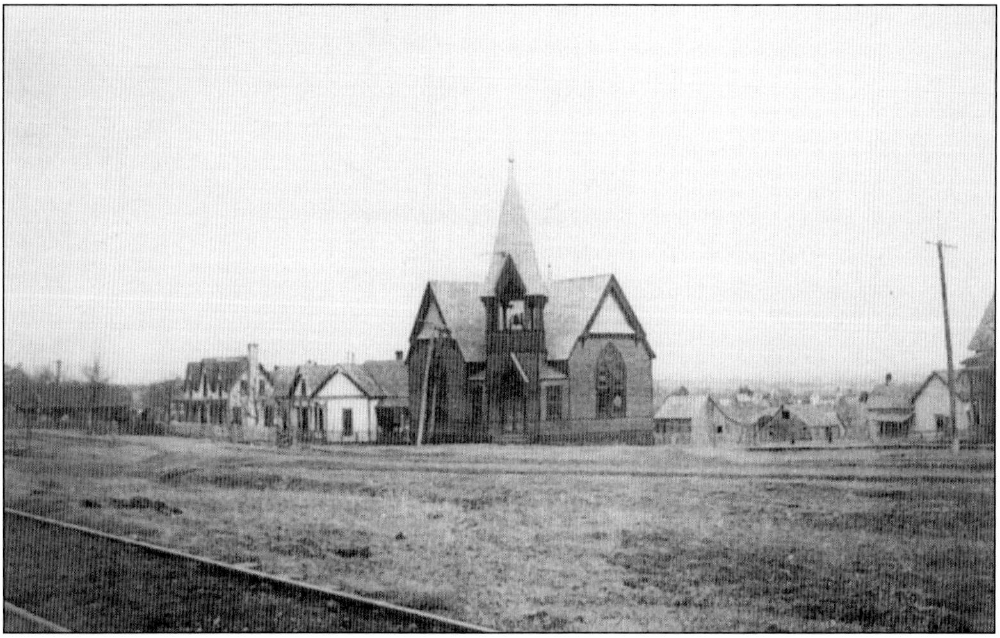

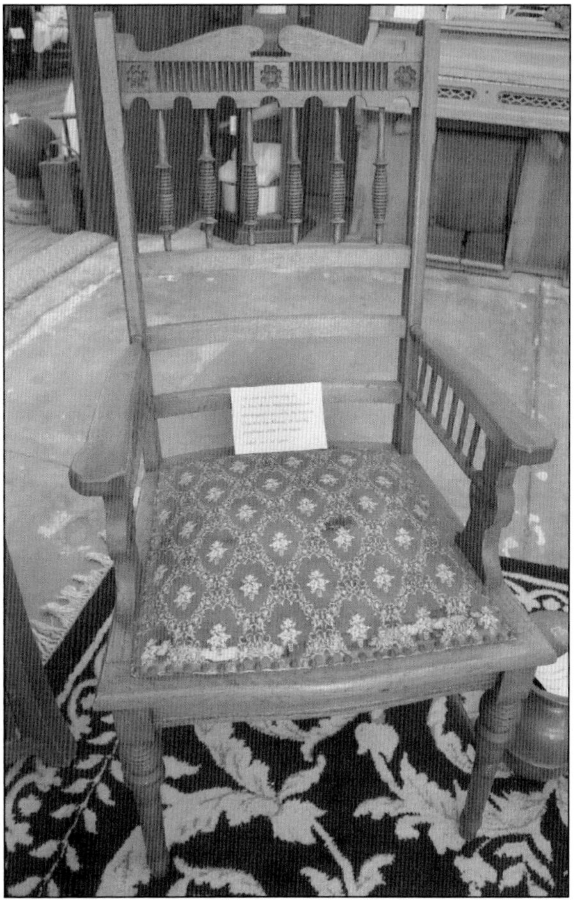

A growing band of Presbyterians purchased the Methodist church at the edge of the cemetery after the Methodists erected a new building west of the tracks in 1893. The Presbyterians moved their church to South West Main Street, where they flourished for more than two decades. A period of decline in the 20th century led to disbandment. (Courtesy of Van Alstyne Historical Society.)

This chair was used in the study of Dr. John Moore, who frequently served the Presbyterian church. Today, the chair is on display in the Van Alstyne Historical Museum. (Photograph by the author.)

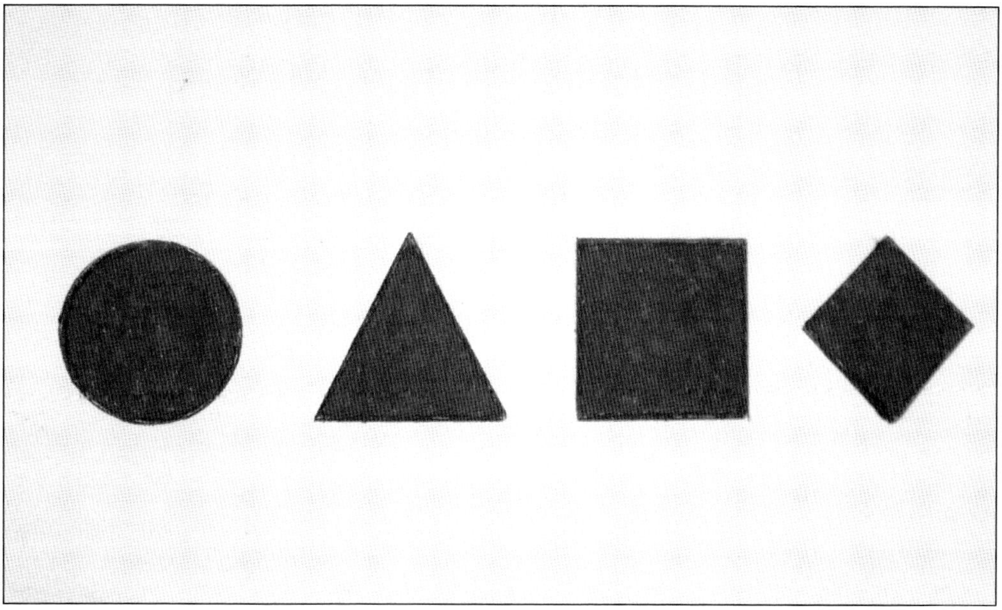

Church music was predominantly Southern gospel, hymns reflecting power and emotion. Four basic shapes produced shape note music, a simplified form of music that could readily be taught to congregations. Publishing companies printed inexpensive paperback hymnals and sheet music. Company representatives provided special music at church services and, following dinner-on-the-grounds, conducted workshops to teach shape note music. The church would purchase sheet music and a set of hymnals. Individuals also would buy hymnals and sheet music for home use, because a favorite family entertainment was to gather around the parlor piano or pump organ and sing hymns or popular songs. (Both photographs by the author.)

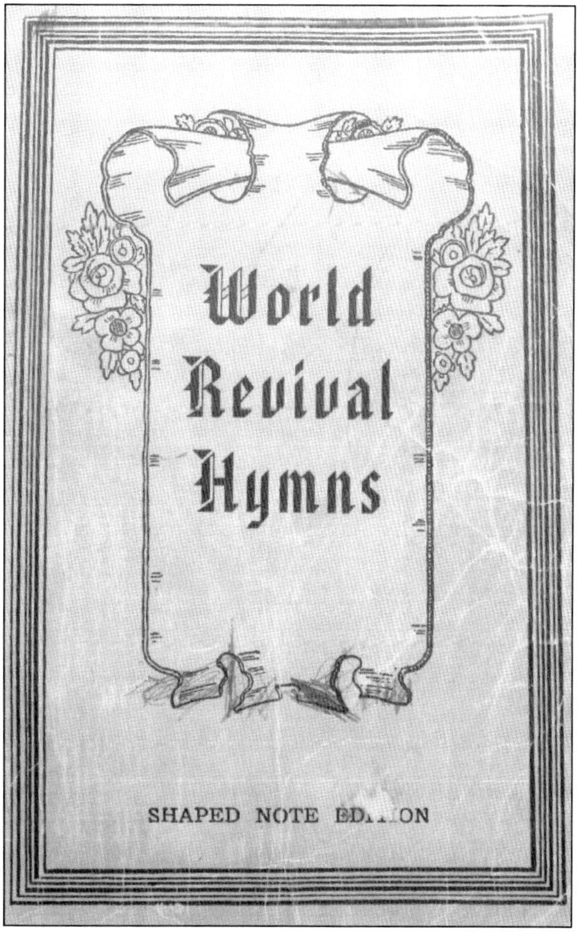

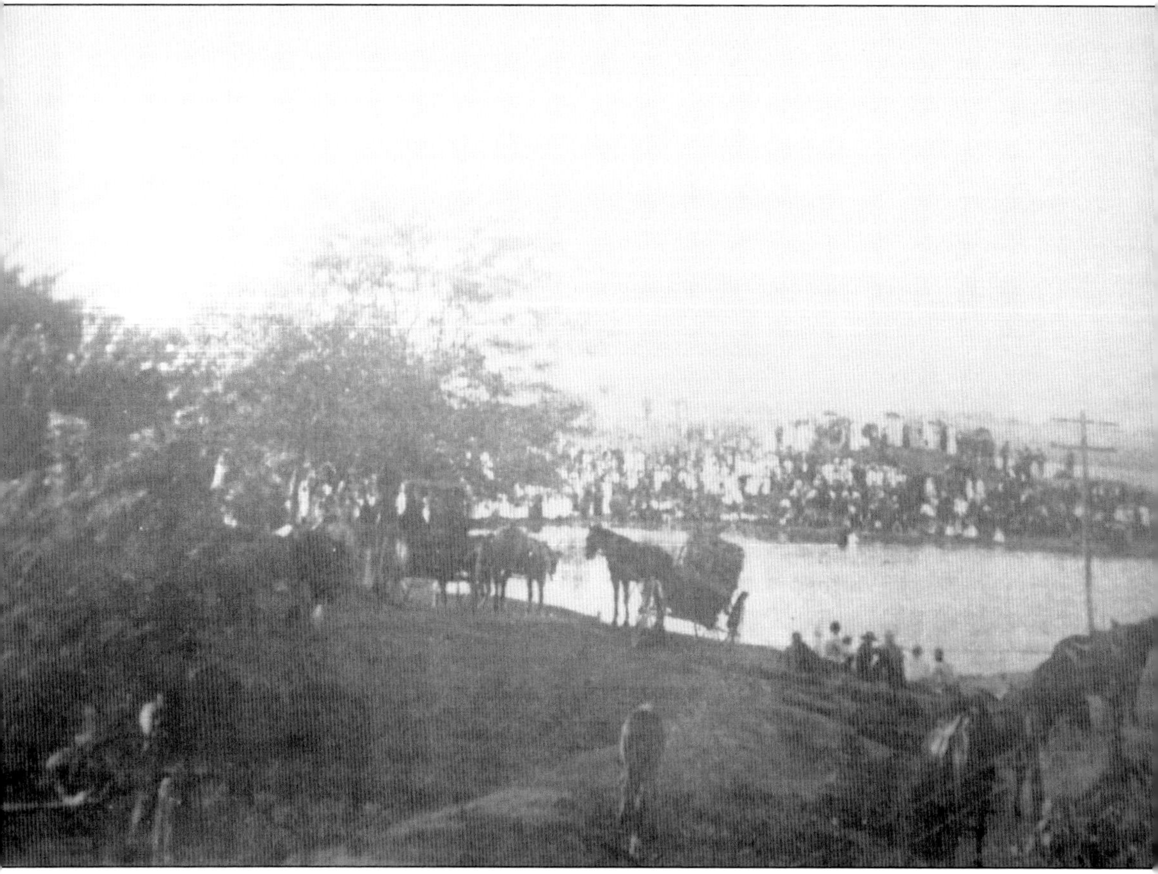

Following a revival, or "protracted meeting," the children and adults who had been converted were baptized at a nearby pond, always before a large and appreciative crowd. (Courtesy of Van Alstyne Historical Society.)

Five

School Days

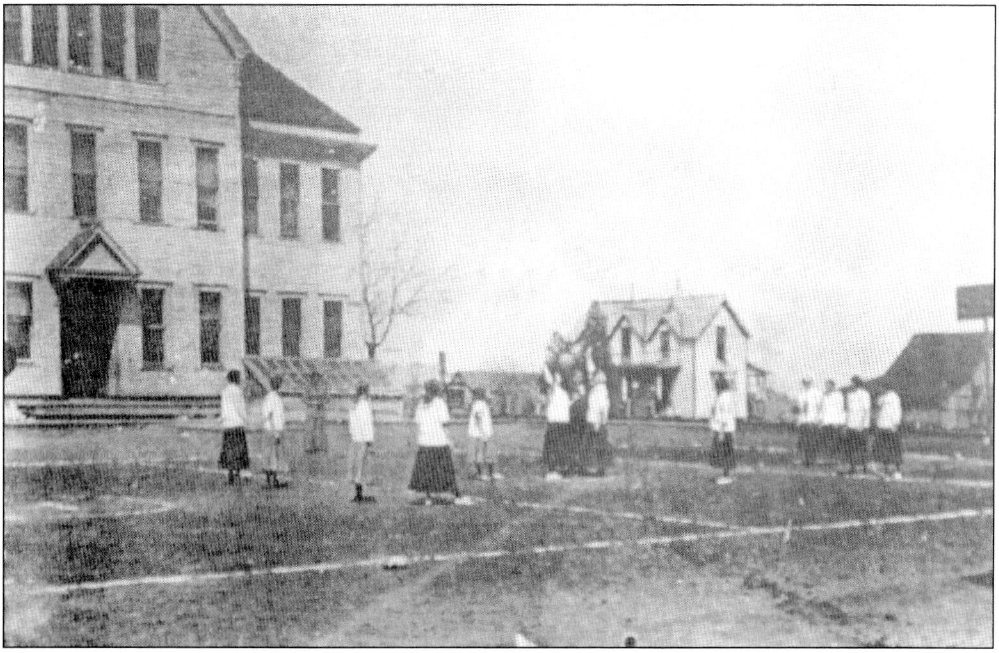

When Van Alstyne was founded, there were few public schools in Texas. Most education was provided by private schools, often housed in one-room buildings and taught by schoolmarms or male professors. Such hit-and-miss education was all that was available in early Van Alstyne until 1889. City leaders and landowners who lived near town formed the Columbia College Association, and $4,000 was raised by selling stock for $25 per share. In July 1890, forty-six acres in the northwest section of town were purchased for $3,750. Funds were raised by selling lots, but four acres were reserved for the college campus. A three-story frame building was erected beside Third Street (now Denton Drive), facing east. There were eight large rooms, including an auditorium with a stage. A dormitory was built north of the main building across Baldwin Street. By the time this photograph was taken in 1913, the old college building was part of the new public school. (Courtesy of Van Alstyne Historical Society.)

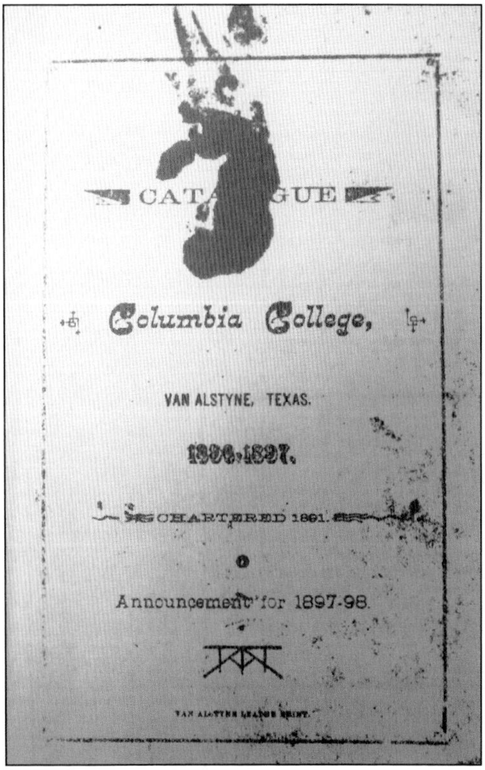
CAT[illegible]GUE

Columbia College,

VAN ALSTYNE, TEXAS.

1896-1897.

CHARTERED 1891.

Announcement for 1897-98.

VAN ALSTYNE LEADER PRINT.

A Columbia College catalogue for the 1896–1897 school year is on display at the Van Alstyne Historical Museum. This invaluable artifact provides a list of faculty members, courses, student members of various departments, student costs, college policies, and numerous other details about the operation of the school. (Courtesy of Van Alstyne Historical Society.)

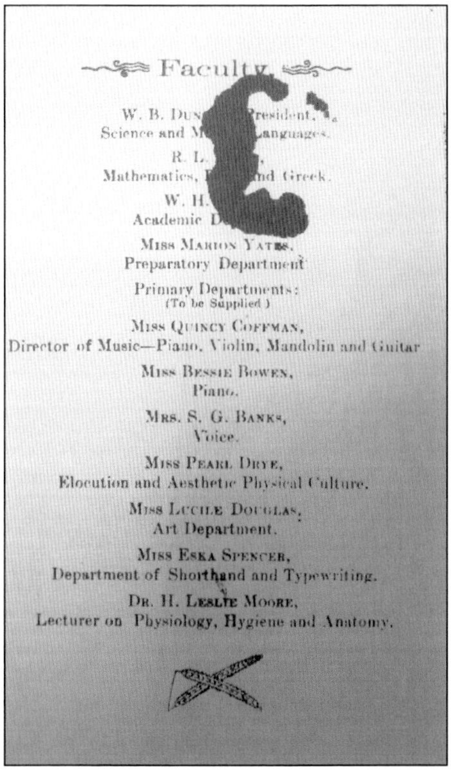
Facult[illegible]

W. B. Dun[illegible] President,
Science and M[illegible] Languages.

R. L. [illegible],
Mathematics, [illegible] and Greek.

W. H. [illegible]
Academic D[illegible]

Miss Marion Yates,
Preparatory Department

Primary Departments:
(To be Supplied.)

Miss Quincy Coffman,
Director of Music—Piano, Violin, Mandolin and Guitar

Miss Bessie Bowen,
Piano.

Mrs. S. G. Banks,
Voice.

Miss Pearl Drye,
Elocution and Aesthetic Physical Culture.

Miss Lucile Douglas,
Art Department.

Miss Eska Spencer,
Department of Shorthand and Typewriting.

Dr. H. Leslie Moore,
Lecturer on Physiology, Hygiene and Anatomy.

Listed in the catalogue are 11 faculty members, along with a Primary Department vacancy "to be supplied." This list reveals the various course offerings. A large smudge mars the top of several pages. (Courtesy of Van Alstyne Historical Society.)

Below the projected calendar is an accreditation statement, dated September 1892, "that Columbia College be affiliated with the University of Texas." (Courtesy of Van Alstyne Historical Society.)

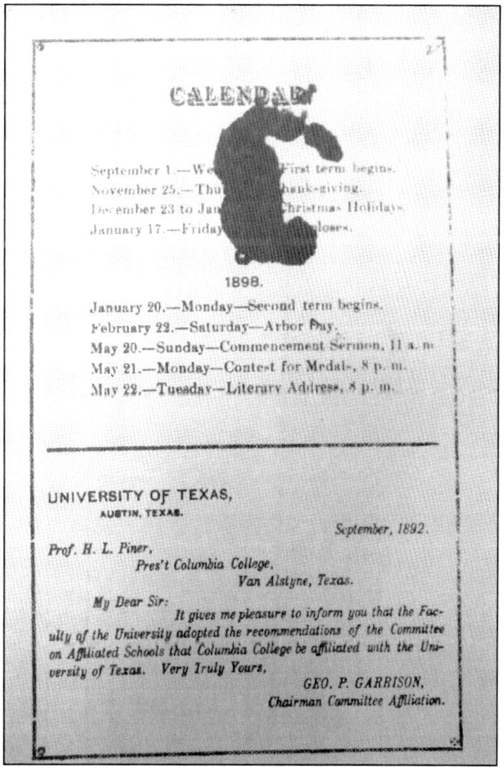

CALENDAR

September 1.—We... First term begins.
November 25.—Thu... hanksgiving.
December 23 to Jan... Christmas Holidays.
January 17.—Friday... loses.

1898.

January 20.—Monday—Second term begins.
February 22.—Saturday—Arbor Day.
May 20.—Sunday—Commencement Sermon, 11 a. m.
May 21.—Monday—Contest for Medals, 8 p. m.
May 22.—Tuesday—Literary Address, 8 p. m.

UNIVERSITY OF TEXAS,
AUSTIN, TEXAS.

September, 1892.

Prof. H. L. Piner,
Pres't Columbia College,
Van Alstyne, Texas.

My Dear Sir:
It gives me pleasure to inform you that the Faculty of the University adopted the recommendations of the Committee on Affiliated Schools that Columbia College be affiliated with the University of Texas. Very Truly Yours,

GEO. P. GARRISON,
Chairman Committee Affiliation.

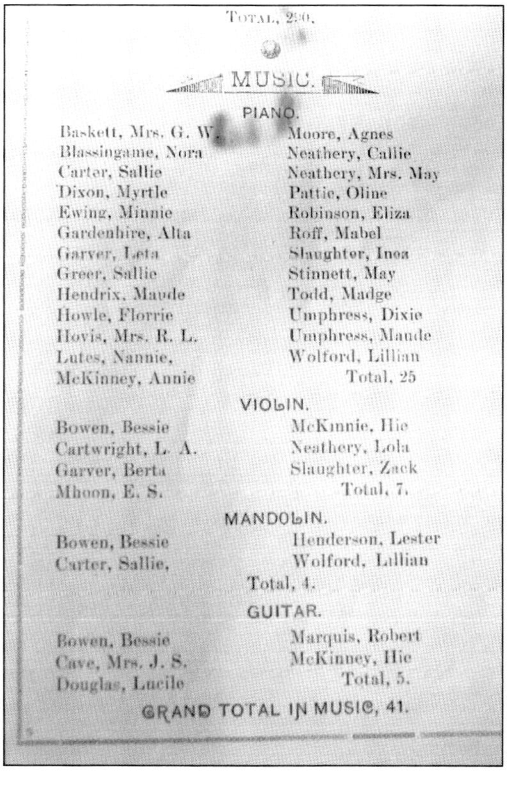

TOTAL, 290.

MUSIC.

PIANO.

Baskett, Mrs. G. W.
Blassingame, Nora
Carter, Sallie
Dixon, Myrtle
Ewing, Minnie
Gardenhire, Alta
Garver, Leta
Greer, Sallie
Hendrix, Maude
Howle, Florrie
Hovis, Mrs. R. L.
Lutes, Nannie,
McKinney, Annie
Moore, Agnes
Neathery, Callie
Neathery, Mrs. May
Pattie, Oline
Robinson, Eliza
Roff, Mabel
Slaughter, Inoa
Stinnett, May
Todd, Madge
Umphress, Dixie
Umphress, Maude
Wolford, Lillian
Total, 25

VIOLIN.

Bowen, Bessie
Cartwright, L. A.
Garver, Berta
Mhoon, E. S.
McKinnie, Hie
Neathery, Lola
Slaughter, Zack
Total, 7.

MANDOLIN.

Bowen, Bessie
Carter, Sallie,
Henderson, Lester
Wolford, Lillian
Total, 4.

GUITAR.

Bowen, Bessie
Cave, Mrs. J. S.
Douglas, Lucile
Marquis, Robert
McKinney, Hie
Total, 5.

GRAND TOTAL IN MUSIC, 41.

A list of music students includes several names of prominent Van Alstyne families of the era. Music students paid $5 tuition per month, plus an annual "Incidental fee" of $1. Fees were the same for most other disciplines, such as "Collegiate," "Art," "Elocution," or "Stenography and Typing." Room and board was available "in the very best homes in the city at from $2.50 to $3.50 per week." (Courtesy of Van Alstyne Historical Society.)

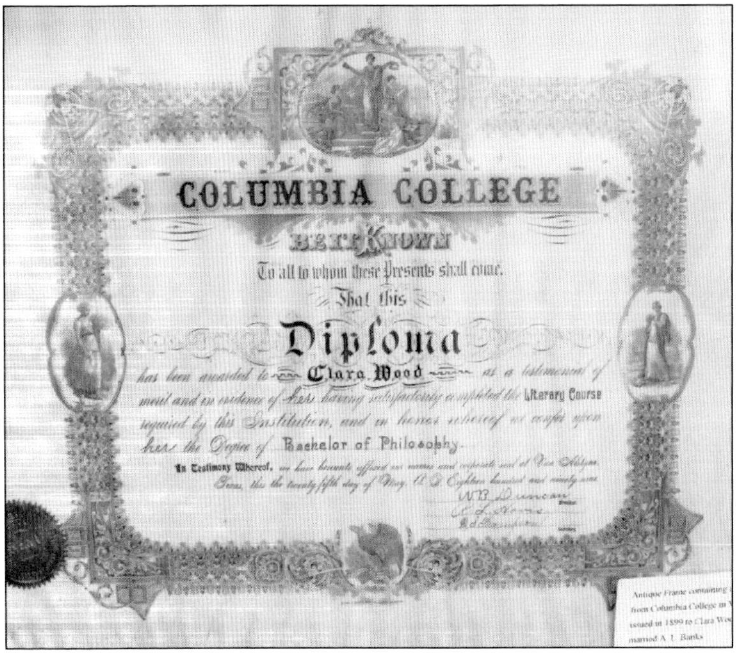

Columbia College accepted students from first graders to college seniors. Vocational education was a growing national trend and would be offered at Columbia College, along with liberal arts. In May 1899, Clara Wood completed the Literary Course and was awarded a bachelor of philosophy degree. (Courtesy of Van Alstyne Historical Society.)

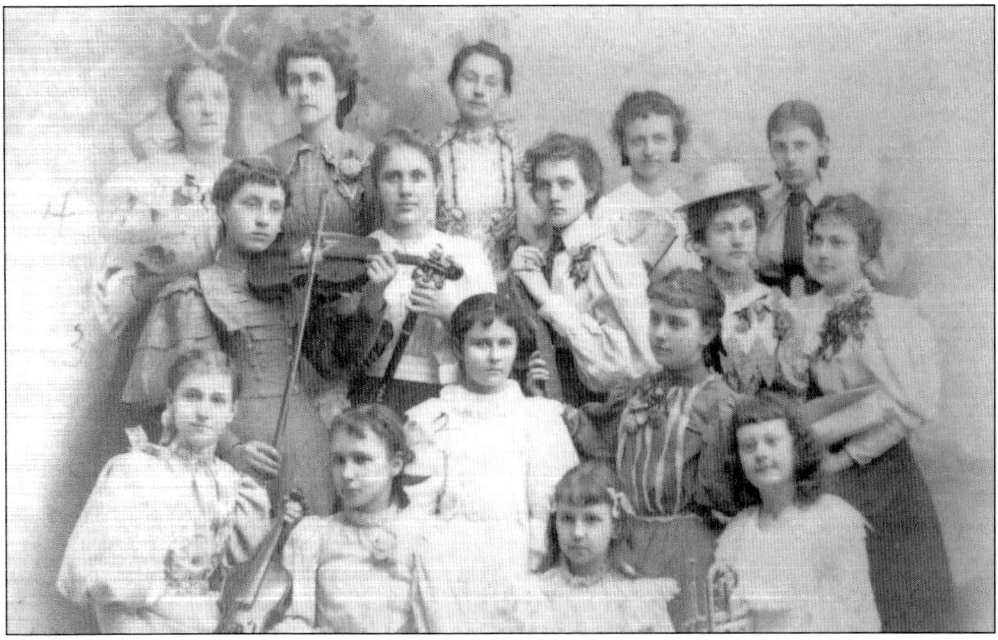

In 1896, the Young Ladies Music Class of Columbia College posed for the camera. Everyone dressed in Victorian finery, and several held their instruments. From left to right are (first row) Inez Slaughter, Dixie Umphrees, Maude Umphrees, and Sallie Mae Carter; (second row) Nannie Golden and Ann McKinney; (third row) Leta Garner, Flora Howell, Una Mount, Pearl Cannon, and Ruth McKinney. Those on the top row cannot be named, although the woman at center has the demeanor of a teacher. (Courtesy of Van Alstyne Historical Society.)

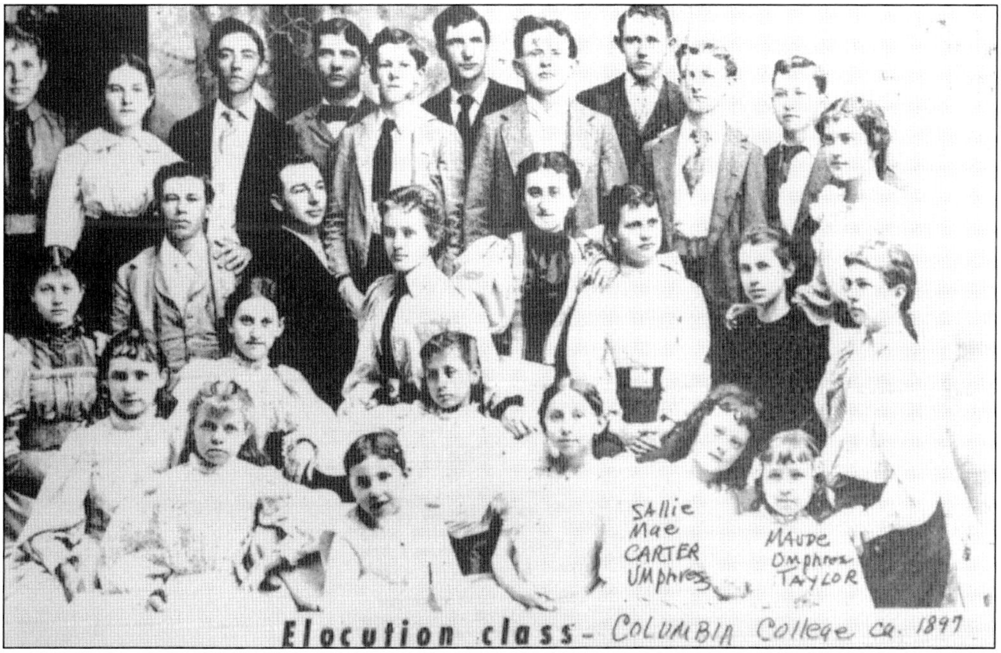

The Columbia College Elocution Class posed for a photograph in 1897. Sallie Mae Carter (bottom row, second from right), George Terrell Baskett (standing third from right), and Fred Smith Kemp (standing fifth from right) would graduate together five years later. (Courtesy of Van Alstyne Historical Society.)

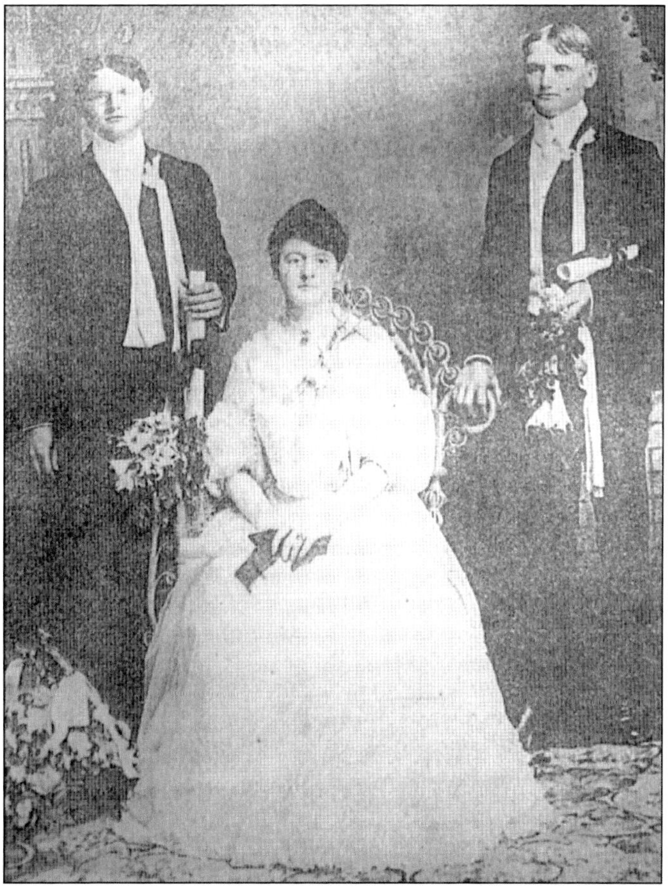

Three members of the Columbia College class of 1902 pose with their degrees in this photograph. Fred Smith Kemp (standing at left) received a bachelor of arts degree. Sallie Mae Carter, who would marry Lyman Umphrees, earned a bachelor's degree in elocution and physical culture. George Terrell Baskett received a bachelor of arts degree, as did the other class member, Eulah Edith Wilson, who is not pictured. (Courtesy of Van Alstyne Historical Society.)

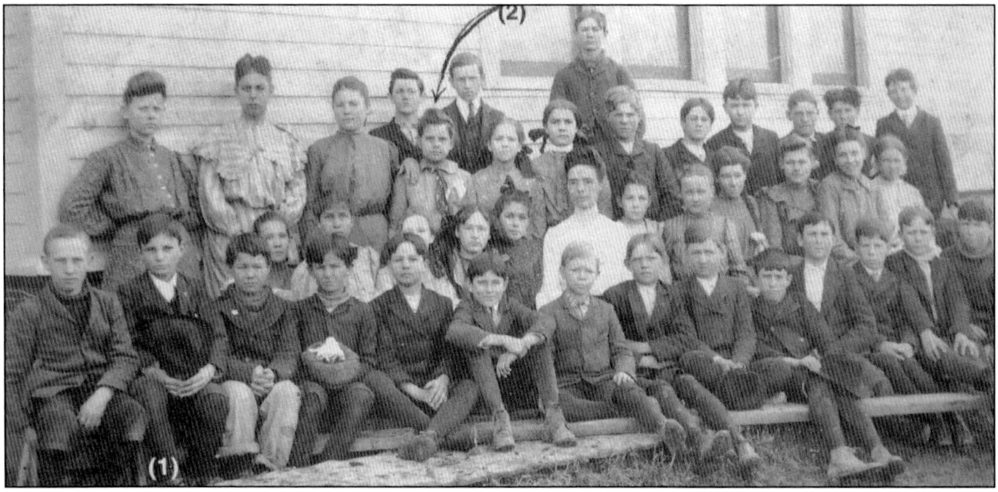

Columbia College students during the 1903–1904 school year tended to be quite young. At this point, the college was in its last chapter. (Courtesy of Van Alstyne Historical Society.)

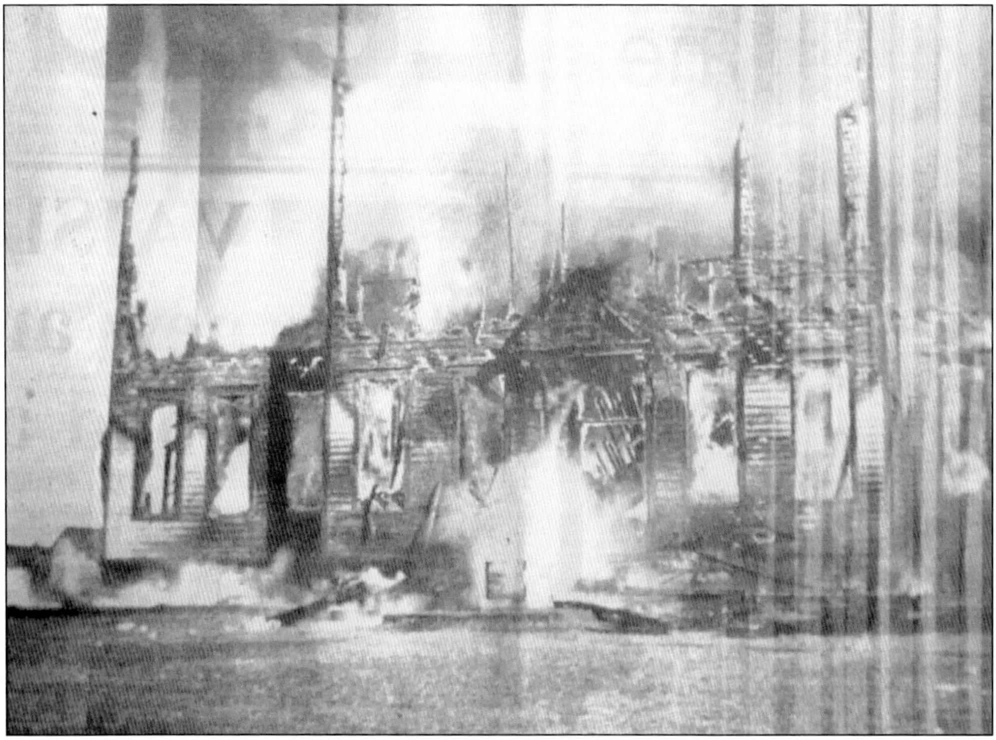

By 1905, Columbia College had closed, but for the next decade, the big structure housed Van Alstyne schoolchildren. A Van Alstyne landmark for 25 years, the old college building burned in 1915. A large crowd came to watch the early-morning fire. The one-time dormitory, half a block to the north, became the home of elementary classes. The former dining room was converted to a classroom. (From a 1915 issue of the Van Alstyne *Leader*.)

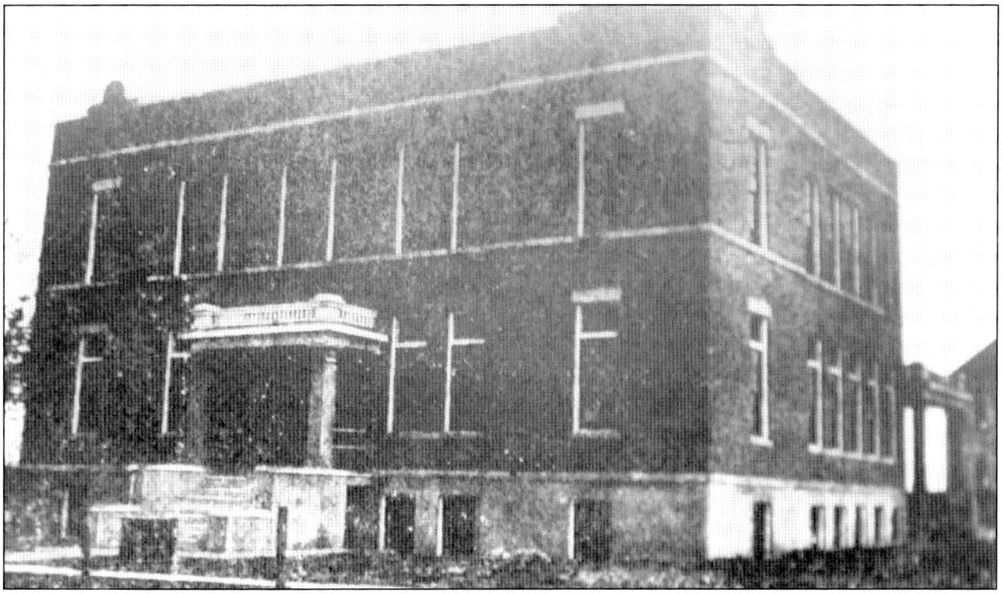

By 1890, there were 2,500 public high schools in the United States, although less than seven percent of young Americans between the ages of 14 and 17 attended high schools. But secondary education accelerated during the 1890s; by 1900, there were 6,000 high schools, and by 1910, there were 14,000. Van Alstyne became part of this extraordinary expansion in 1906, when old Columbia College was converted to a free public school. Roscoe Garver and Earl McComb were the first two graduates of Van Alstyne High School (VAHS) as the class of 1907. Two years later, the city voted a bond issue to purchase the college campus and to erect a three-story brick school south of the frame college building. The new school opened in 1910 and included an auditorium that featured theater seating and background stage scenery. (Both, courtesy Van Alstyne Independent School District [ISD].)

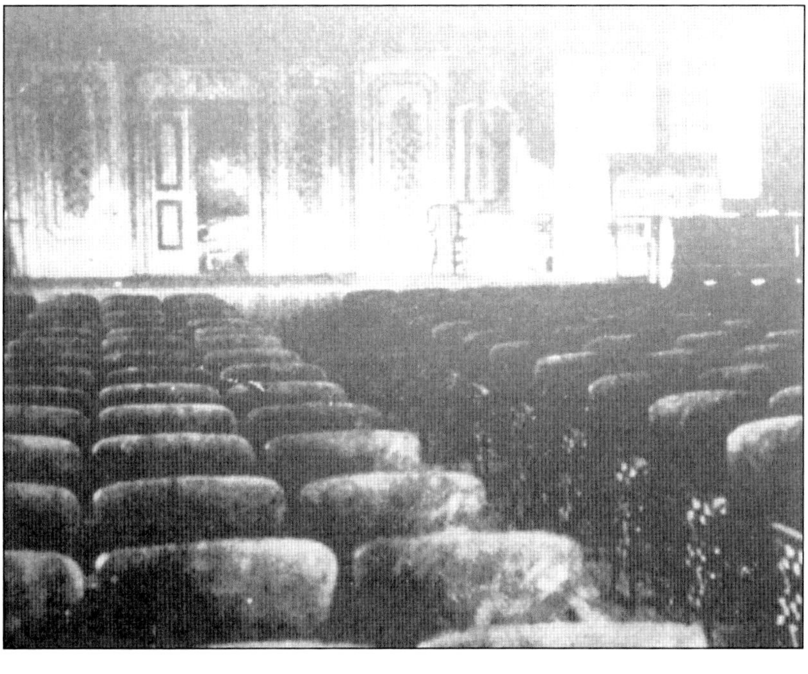

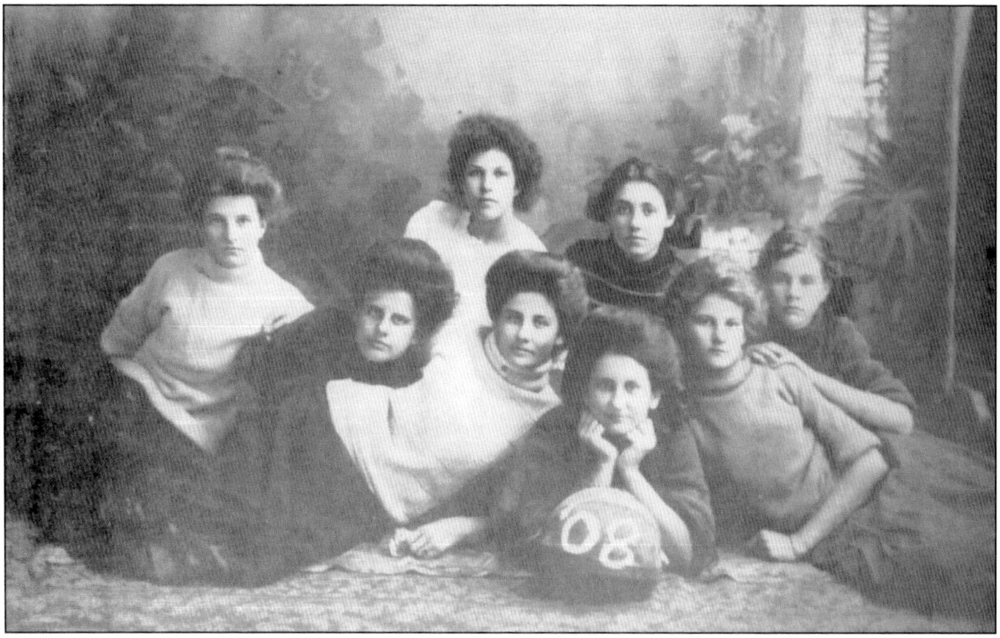

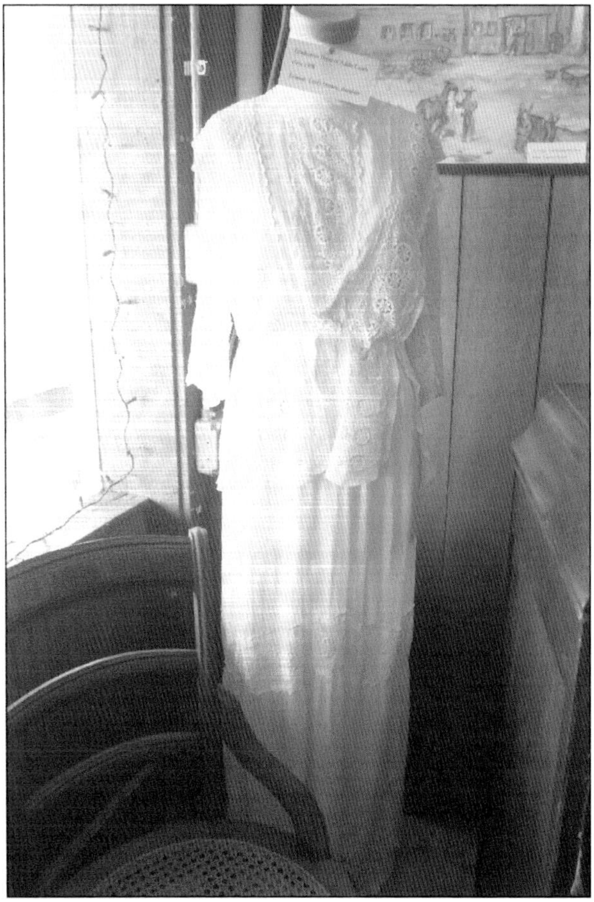

Basketball was invented in 1891 as a winter sport by Dr. James Naismith at Springfield College in Springfield, Massachusetts. The game spread rapidly to colleges and high schools, including Van Alstyne High School in 1908. As in most other small town high schools, Van Alstyne basketball was played on outdoor courts. (Courtesy Van Alstyne Historical Society.)

The second Van Alstyne High School graduating class boasted five members, and the school staged proper commencement exercises. Baccalaureate services were held at the First Christian Church. The first senior play was staged at the Carter Opera House, where a crowd again gathered on Monday night, May 4, 1908, for graduation ceremonies. The lovely graduation dress of Addie Leach is on display at the Van Alstyne Historical Museum. (Photograph by the author.)

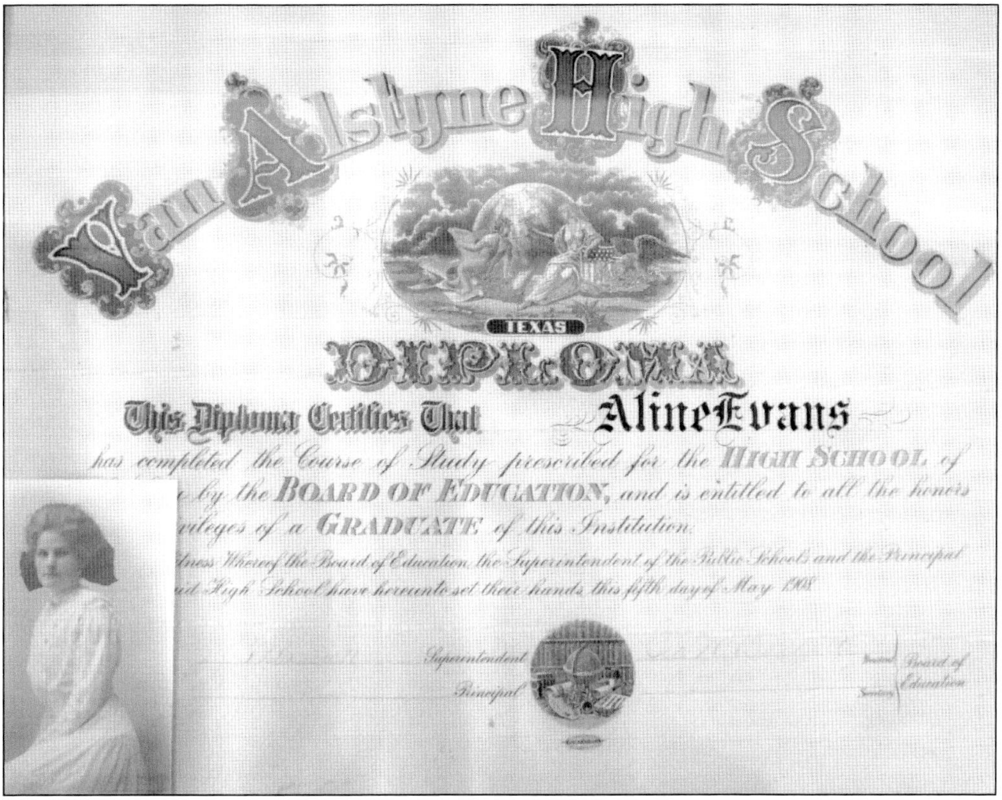

Aline Evans was a member of the class of 1908, and her high school diploma and a graduation photograph are on display at the Van Alstyne Historical Museum. (Courtesy of Van Alstyne Historical Society.)

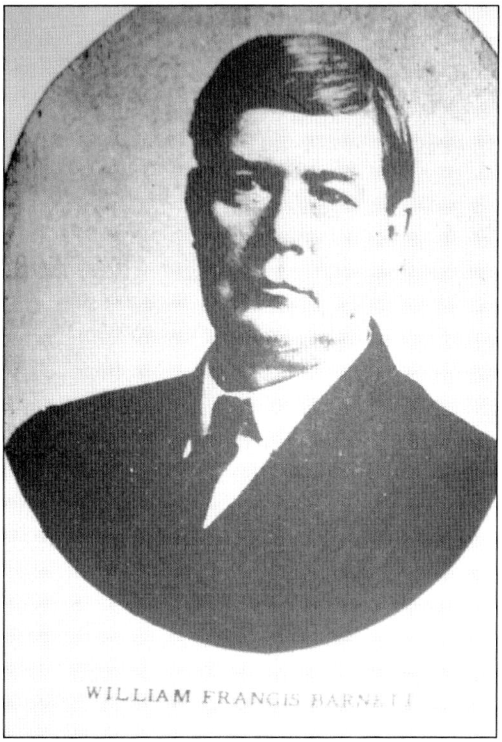

William Francis Barnett was a progressive educator who served Van Alstyne as superintendent. Barnett started a high school football team, began an annual, and also organized the area's first Boy Scout troop. (From the 1913 Van Alstyne High School annual.)

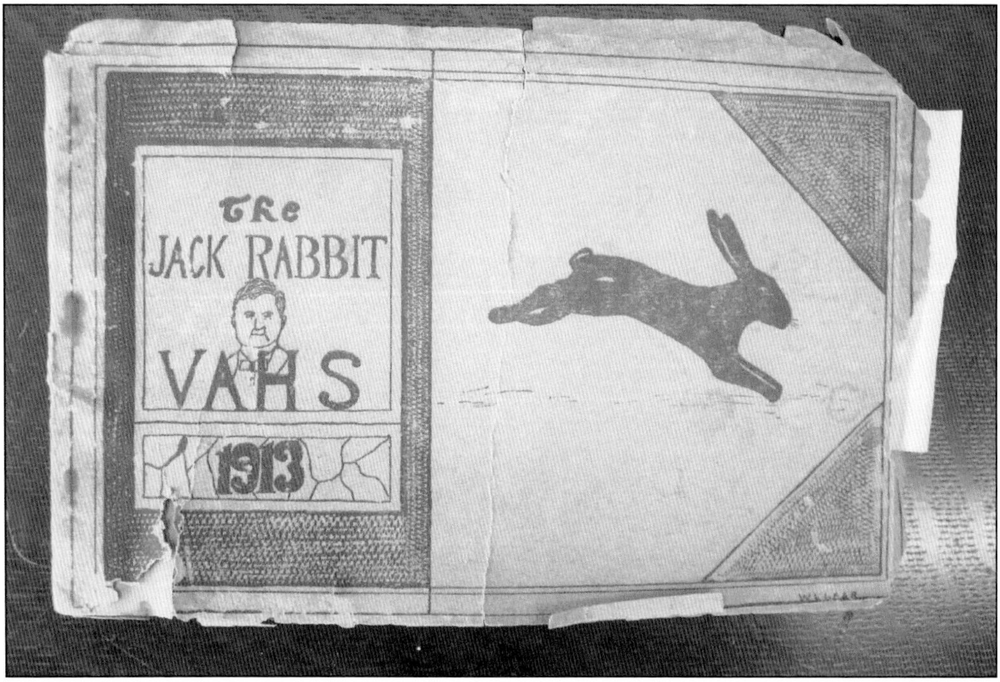

The first high school annual was the *Jack Rabbit* in 1913. (Photograph by the author.)

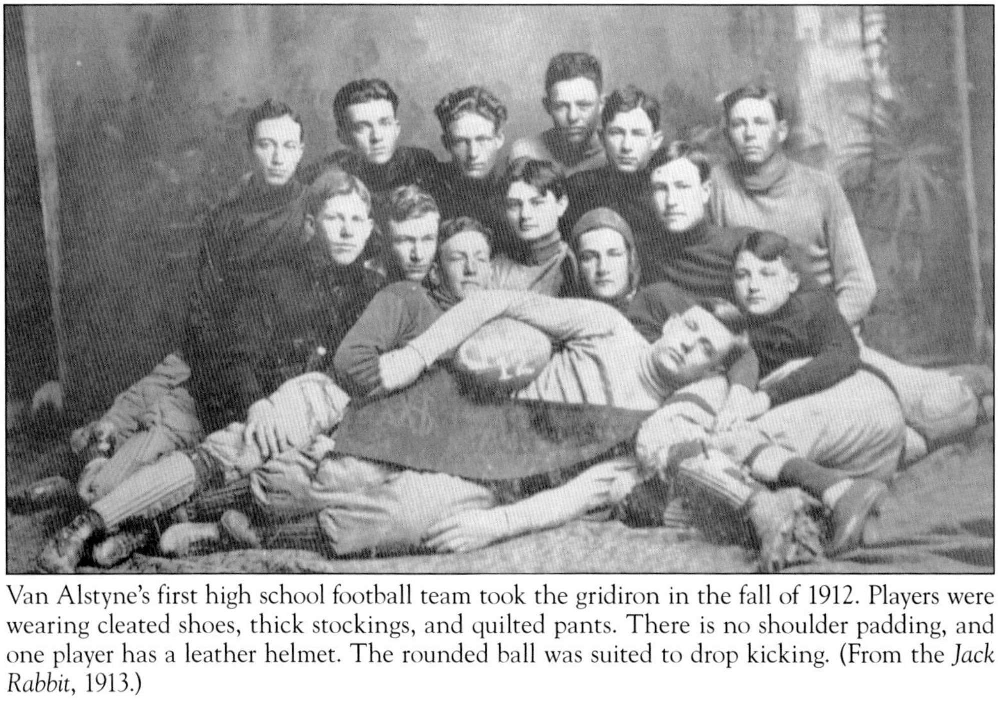

Van Alstyne's first high school football team took the gridiron in the fall of 1912. Players were wearing cleated shoes, thick stockings, and quilted pants. There is no shoulder padding, and one player has a leather helmet. The rounded ball was suited to drop kicking. (From the *Jack Rabbit*, 1913.)

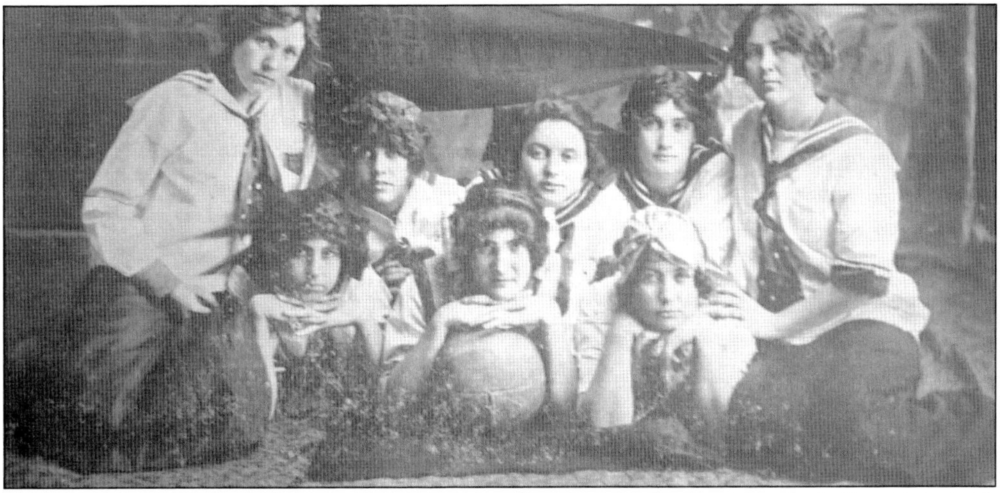

Van Alstyne girls wore the customary skirts and neckerchiefs while playing basketball in 1912–1913. (From the *Jack Rabbit*, 1913.)

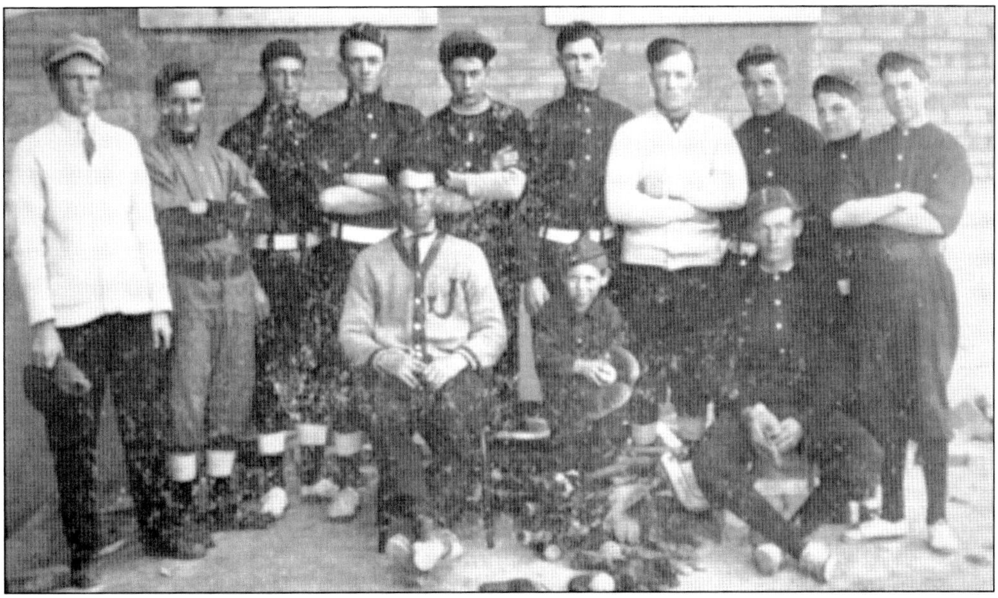

The 1913 baseball team wore dark uniforms, and some players sported fashionable white belts. (From the *Jack Rabbit*, 1913.)

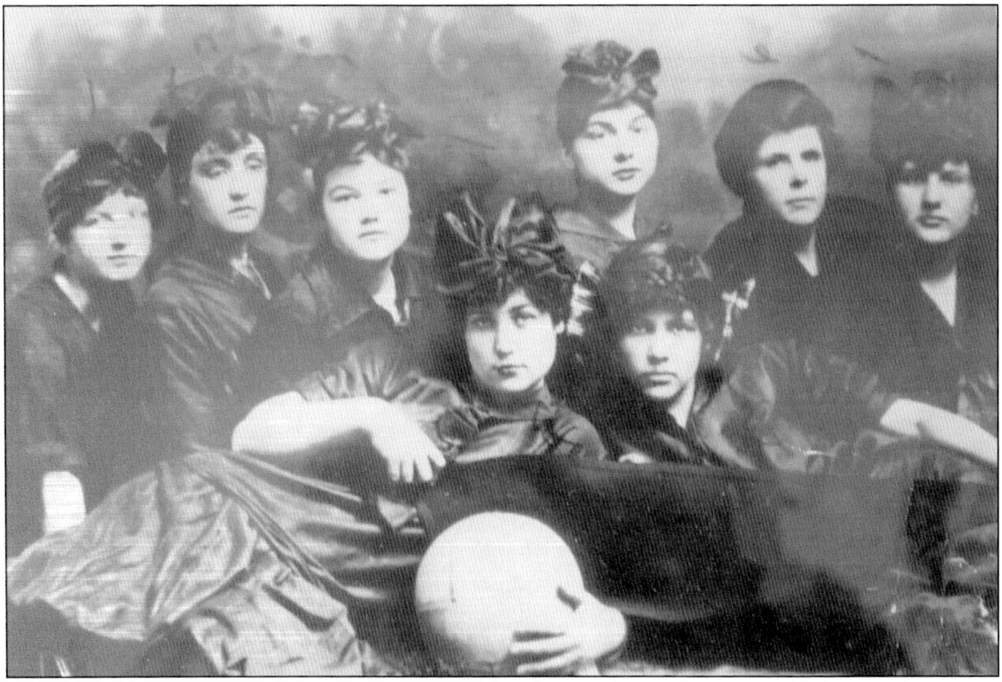

The VAHS girls' basketball team of 1915–1916 was undefeated. Although not many games were played in a season, the 1915–1916 squad was the sixth consecutive team to go undefeated. (Courtesy of Van Alstyne Historical Society.)

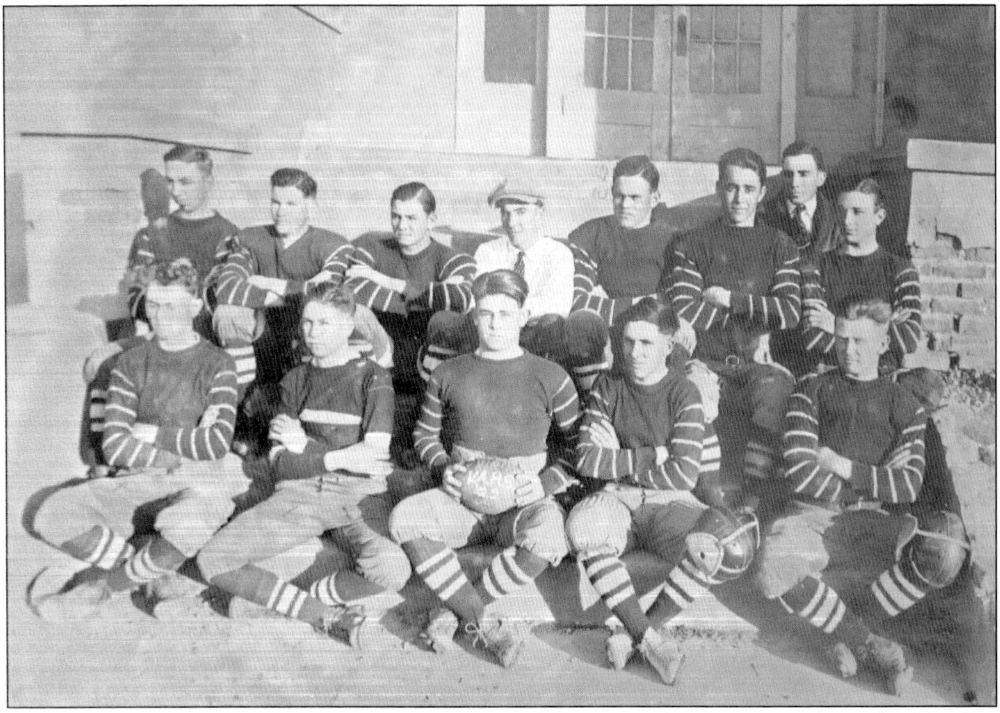

The 1922 football squad boasted jerseys with striped sleeves, and at least two players had leather helmets. (Courtesy of Van Alstyne Historical Society.)

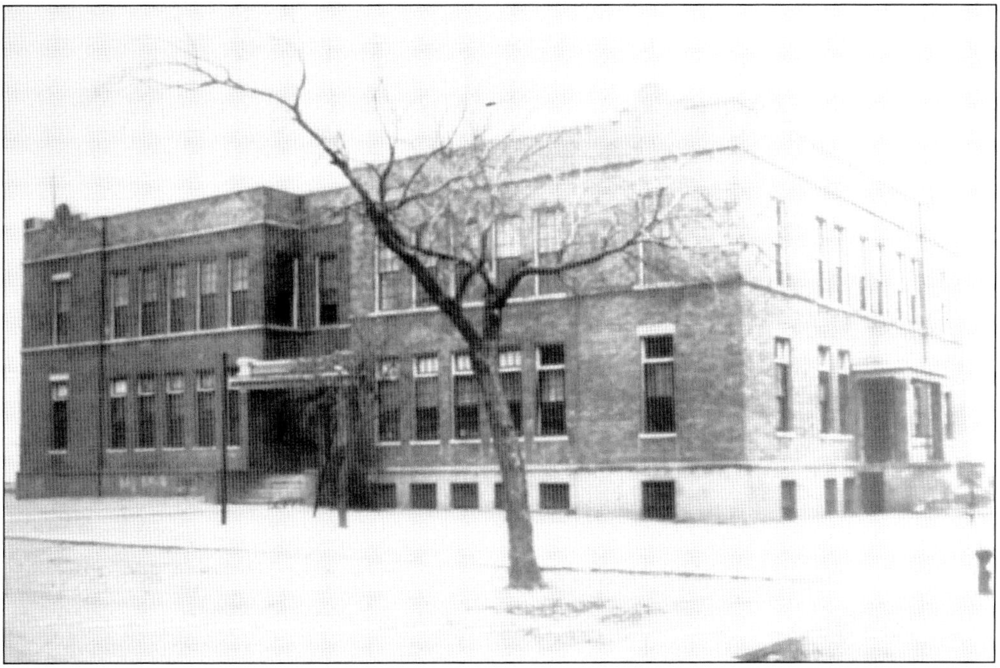

After the old Columbia College building burned in 1915, the 1910 brick high school soon was expanded to house all 12 grades. (Courtesy of Van Alstyne ISD.)

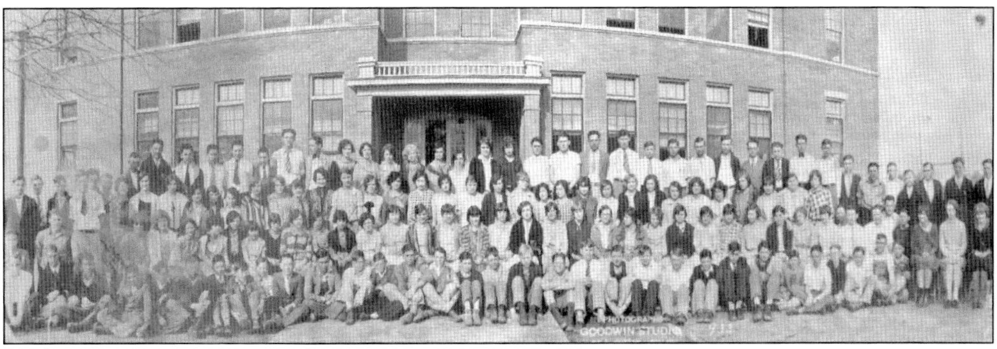

In 1929, the entire student body of Van Alstyne High School posed in front of its big brick school for a panoramic photograph. More than 130 students are pictured, along with several teachers and administrators. This fine old photograph is on display in the Van Alstyne Historical Museum. (Courtesy of Van Alstyne Historical Society.)

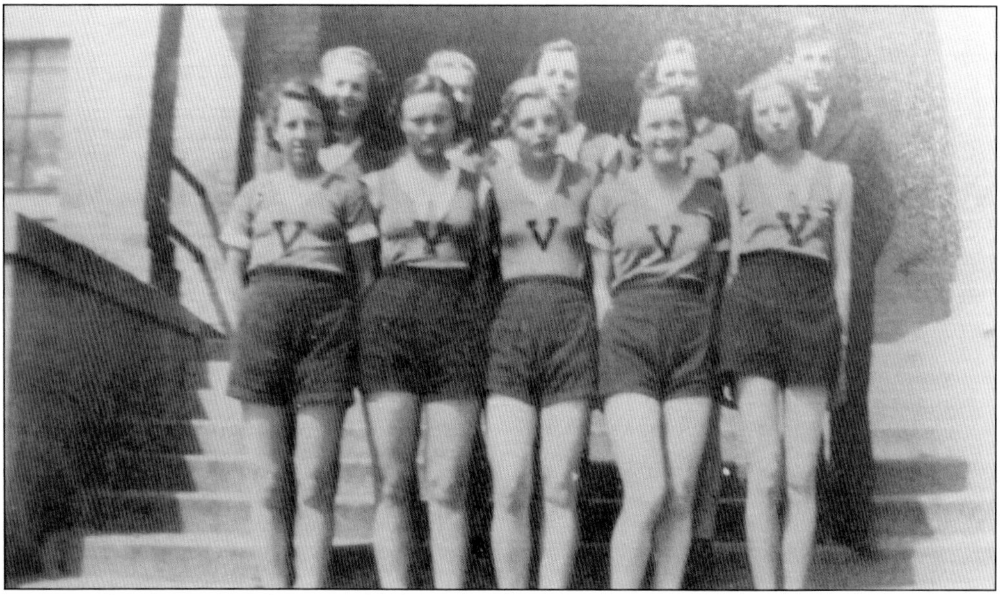

By the early 1930s, Van Alstyne girls played basketball and volleyball in uniforms that permitted free movement, unlike earlier uniforms with skirts and ties. (Courtesy of Van Alstyne ISD.)

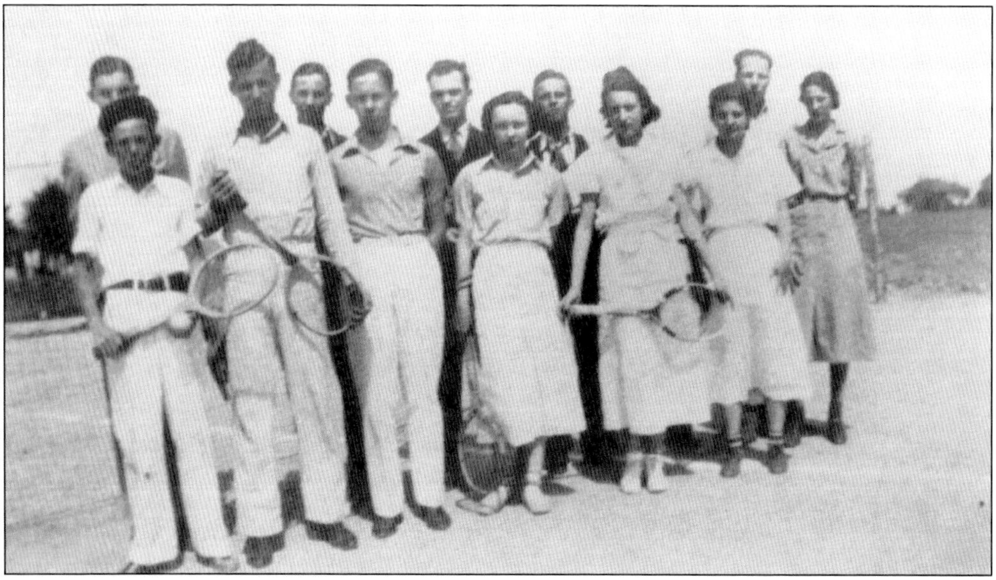

During the 1920s, Van Alstyne High School students often formed a tennis club, playing, in the fashion of the time, in light-colored trousers and skirts. (Courtesy of Van Alstyne ISD.)

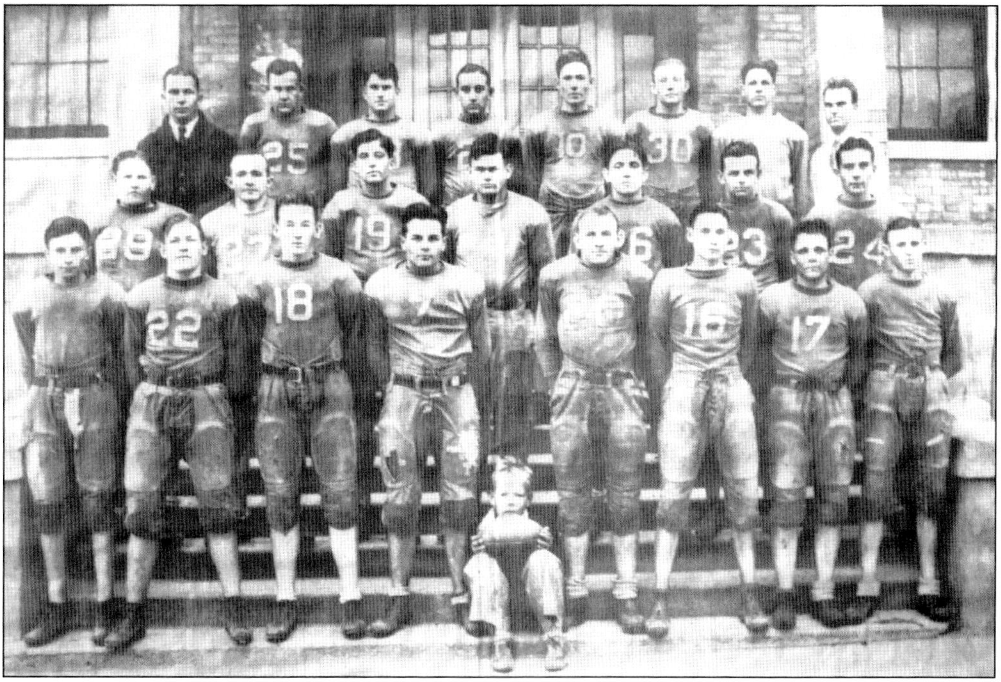

The 1931 Panther football squad posed for a team photograph at the front entrance to the school. By the 1930s, football pants held thigh guards and kneepads, and everyone wore light shoulder pads beneath their jerseys. No one wears a number higher than 30. It would be years before ends wore numbers in the 80s, tackles in the 70s, guards in the 60s, etc. The thick, high stockings of earlier years have been discarded, leaving ankles bare. (Courtesy of Van Alstyne ISD.)

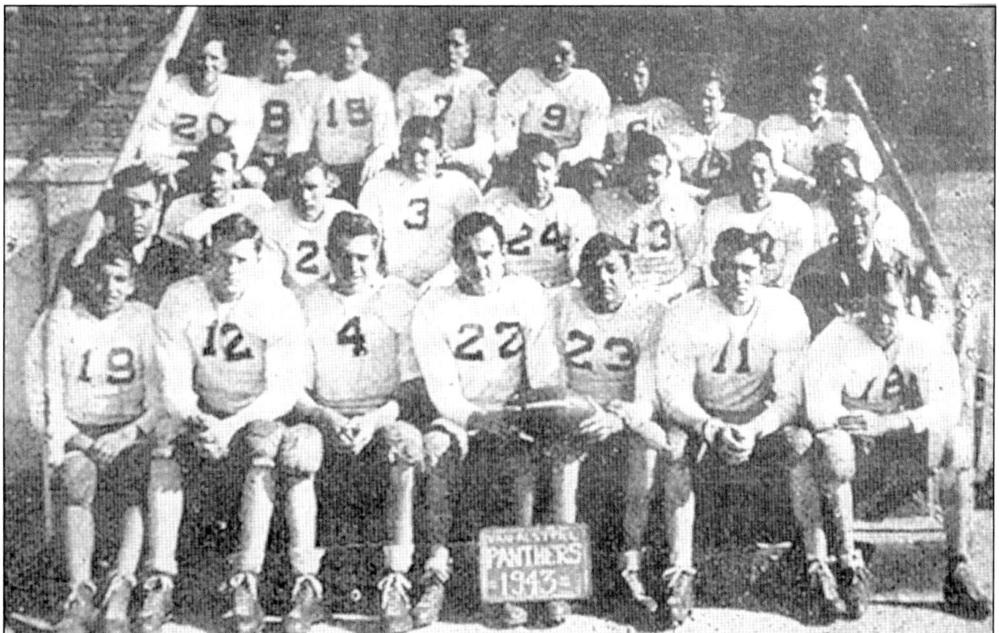

During the war year of 1943, the Panthers had a strong football team. But within a year or so, most of the senior players would be wearing military uniforms. (Courtesy of Van Alstyne ISD.)

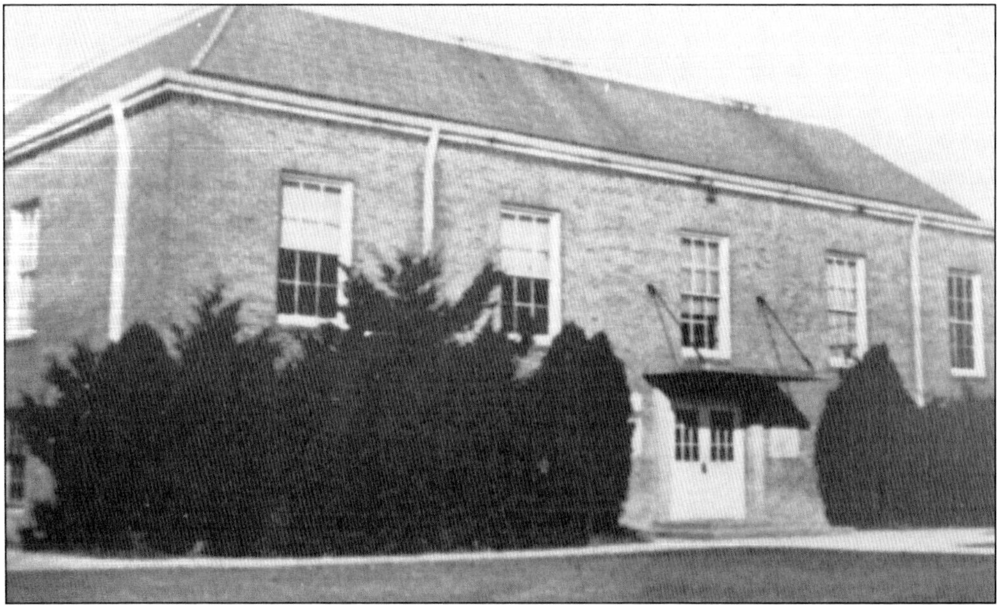

During the 1930s, the Works Progress Administration built the first indoor gymnasiums in communities across the United States. Van Alstyne's brick gym was erected near the site of the old Columbia College building. (Courtesy of Van Alstyne ISD.)

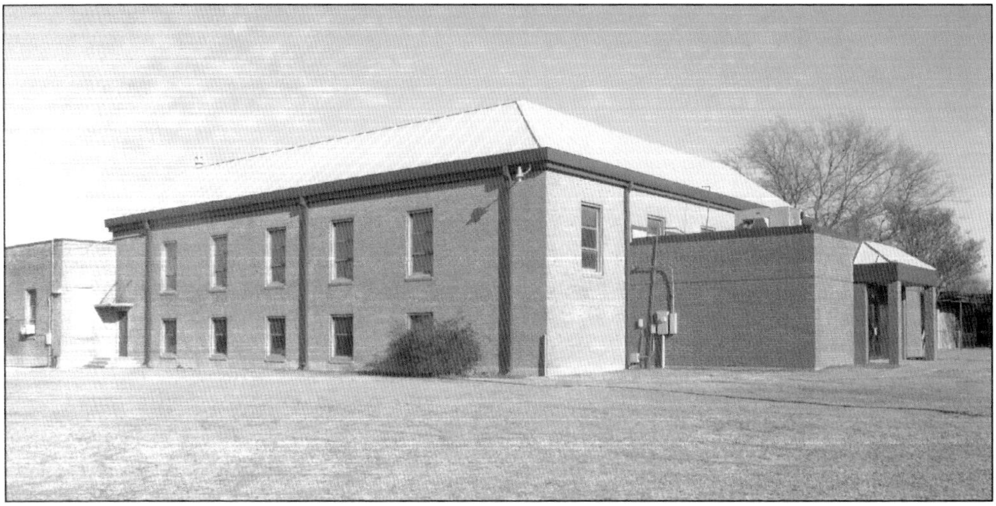

The VAHS gymnasium was expanded by the later addition of a new entrance. The sturdy old gym still stands as a nostalgic reminder of countless basketball and volleyball games played within its walls. (Photograph by the author.)

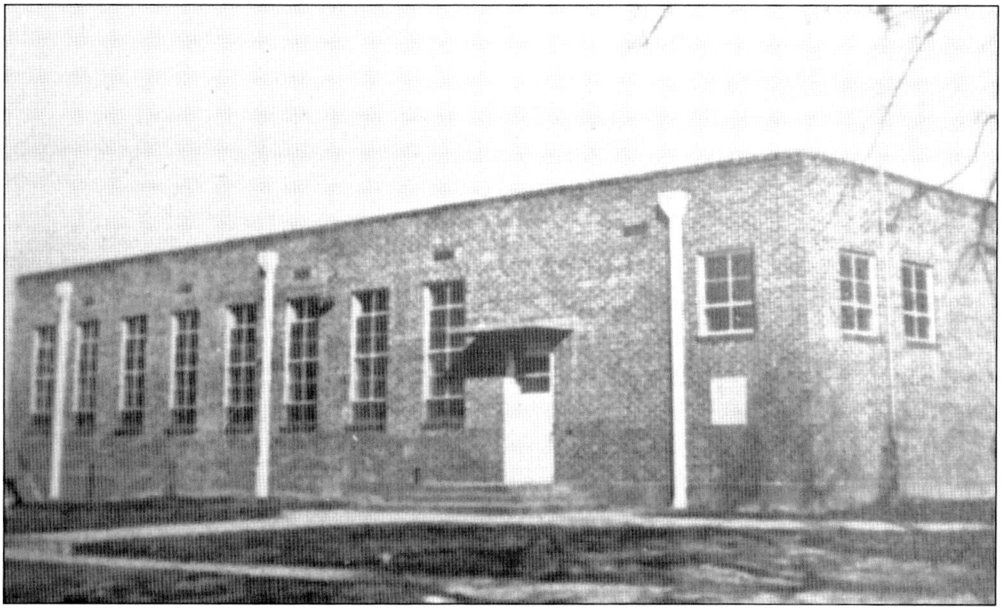

In 1946, a cafeteria was built at the southwest corner of the school campus. The building was later converted to other purposes and still stands. (Photograph by the author.)

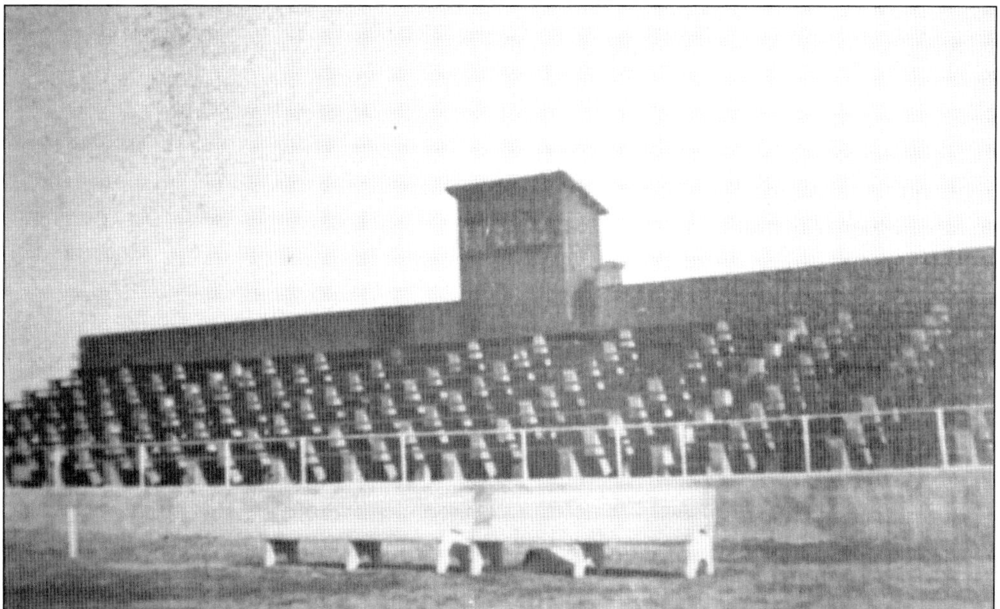

Panther football was played at a stadium north of the campus. The main grandstand was one of the finest among the small schools in the area. (Courtesy of Van Alstyne ISD.)

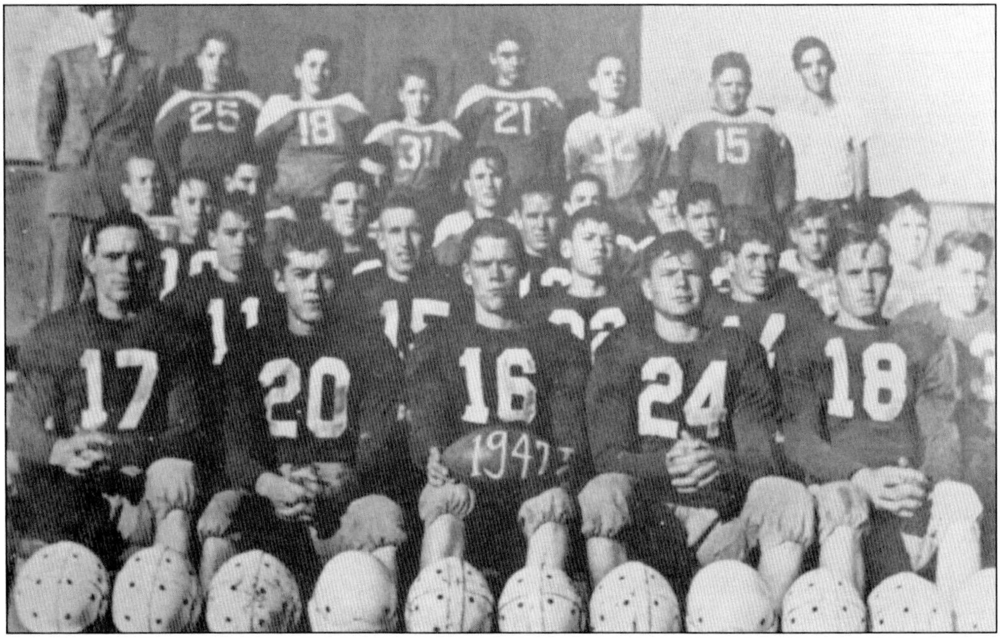

The 1947 Panthers won the first district championship in the history of Van Alstyne football. (Courtesy of Van Alstyne ISD.)

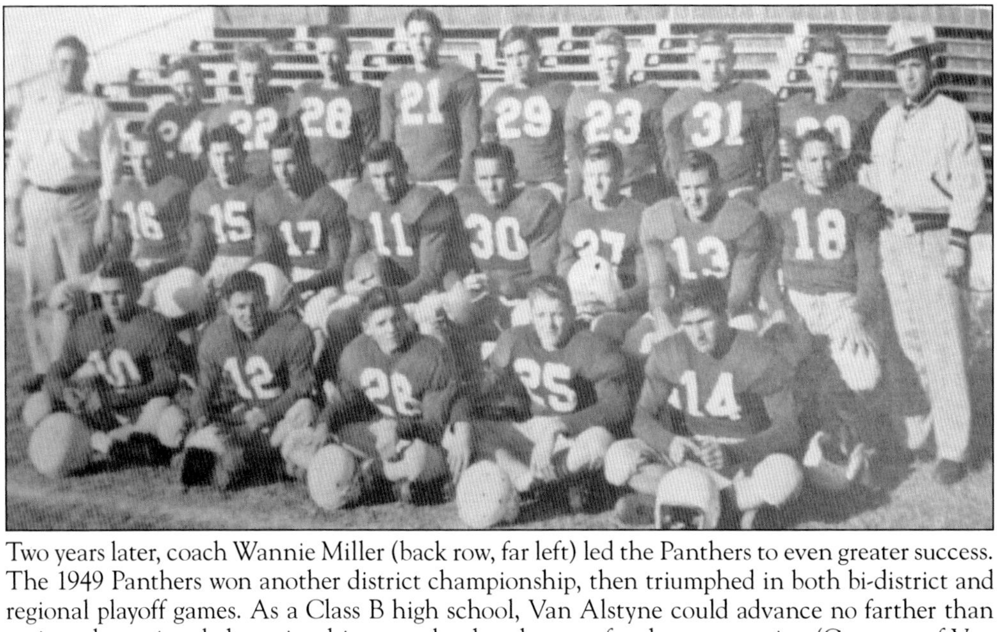

Two years later, coach Wannie Miller (back row, far left) led the Panthers to even greater success. The 1949 Panthers won another district championship, then triumphed in both bi-district and regional playoff games. As a Class B high school, Van Alstyne could advance no farther than region; the regional championship was a landmark event for the community. (Courtesy of Van Alstyne ISD.)

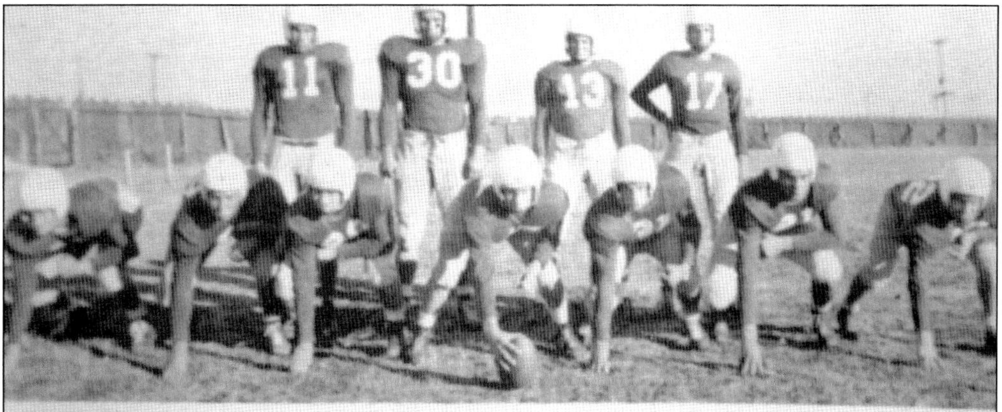

STARTING LINEUP

The starting 11 of the 1949 Region IV champs posed for a photograph on their home field. (Courtesy of Van Alstyne ISD.)

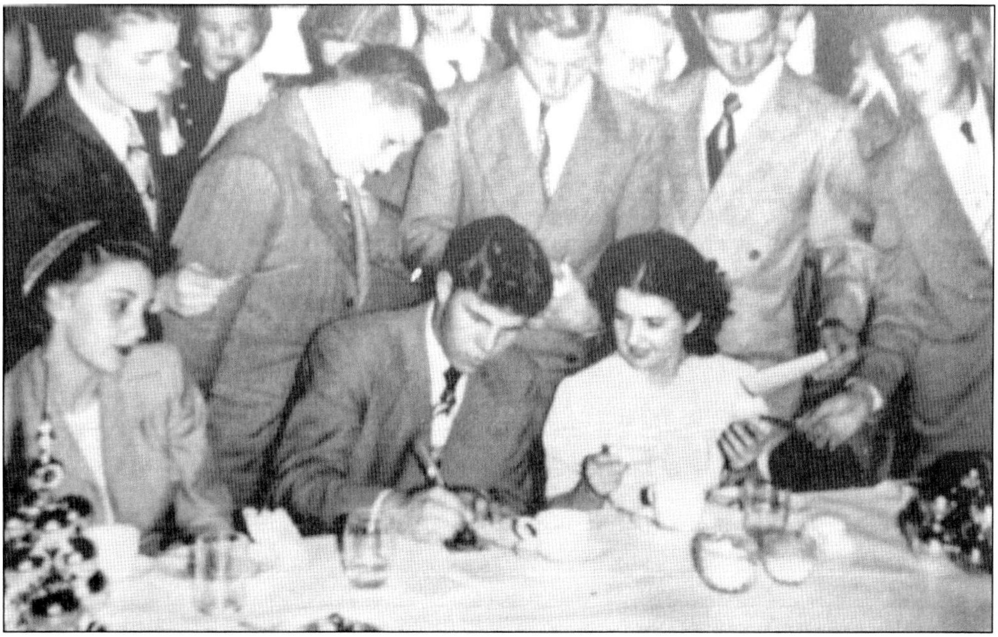

The featured speaker at the football banquet honoring the regional champs was Southern Methodist University star Kyle Rote, a future All-American and NFL standout. Rote graciously signed autographs for a legion of admirers. (Courtesy of Van Alstyne ISD.)

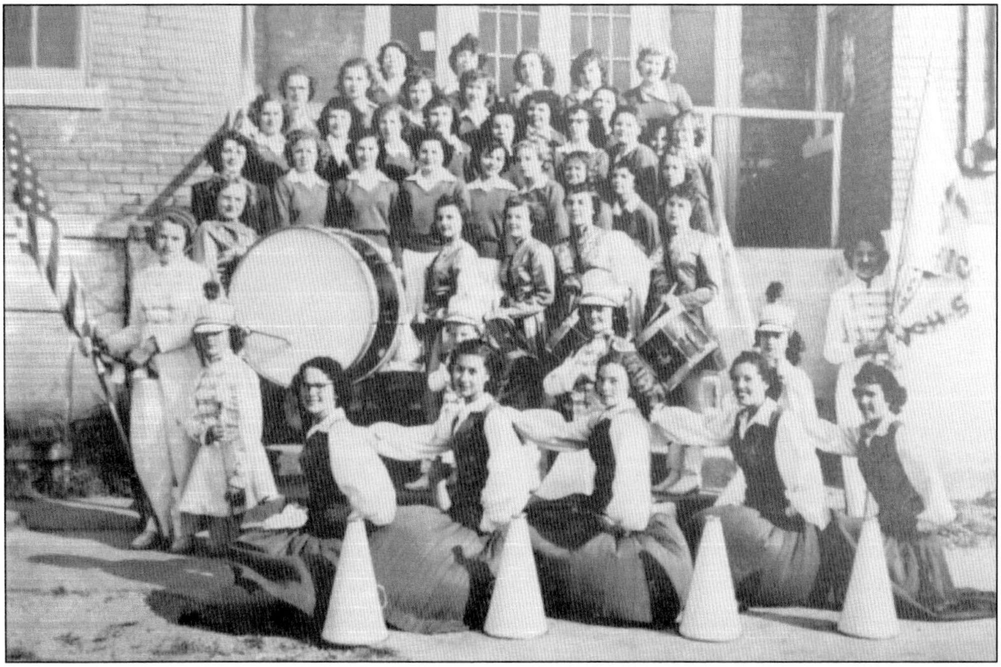

The 1949 Panther Pep Squad included cheerleaders, majorettes, flag-bearers, and nearly 30 squad members. (Courtesy of Van Alstyne ISD.)

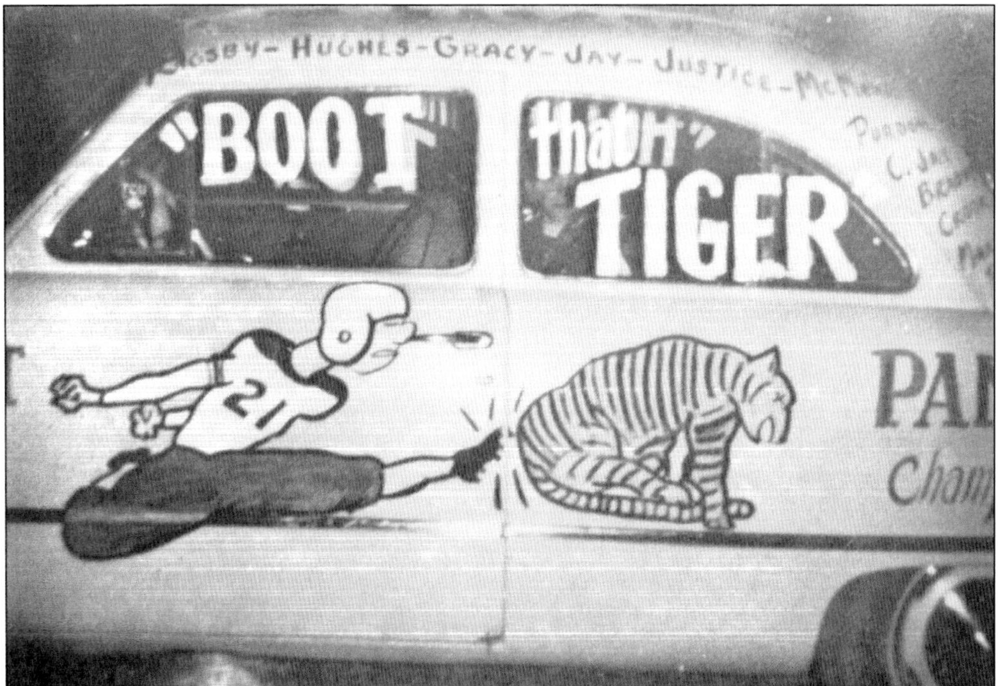

With school spirit at a fever pitch, a car was profusely decorated for a key game against the Whitewright Tigers. (Courtesy of Van Alstyne ISD.)

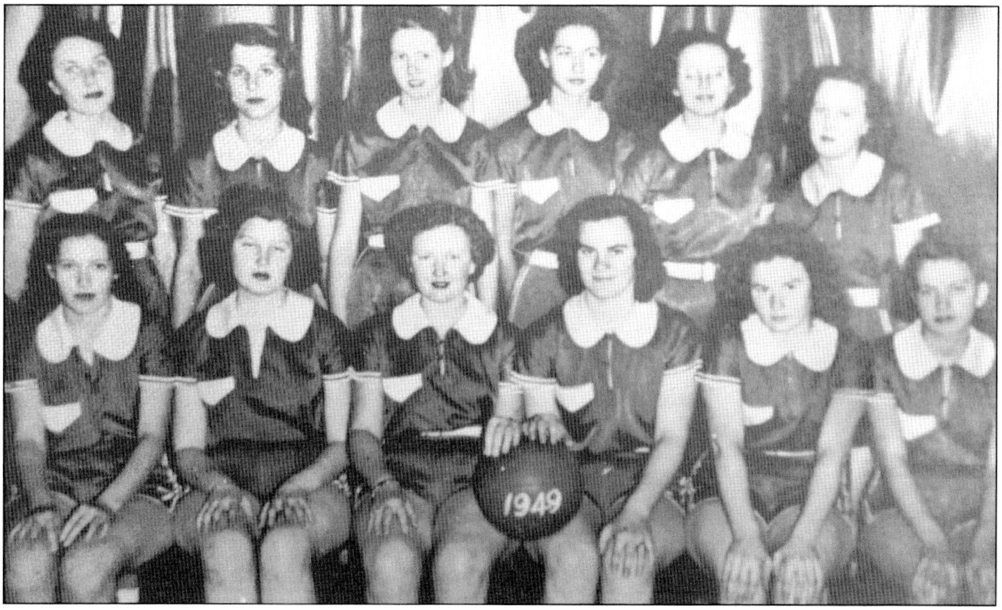

The 1949 Pantherette basketball team posed for a team photograph in the satin uniforms popular during the 1940s. Girls' basketball in Texas was played with six starters: three players were defenders and three others tried to score, and each trio stayed on its own half of the court. (Courtesy of Van Alstyne ISD.)

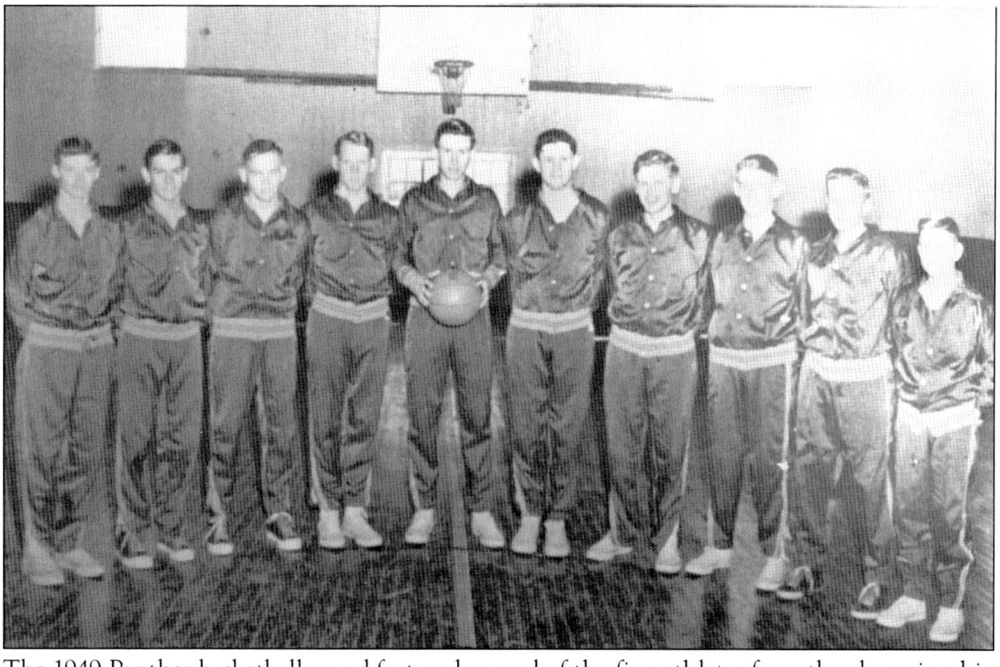

The 1949 Panther basketball squad featured several of the fine athletes from the championship football team. (Courtesy of Van Alstyne ISD.)

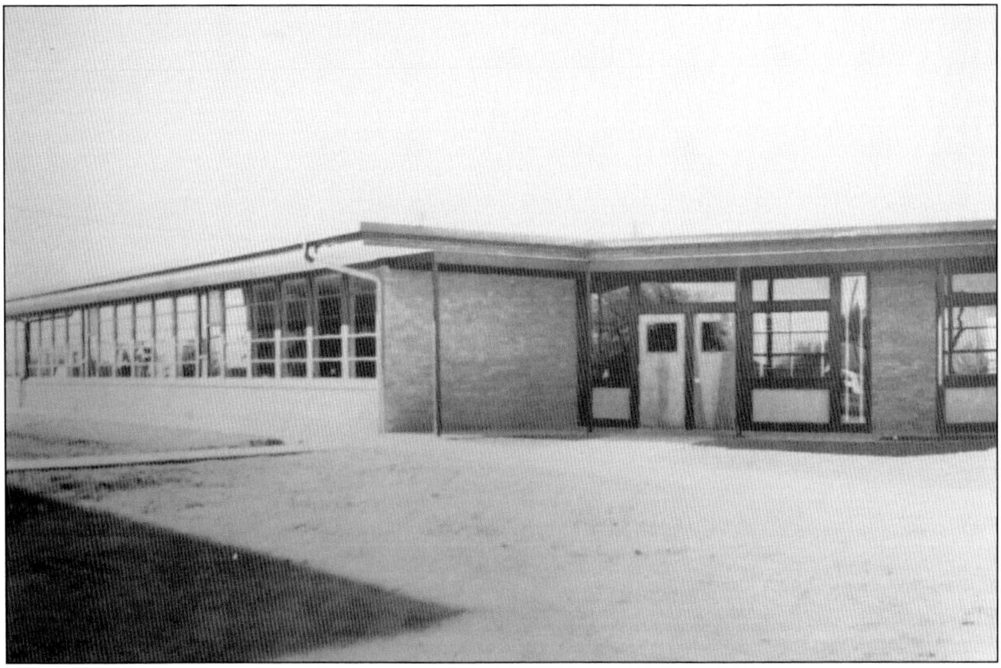

In 1954, Van Alstyne secondary students moved into a new building, located just north of the gymnasium. A classic 1950s school, the long building featured a flat roof, light-colored brick, and a great deal of glass. Offices were to the right of the entrance, while classrooms opened off a long hallway to the west, or left. (Courtesy of Van Alstyne ISD.)

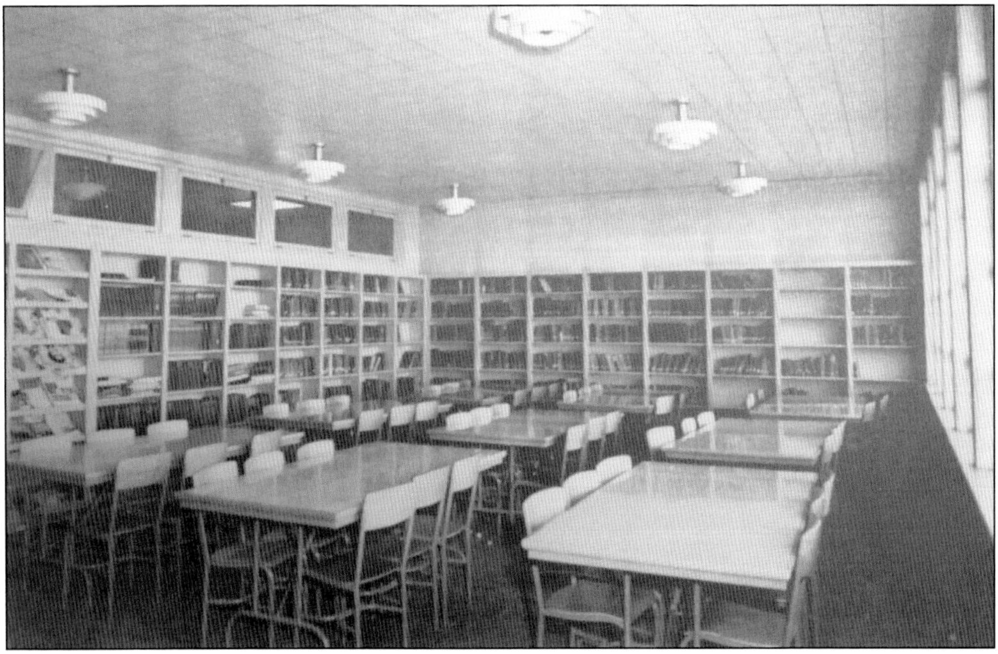

This library became a center of academic activity. (Courtesy of Van Alstyne ISD.)

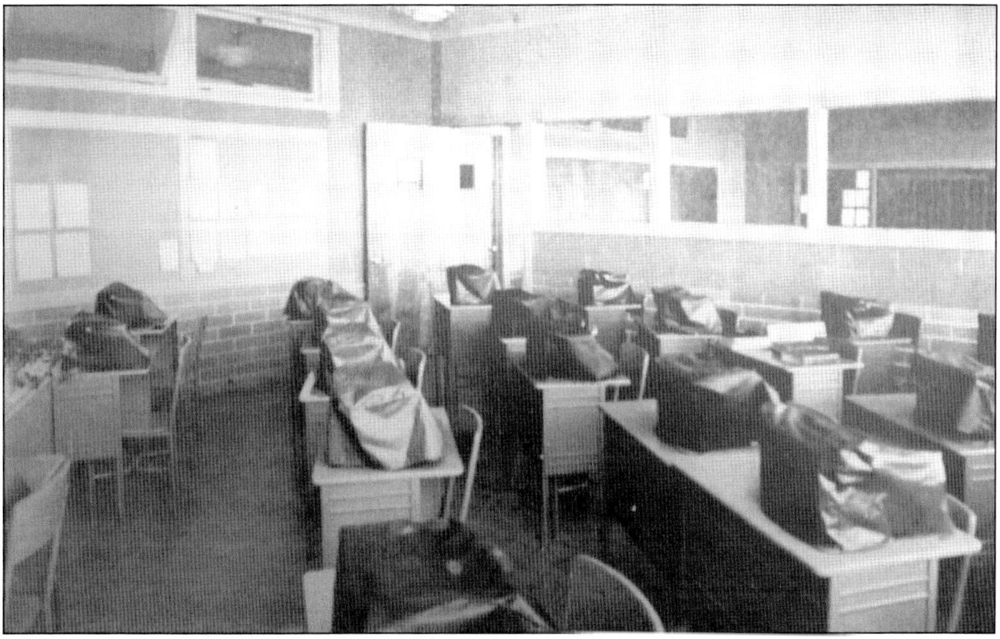

The business classroom was equipped with the latest typewriters, along with other office machines. (Courtesy of Van Alstyne ISD.)

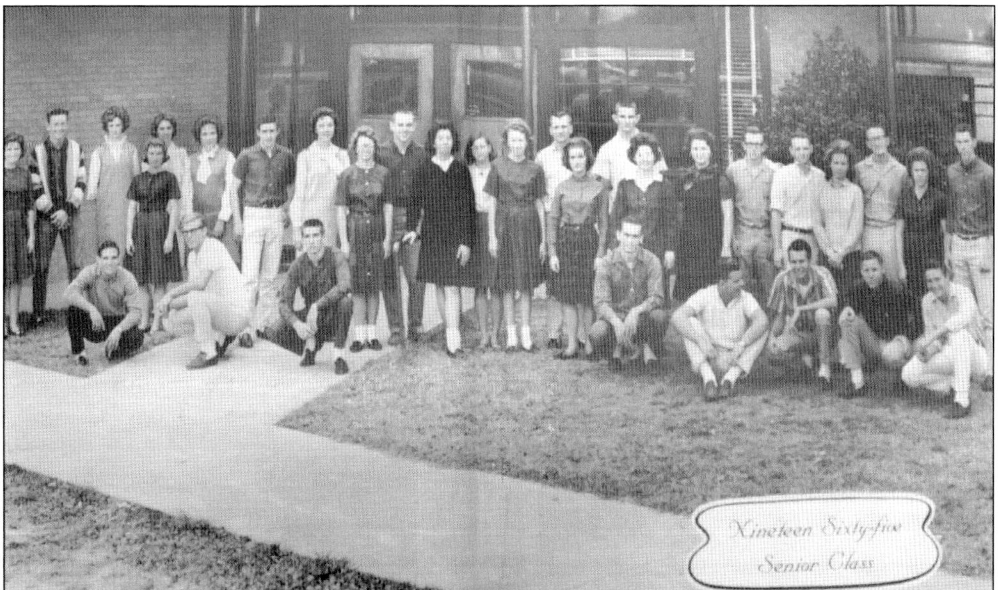

The 1965 senior class of VAHS posed in front of its high school for this photograph. (Courtesy of Van Alstyne ISD.)

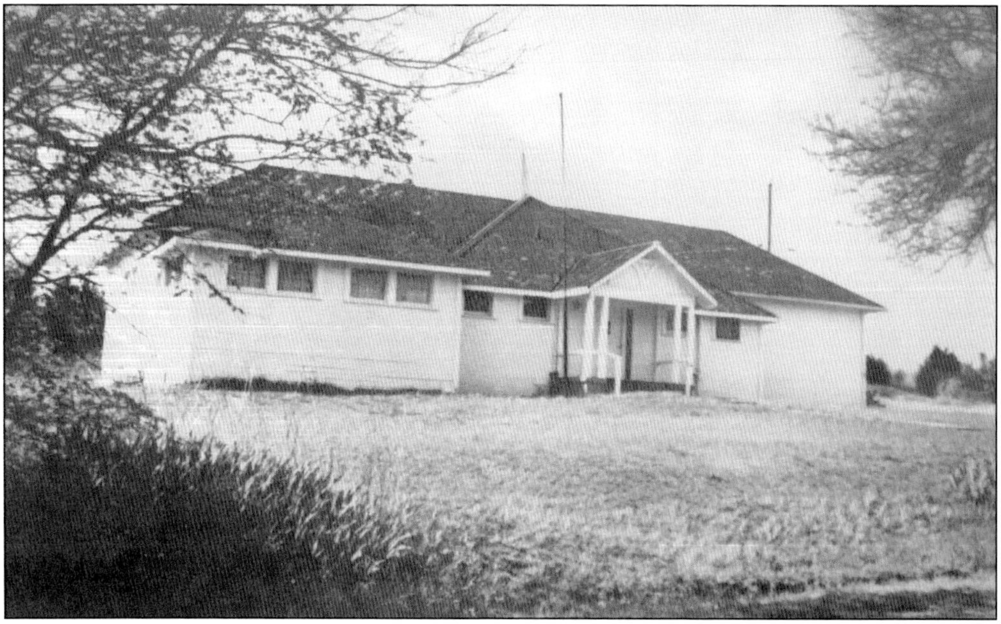

With segregation the rule in Texas public schools, the small black population of Van Alstyne had always attended a separate school. In 1936, a new frame building for black students was built atop a hill in the east part of town. In 1956, following a 1954 US Supreme Court decision, integration was enforced at the public schools of Mansfield, a farm town roughly the size of Van Alstyne in the 1950s and located southeast of Fort Worth. Integration began to spread throughout the public schools of Texas. Following the integration of Van Alstyne public schools in 1965, the old frame school became the home of Sardis Baptist Church. (Both, courtesy of Van Alstyne ISD.)

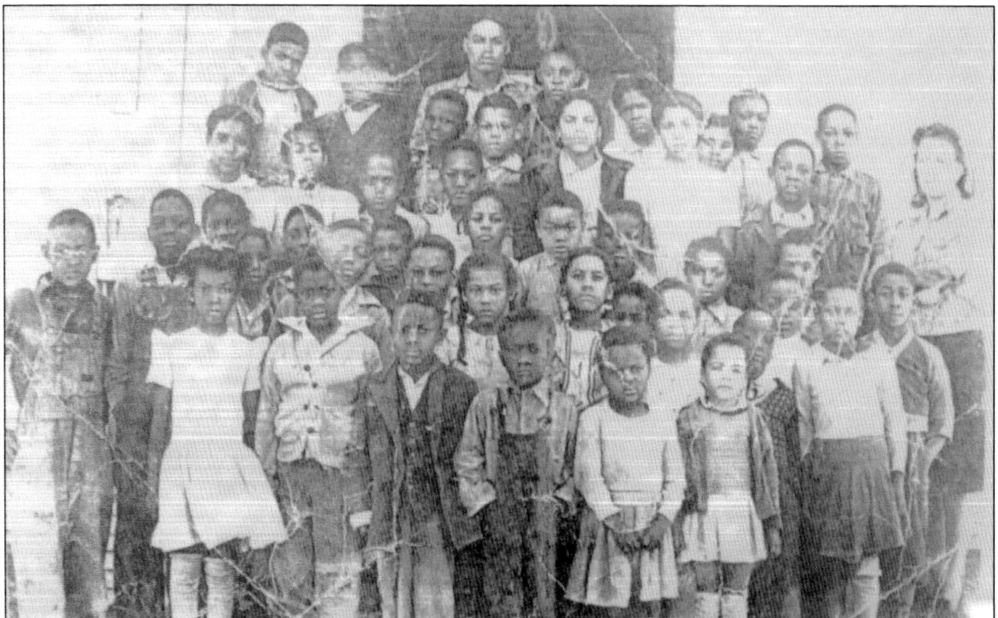

Six

HEARTLAND COMMUNITY

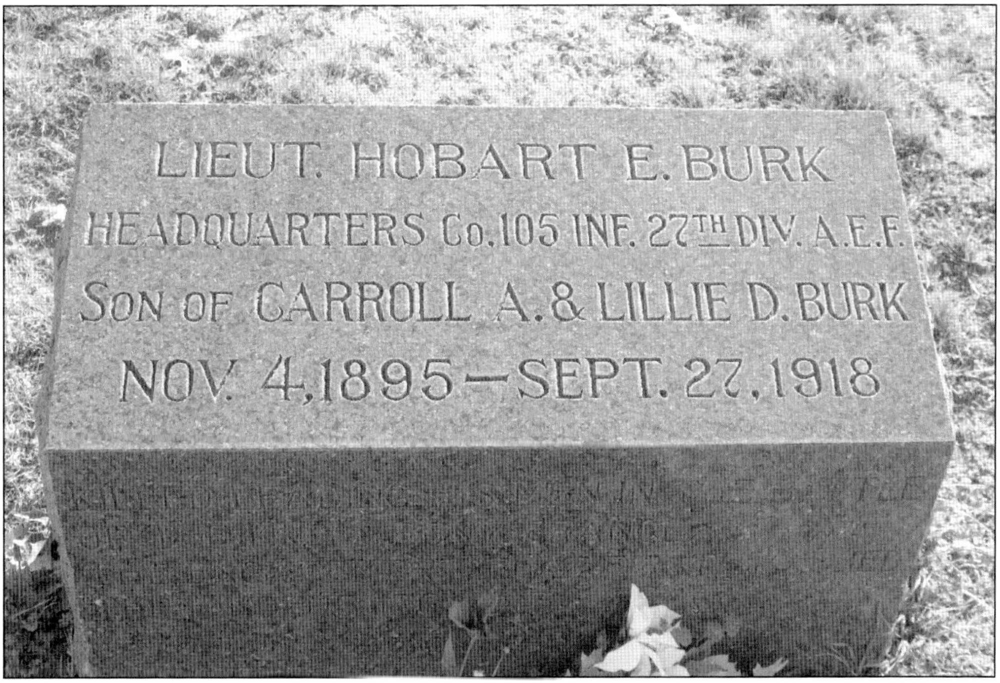

More than 197,000 Texans donned uniforms during the First World War, and over 5,000 lost their lives. Lt. Hobart Burk was the only Van Alstyne soldier to be killed in action. The son of Carroll and Lillie Burk (who died when her son was seven), Hobart was a 1913 graduate of VAHS. He joined the Texas National Guard and served during the 1916 punitive campaign against Mexico before being sent to France as part of the American Expeditionary Force. On September 27, 1918, Lieutenant Burk led his men in a charge against the Hindenburg Line near Bony, France. Slain at the age of 22, Burk was buried in a nearby military cemetery. Three years later, he was brought home and interred beside his mother in the Van Alstyne Cemetery. More than 1,500 citizens attended funeral services at the First Christian Church and at the graveside. (Photograph by the author.)

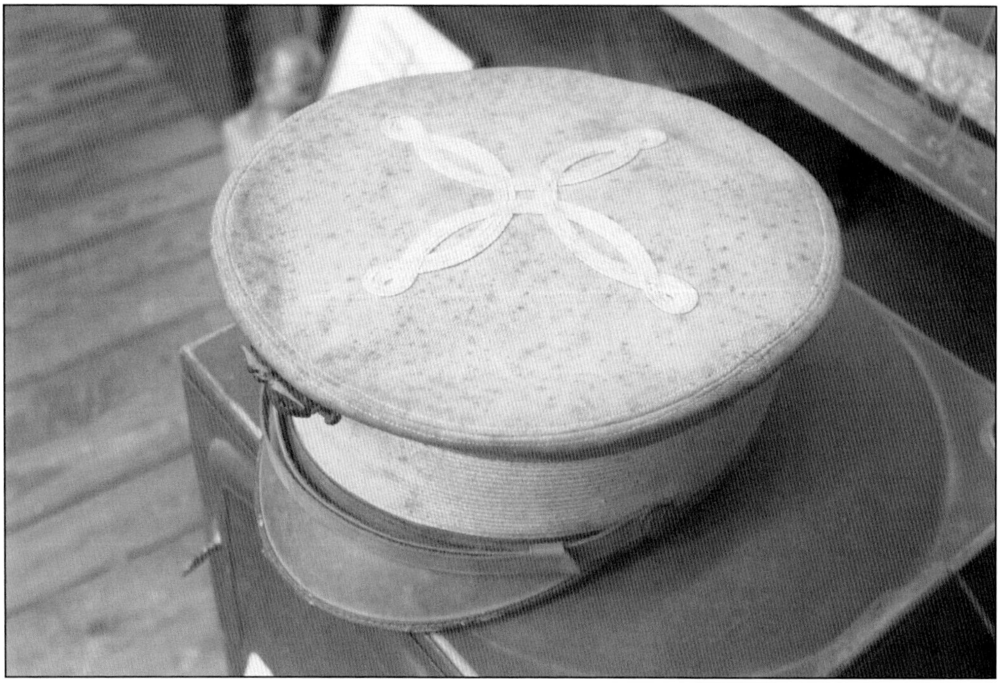

Henry D. Hynds was born in 1896 in McKinney. During World War I, he served as a lieutenant in the US Marine Corps; pictured above is his uniform cap (now on display in the Van Alstyne Historical Museum). After the war, Hynds worked in the family cotton business in Oklahoma until his marriage in 1921 to Helen Umphrees. Henry and Helen were wed in Van Alstyne, where they would make their home and raise two sons and a daughter. (Photograph by the author.)

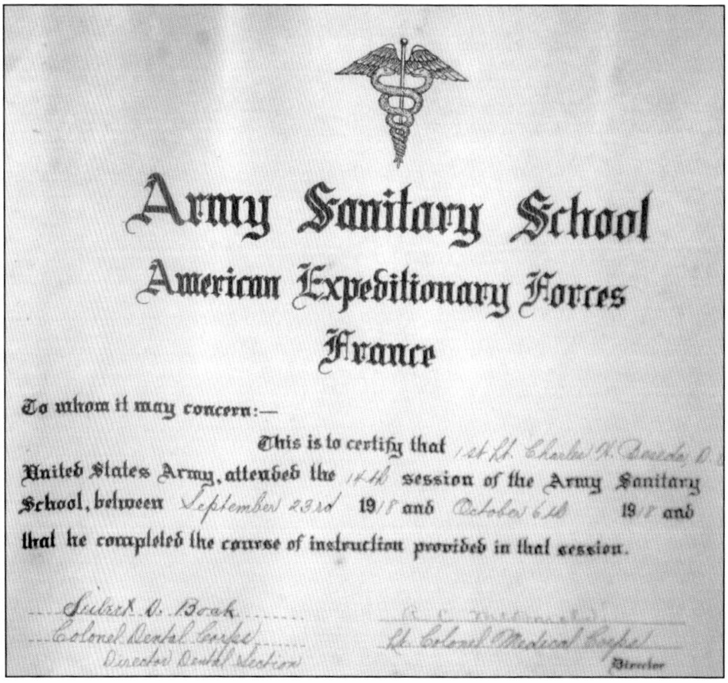

Army Sanitary School
American Expeditionary Forces
France

To whom it may concern:—

This is to certify that 1st Lt. Charles H. Beseda United States Army, attended the 14th session of the Army Sanitary School, between September 23rd 1918 and October 6th 1918 and that he completed the course of instruction provided in that session.

Colonel Dental Corps
Director Dental Section

Lt. Colonel Medical Corps
Director

In France, 1st Lt. Charles Beseda was a dentist in the Medical Corps, and his certificate of completion of a two-week session of the Army Sanitary School is on display at the Van Alstyne Historical Museum. After the war, Dr. Beseda married Ruth Kesler, a graduate of VAHS, and practiced dentistry in Van Alstyne for 40 years while actively serving as a community leader. (Courtesy of Van Alstyne Historical Society.)

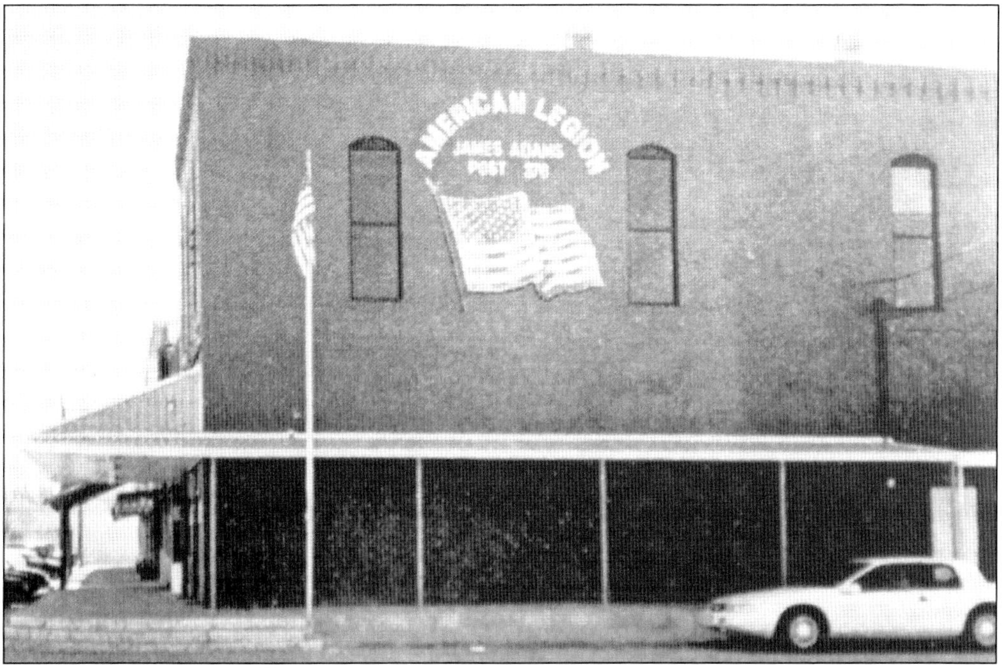

When an American Legion post was established in Van Alstyne in 1922, it was named after fallen hero Lt. Hobart Burk. But the post disbanded in 1928 from lack of interest. In 1938, a new American Legion post was organized and named after another Van Alstyne patriot, Lt. James Adams of the US Army. (Courtesy of Van Alstyne Historical Society.)

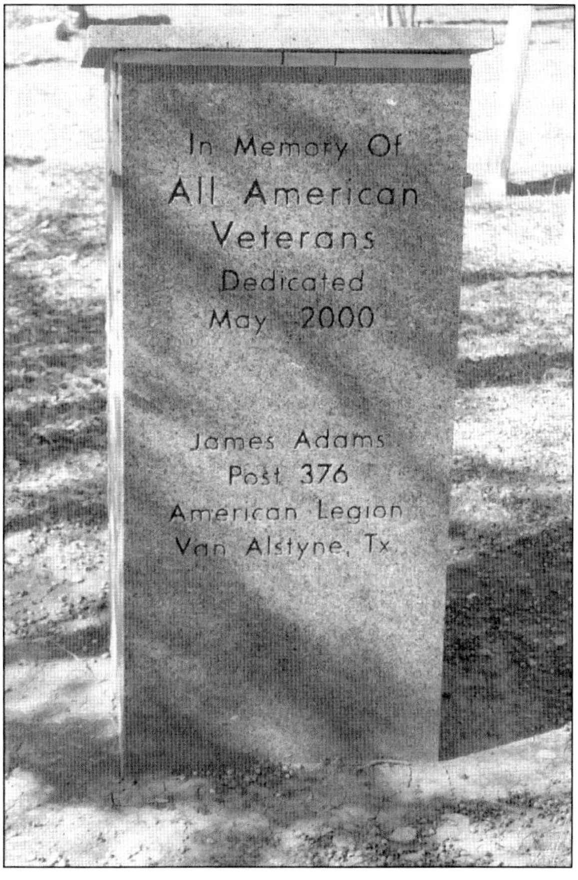

The James Adams Post 376 of the American Legion dedicated a monument "In Memory of All American Veterans" in 2000. (Photograph by the author.)

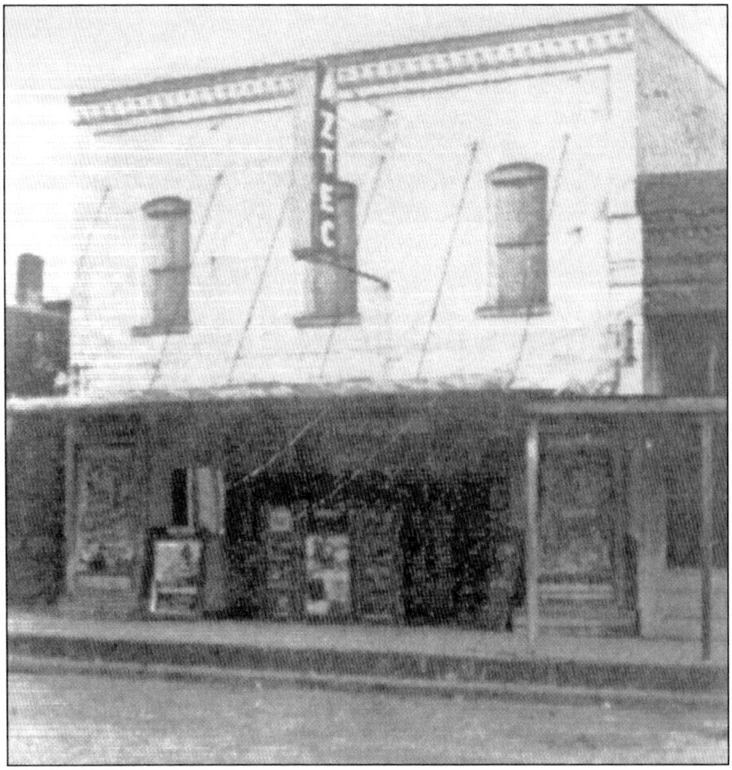

During the early 1900s, motion pictures became an enormously popular form of entertainment throughout America. By the mid-1920s, there were 20,000 movie theaters across the United States, and in 1946, one hundred million Americans went to the movies weekly. The Aztec, pictured at left, opened in 1936. The Aztec became Van Alstyne's third downtown theater, alongside the Lyric and the Ritz. (Courtesy of Van Alstyne Historical Society.)

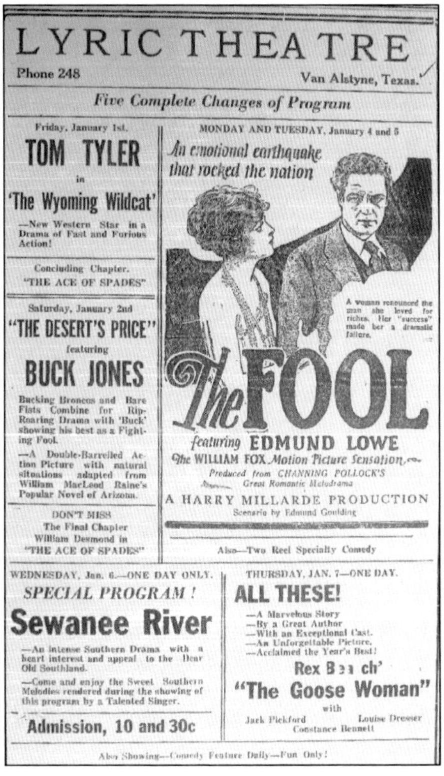

Theaters changed films every couple of days—indeed, sometimes there was a daily change of programs. There were double features and 13-week serials that played each Saturday for juvenile audiences, as well as cartoons and newsreels and other short features. This ad for the Lyric Theatre ran in the *Leader* in January 1926. (Author's collection.)

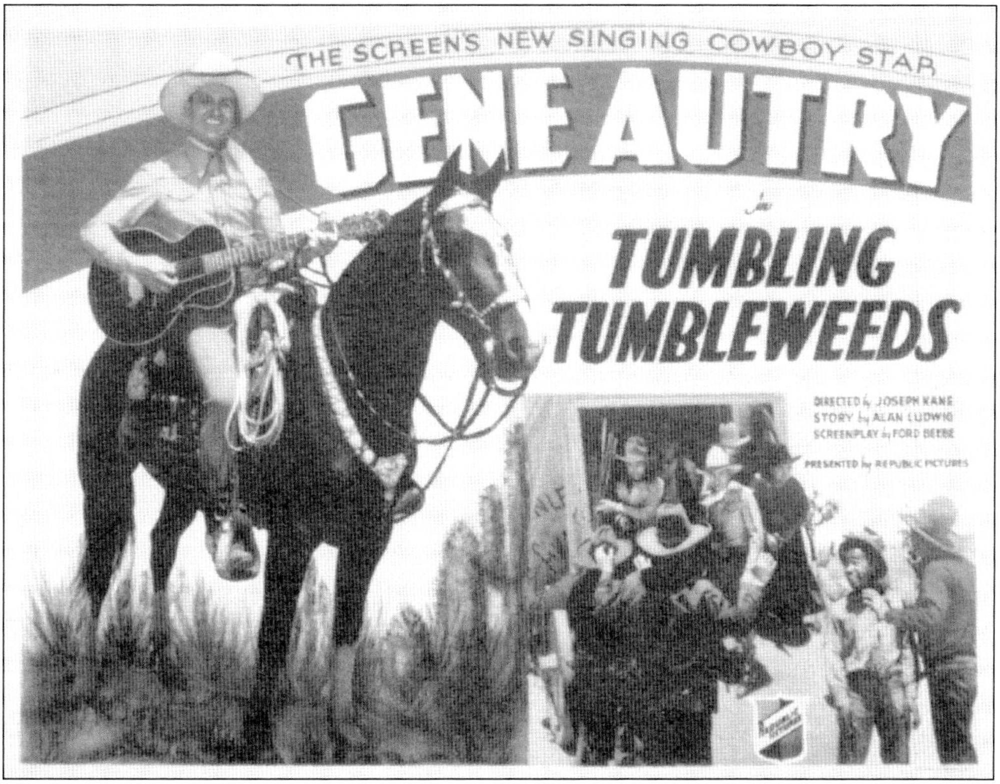

Western movies enjoyed great popularity in Van Alstyne, and no cowboy star had a greater following than Gene Autry. Gene was a schoolboy at Tioga, a little Grayson County farm town located about 20 miles west of Van Alstyne. As a young man, Gene pursued a singing career, and in 1935, he vaulted to stardom as Hollywood's first "Singing Cowboy." (Author's collection.)

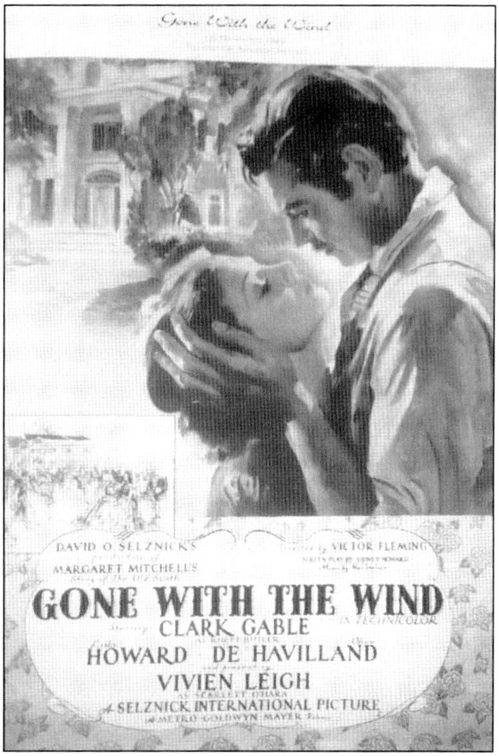

In 1939, the Aztec Theater featured one of the greatest hits in motion picture history, *Gone with the Wind*. Held over for three consecutive three-day runs, every showing of the movie was a sellout. (Author's collection.)

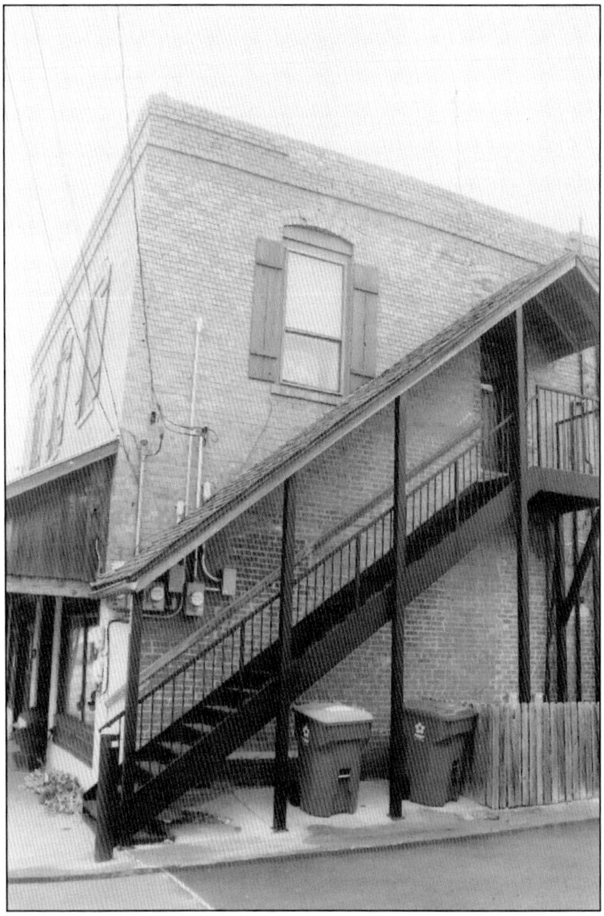

Chief of police Will Echols habitually patrolled the streets of Van Alstyne after midnight. About 2:40 a.m. on Thursday, March 21, 1929, one or more criminals opened fire on him from an alley that opened onto Preston between Jefferson and Cooper Streets. Chief Echols was hit twice. He promptly returned fire, but after two rounds, his Colt .45 revolver, damaged by a bullet, would not work. (Photograph by the author.)

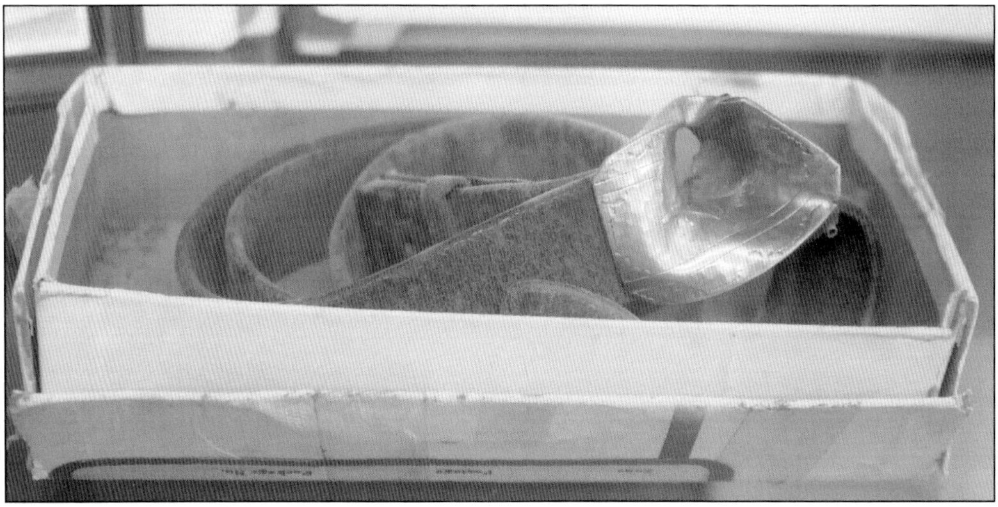

One bullet penetrated the chief's belt buckle. The criminals fled and escaped town. Chief Echols staggered to a doctor's office a block away and was taken to a Sherman hospital. The 67-year-old officer died of his wounds two days later. The damaged buckle and belt are on display at the Van Alstyne Historical Museum. (Photograph by the author.)

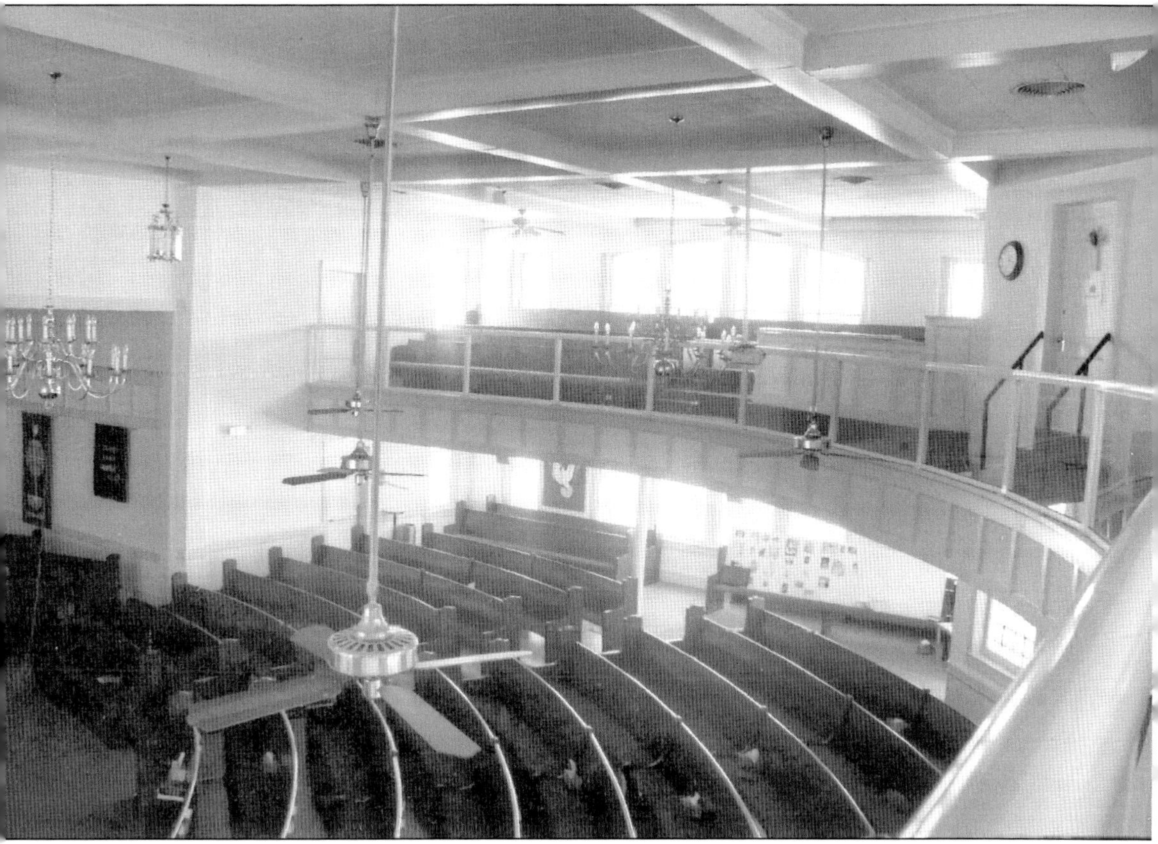

Chief Echols was survived by his wife of 22 years, Ethel, and their sons, Bill and Keith. Funeral services were held at the Methodist church, which the family attended, and at the graveside. No Van Alstyne funeral has ever attracted such a crowd, estimated at 2,500 to 3,000 mourners. Someone counted 432 automobiles. The president and dean of North Texas State Teachers College, where Bill and Keith were students, came from Denton, along with the head football coach and 14 of Bill's teammates. (Photograph by the author.)

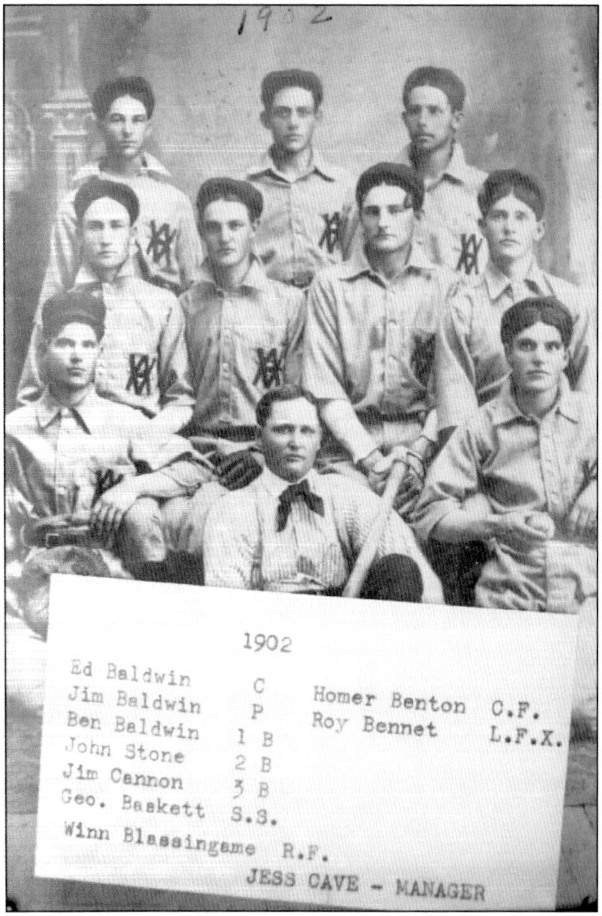

"Base ball" was a popular sport in Van Alstyne during the late 1800s. By 1902, the town was represented by the Grays, a crack nine managed by Jess Cave (front center, with a bat). Clad in flannel uniforms and dark, short-billed caps, these young athletes sported the center-parted hair fashionable at the turn of the century. (Courtesy of Van Alstyne Historical Society.)

In 1936, the Van Alstyne Grays moved into a new 600-seat ballpark, which featured a covered grandstand with a field house beneath. Located north of the school campus, the park was named after Gus Thomasson, a Van Alstyne native who was district director of the Works Progress Administration. Thomasson's WPA headed construction efforts. The Van Alstyne Oil Burners, an African American team, also played in the new park. (Courtesy of Van Alstyne Historical Society.)

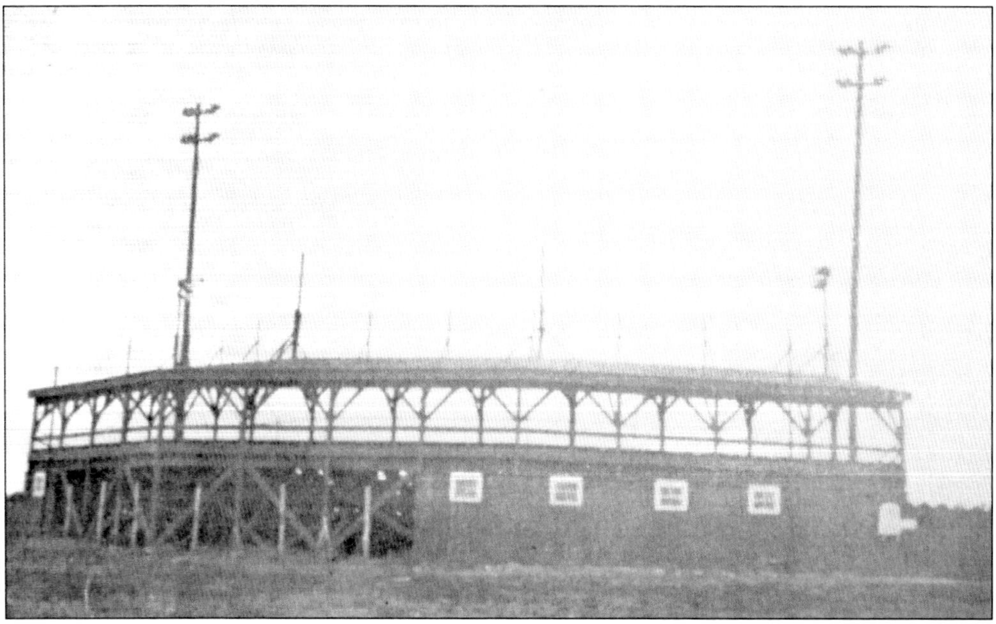

Samuel "Dolly" Gray was born in Van Alstyne in 1897. A right-handed pitcher, he advanced from the local team to the Texas League, playing for the Fort Worth Cats in back-to-back championship seasons in 1922 and 1923. In 1924, he went up to the American League, pitching for the Philadelphia Athletics for four seasons before being traded to the St. Louis Browns. In 1928, Gray was 20-12 for the Browns. The next year, he went 18-15 and led the league in games started (37), innings pitched (305), and shutouts (4). He pitched 10 years in the AL and then spent a couple more years in the minor leagues before returning home to play for the Grays. The former big-leaguer died in 1953 in McKinney. (Right, courtesy of Van Alstyne Historical Society; below, author's collection.)

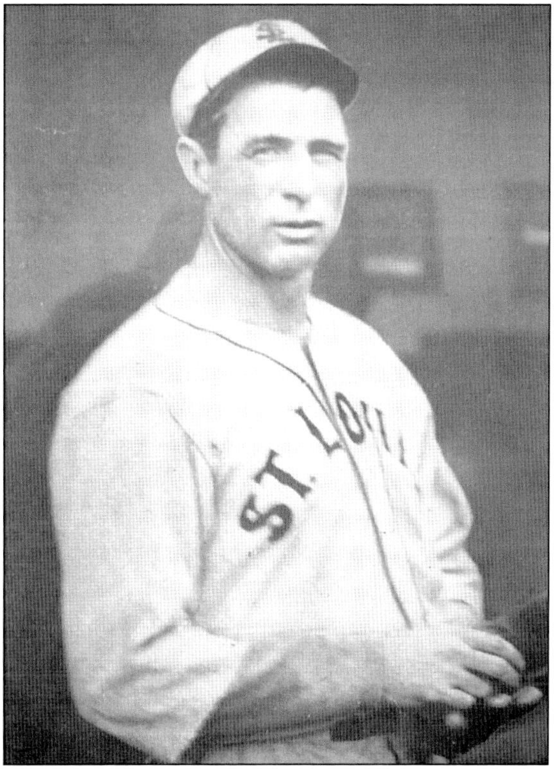

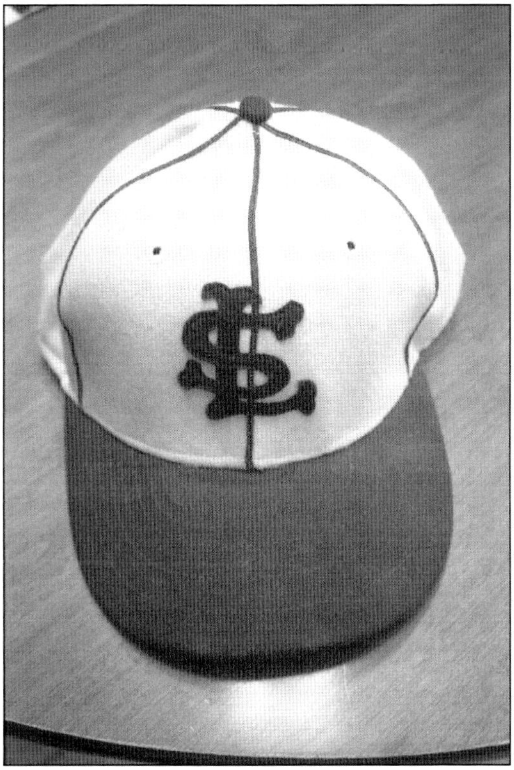

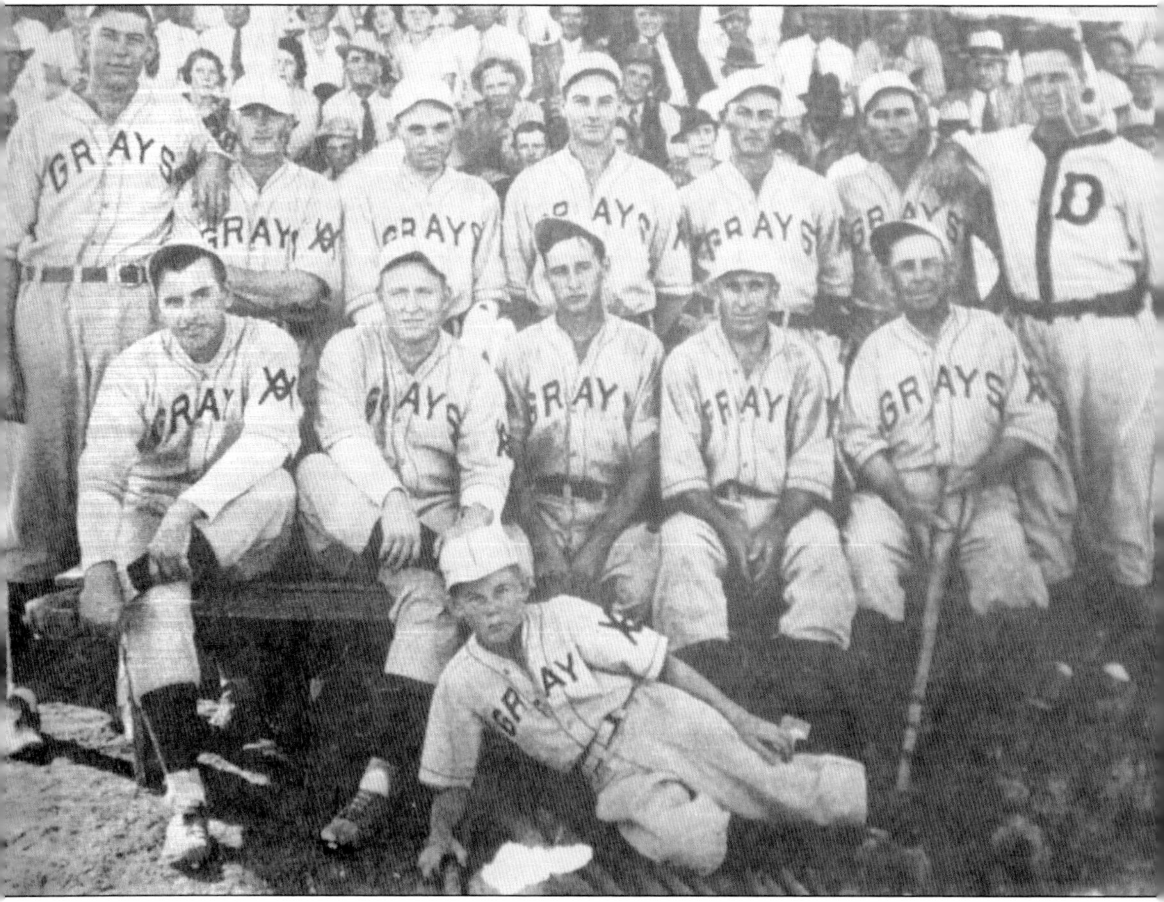

The Van Alstyne Grays enjoyed winning seasons and strong fan support throughout the 1930s. Beginning in 1931, the Grays won four championships in five years in the semi-pro Red River Valley League, playing on Sundays against clubs from nearby Sherman, McKinney, Gunter, Leonard, Whitesboro, and Bonham. Half of the roster of the 1932 Grays, pictured above, was talented enough to play professionally: Monty Stratton (standing at far left) pitched for the White Sox and became an All-Star; John Whitehead (standing far right) also played for the White Sox and for Dallas in the Texas League; Kenneth Williams (standing beside Whitehead), Doak Grider (seated middle), and Carl McMahon (seated second from right) all played in the minor leagues; and Perry Hunter (seated far left) was a Texas League umpire for eight years. (Courtesy of Van Alstyne Historical Society.)

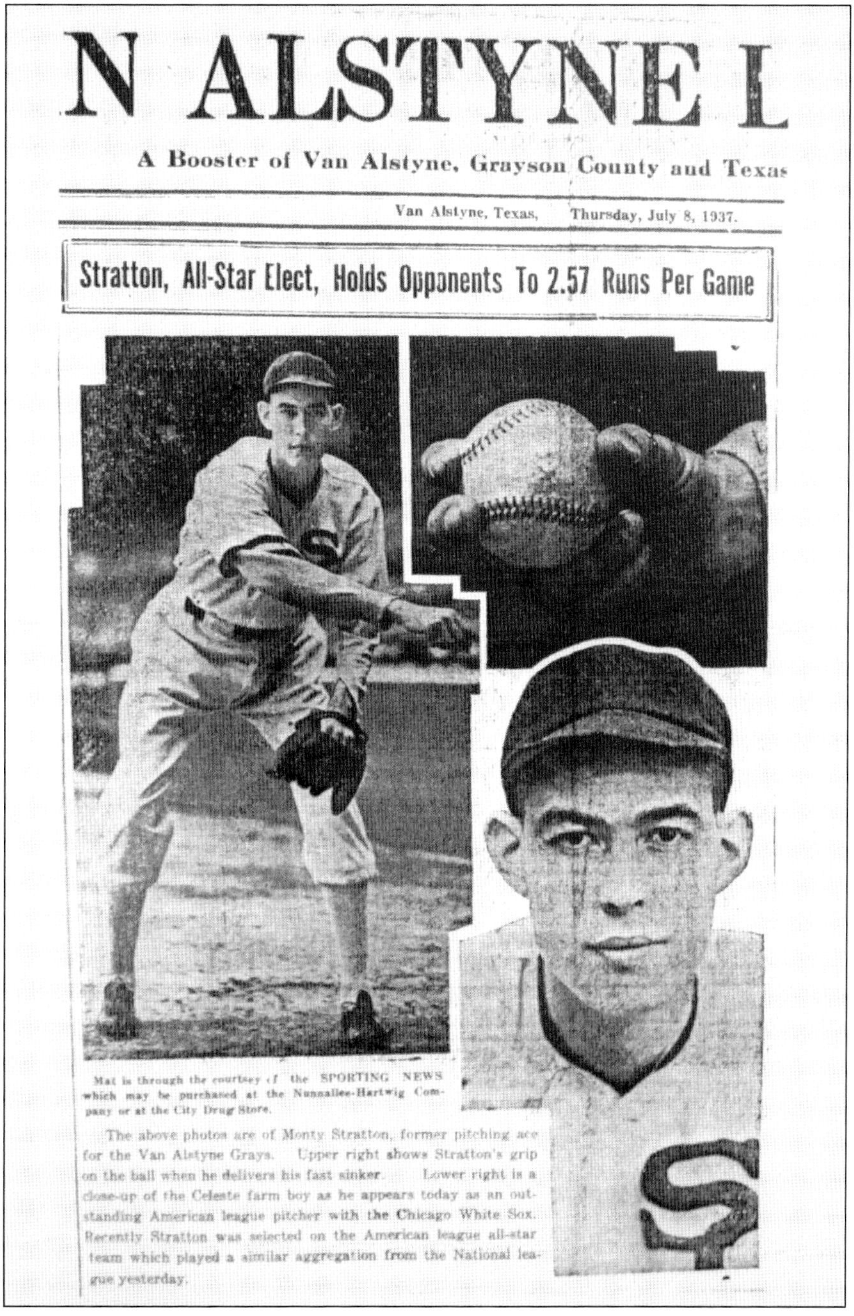

N ALSTYNE I

A Booster of Van Alstyne, Grayson County and Texas

Van Alstyne, Texas, Thursday, July 8, 1937.

Stratton, All-Star Elect, Holds Opponents To 2.57 Runs Per Game

Mat is through the courtesy of the SPORTING NEWS which may be purchased at the Nunnallee-Hartwig Company or at the City Drug Store.

The above photos are of Monty Stratton, former pitching ace for the Van Alstyne Grays. Upper right shows Stratton's grip on the ball when he delivers his fast sinker. Lower right is a close-up of the Celeste farm boy as he appears today as an outstanding American league pitcher with the Chicago White Sox. Recently Stratton was selected on the American league all-star team which played a similar aggregation from the National league yesterday.

In 1932 and 1933, Monty Stratton, a six-foot-five farm boy from Hunt County, pitched for the Grays. A talented right-hander with a wicked curveball, Stratton pitched briefly with the Chicago White Sox in 1934, and by 1937, he was 15-5 and a member of the American League All-Star team. Another 15-win performance followed in 1938, but after the season, he lost his right leg in a hunting accident. Courageously launching a comeback, Stratton pitched brilliantly in 1946, posting an 18-8 record with Sherman in the Class C East Texas League. Van Alstyne fans were able to see him perform in nearby Sherman, and in 1949, they could watch James Stewart play Monty at the Aztec Theater in *The Stratton Story*. (Courtesy of Van Alstyne Public Library.)

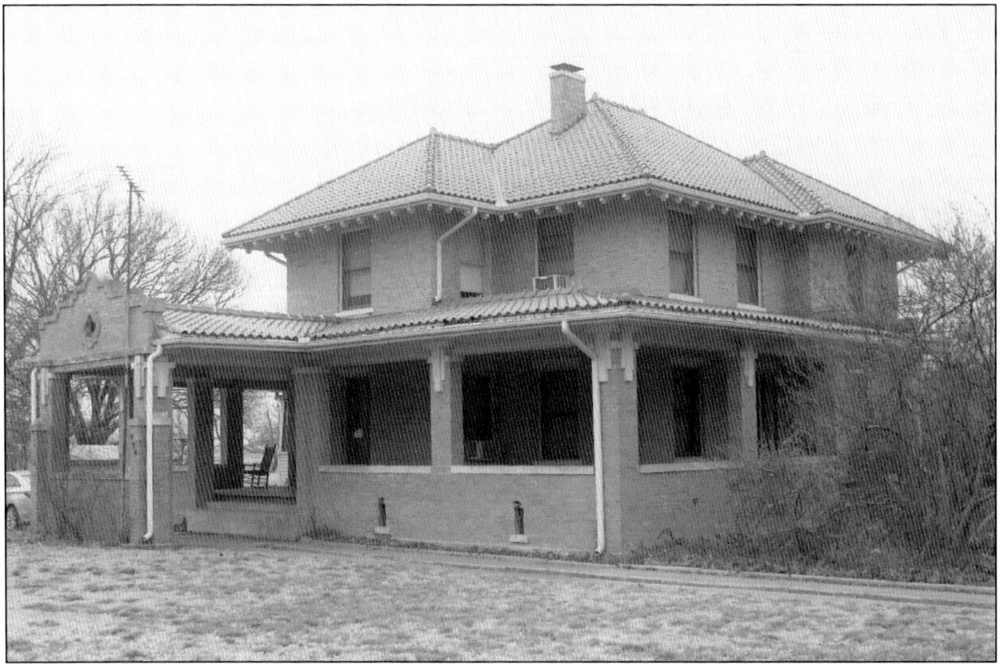

The first brick home in Van Alstyne was built by Creed and Alline Taylor in 1911. The Mission-style residence features a Spanish tile roof and still stands on Highway 5. (Photograph by the author.)

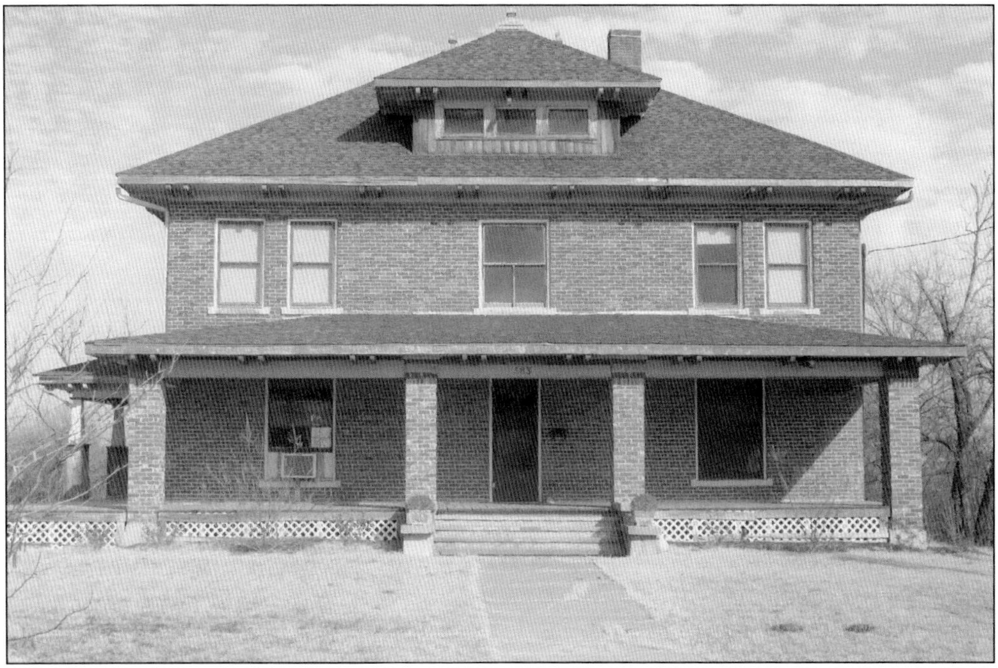

Dr. Stephen Douglas Moore used his spacious brick home, located on South West Main Street, for his medical practice. The front door provided access to the living room, on the right, which was used as the reception area. At left, the room built as a dining room was where Dr. Moore focused his medical efforts, including the birth of hundreds of babies. (Photograph by the author.)

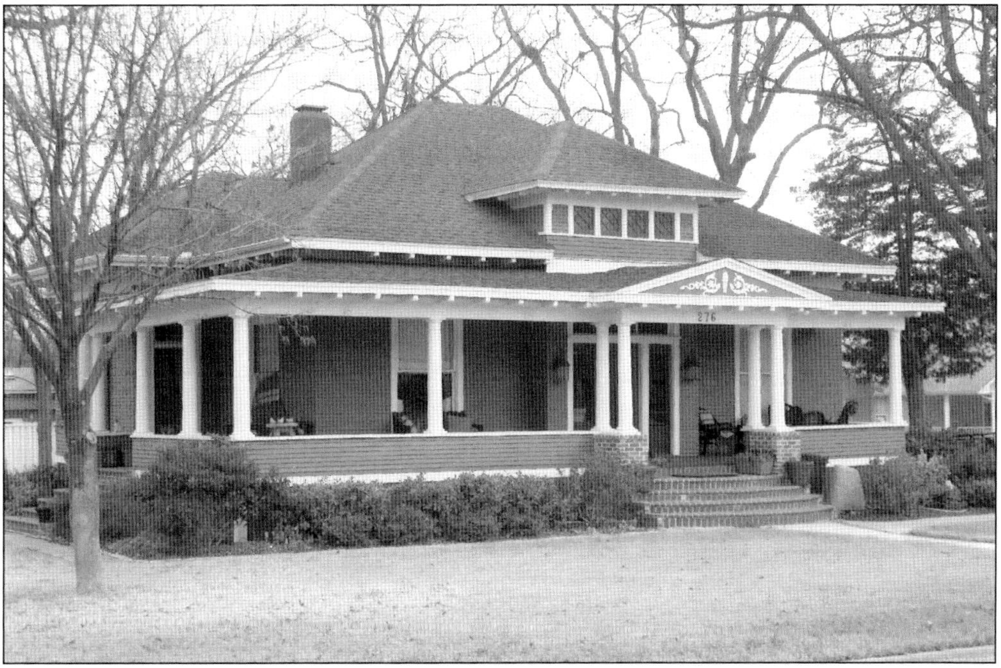

This bungalow-style residence was built in the 1920s for L.A. and Vera Webb Cartwright. Cartwright was the longtime vice president of the First National Bank, while Vera taught in Van Alstyne's elementary school. (Photograph by the author.)

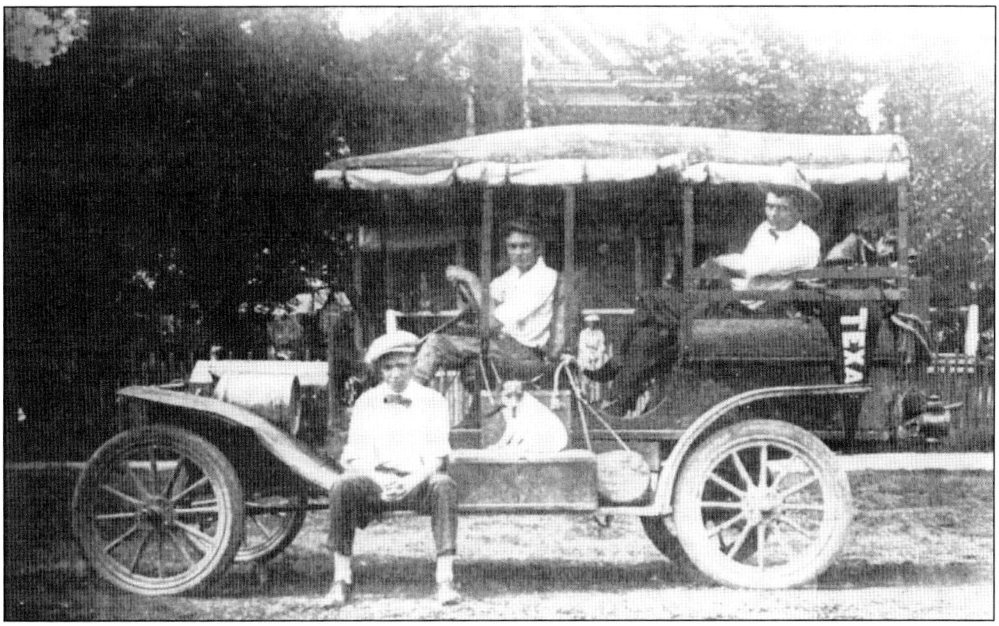

At the wheel of this 1914 Ford Model T converted to a truck was Dave Gray. Dave's brother, John Gray, sits on the running board, while Roy Cotten is in the back. The Ford is parked on unpaved Jefferson Street, with the Gray home in the background. The "Texas" pennant suggests that at least one of these young men attended the state university. (Courtesy of Van Alstyne Historical Society.)

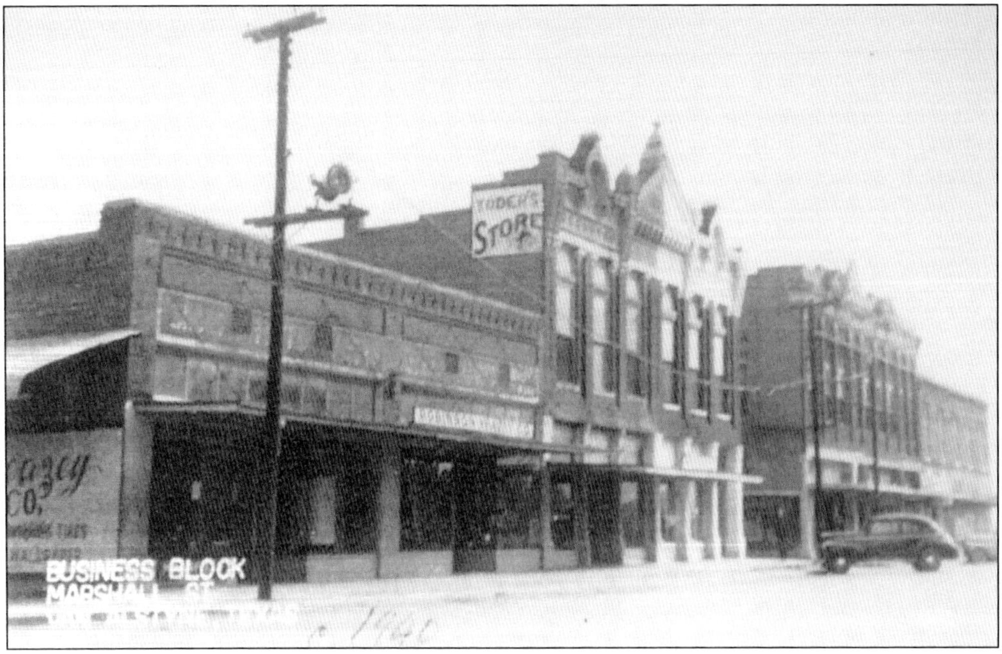

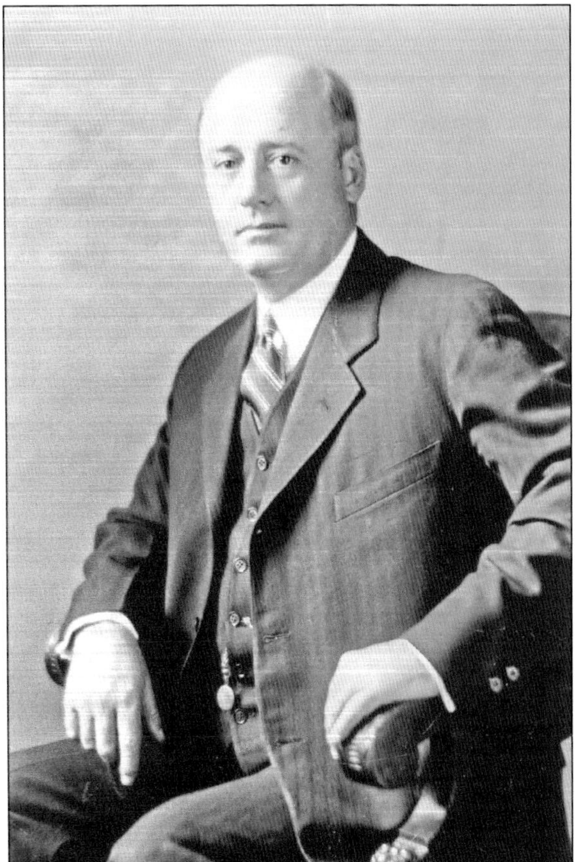

This downtown scene from the 1940s exhibits the paved thoroughfares that finally replaced the longtime dirt and mud streets. Above is the north side of Marshall Street, with the former opera house at right. After 65 years with unpaved streets, Van Alstyne citizens approved the sale of $20,000 in bonds for street pavement in 1937. The Works Progress Administration provided $32,000, and by July 1938, eight city blocks were paved. Congressman Sam Rayburn, pictured at left, had triggered WPA support of the project, and "Mr. Sam" led the ribbon-cutting ceremony on July 26, 1938. A record crowd of 12,000 enjoyed a parade and exuberant celebration along the newly paved streets. (Above, courtesy of Griff Servati; left, author's collection.)

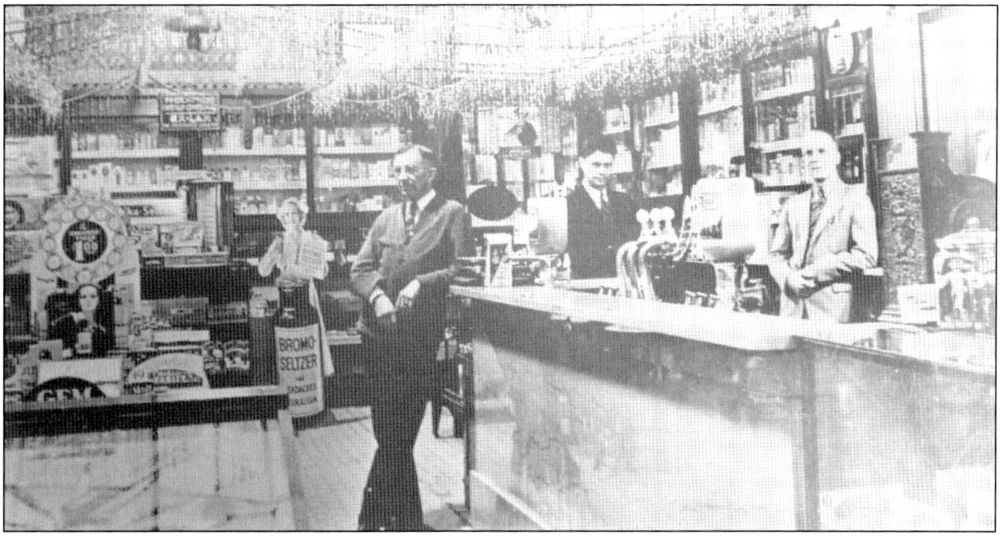

Druggist Luther Kinard, seen here leaning on the counter of his soda fountain, owned the City Drug Store in the mid-1930s. At right is druggist Charlie Williford, and in the dark suit at center is jeweler Foy Bellows. The City Drug Store is in the same Jefferson Street location today, owned by druggist David Schatz, who also owns other properties around town, including the old Carter Opera House building. (Courtesy of Van Alstyne Historical Society.)

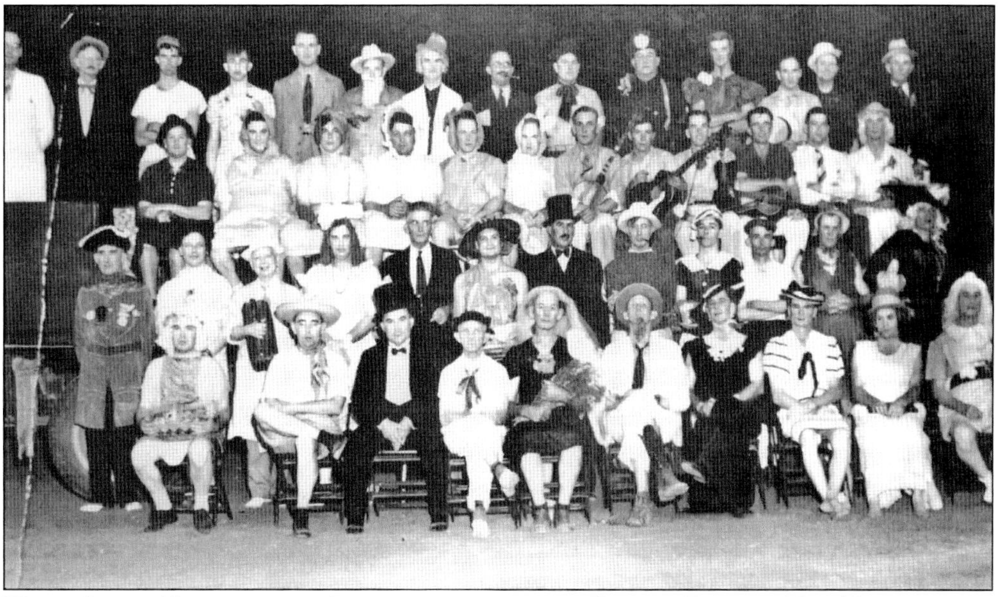

Womanless weddings were popular entertainments in small towns. For years, Van Alstyne citizens staged womanless weddings in the brick gym built by the Public Works Administration. These entertainments were staged as fundraisers for civic projects. The costumed group pictured above performed in 1951. (Courtesy of Van Alstyne Historical Society.)

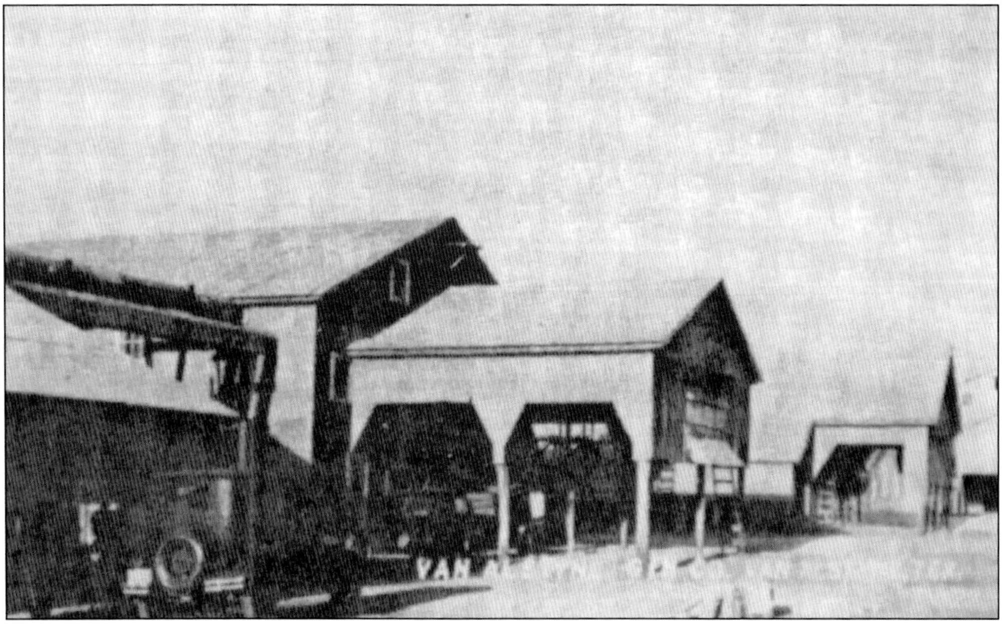

Cotton production remained high during the 1920s and even during the Great Depression, so the cotton gins of Van Alstyne were as busy as ever, providing steady employment for men of the community. (Courtesy of Van Alstyne Historical Society.)

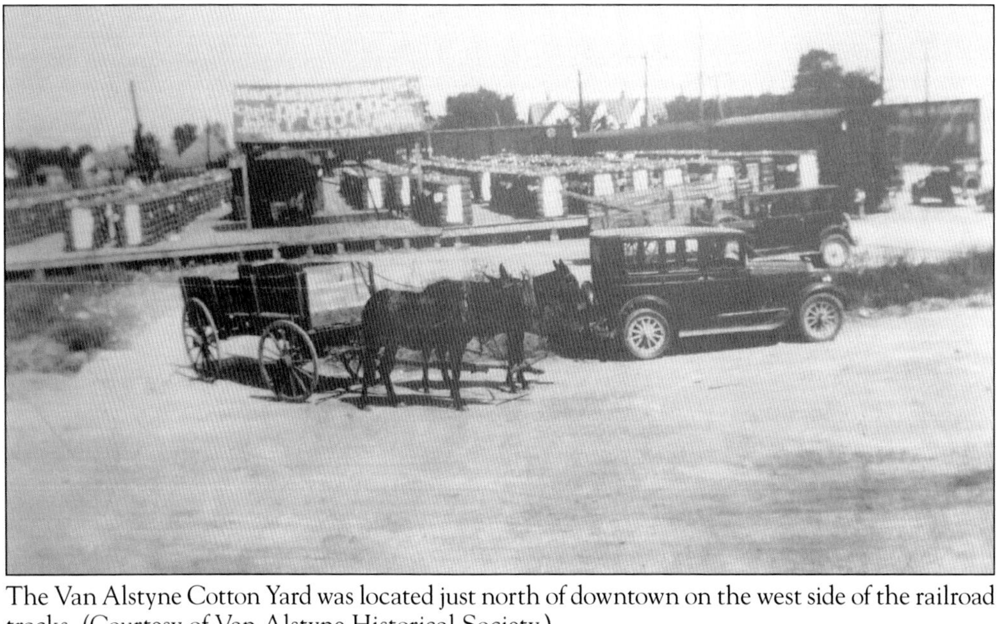

The Van Alstyne Cotton Yard was located just north of downtown on the west side of the railroad tracks. (Courtesy of Van Alstyne Historical Society.)

In 1929, this wooden oil derrick was erected with great hope in northeast of Van Alstyne. The well did not produce, and in 1936, the heavy timbers were used in construction of the grandstand at the new baseball park. (Courtesy of Van Alstyne Historical Society.)

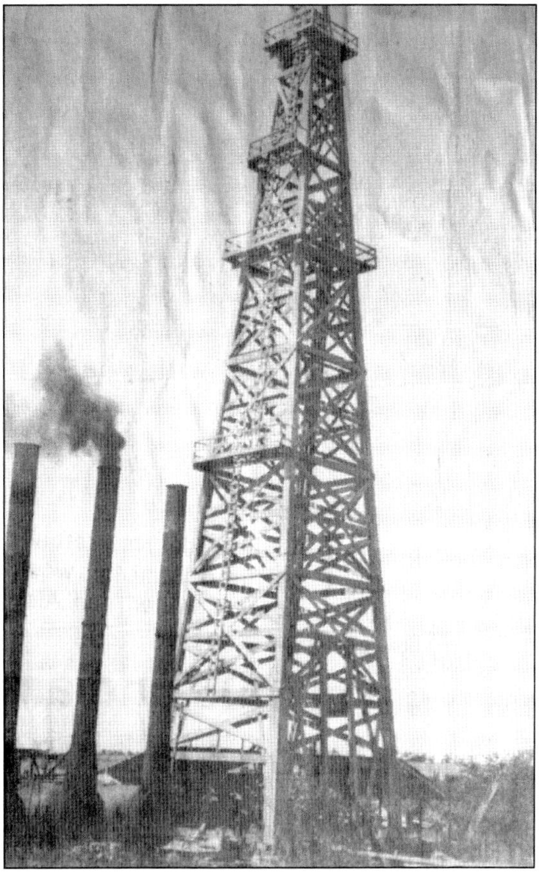

In 1936, a Van Alstyne youngster drove a small wagon pulled by two goats to the Yoder Motor Company. Perhaps the lad had a trade-in in mind. (Courtesy of Van Alstyne Historical Society.)

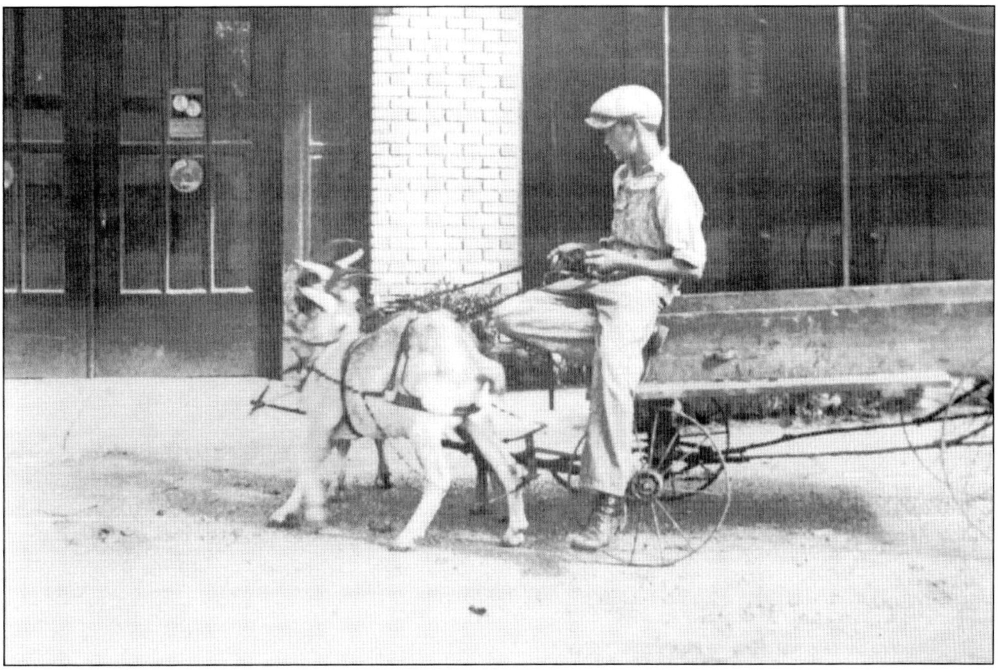

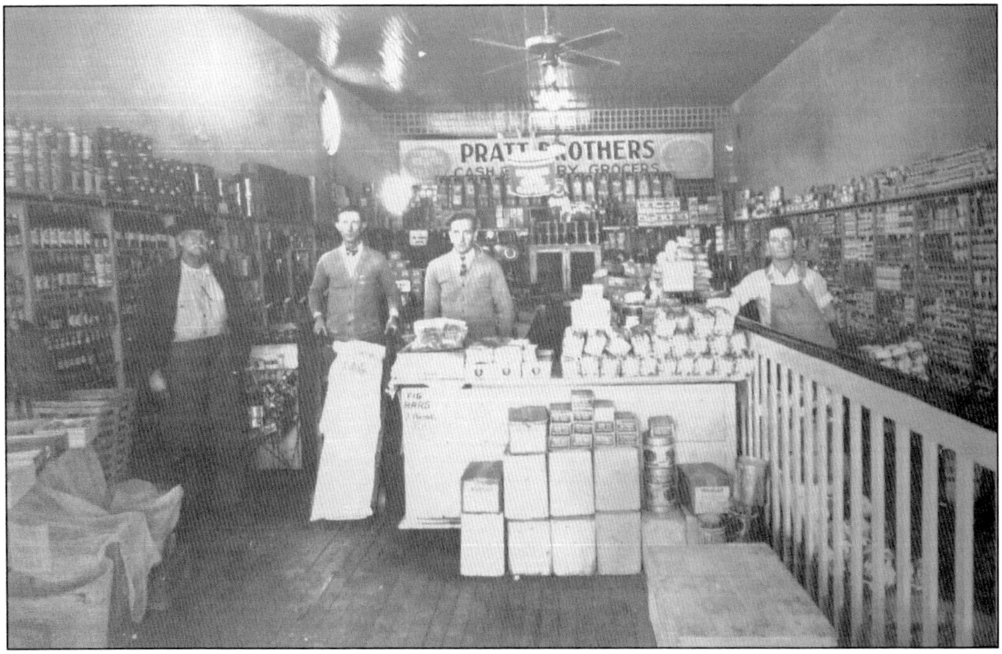

The Pratt Brothers Grocery Store, show here around 1930, was typical of the downtown grocery stores which long served the needs of Van Alstyne citizens. Downtown commercial buildings were long and narrow, and stock had to be arranged accordingly. Ceiling fans were in all stores, keeping the air moving on warm days. (Courtesy of Van Alstyne Historical Society.)

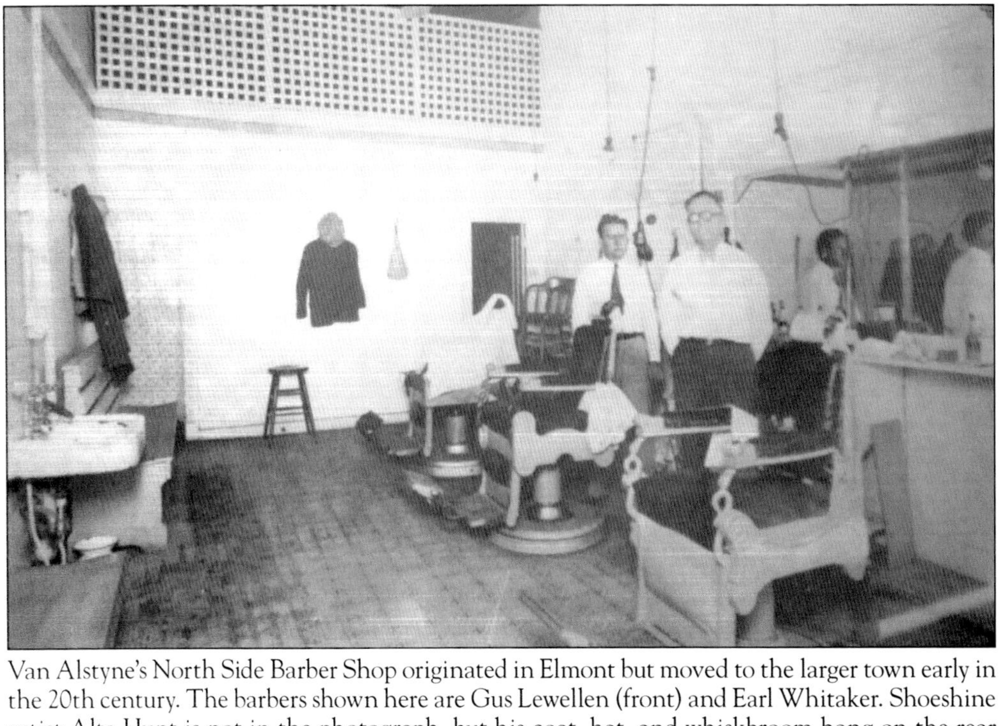

Van Alstyne's North Side Barber Shop originated in Elmont but moved to the larger town early in the 20th century. The barbers shown here are Gus Lewellen (front) and Earl Whitaker. Shoeshine artist Alto Hunt is not in the photograph, but his coat, hat, and whiskbroom hang on the rear wall. (Courtesy of Van Alstyne Historical Society.)

On September 10, 1935, the Texas State Board of Embalming awarded a funeral directing license to Inez Jones of Van Alstyne. Inez was the first woman to be licensed in Texas, and she remained affiliated with the Felsher Funeral Home the rest of her career. (Courtesy of Texas Women's University.)

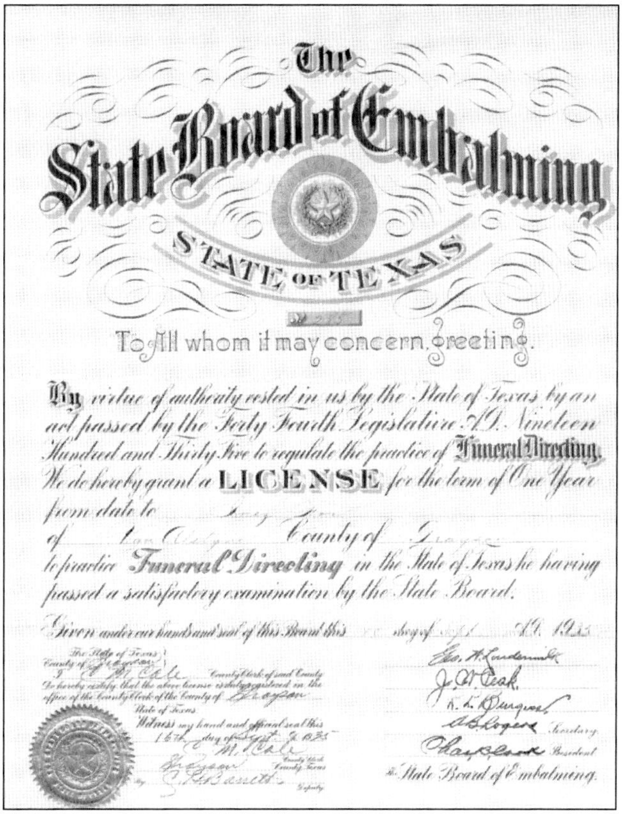

The State Board of Embalming

State of Texas

To All whom it may concern, greeting.

By virtue of authority vested in us by the State of Texas by an act passed by the Forty Fourth Legislature A.D. Nineteen Hundred and Thirty Five to regulate the practice of Funeral Directing. We do hereby grant a LICENSE for the term of One Year from date to [illegible] of [illegible] County of [illegible] to practice Funeral Directing in the State of Texas he having passed a satisfactory examination by the State Board.

Given under our hand and seal of this Board this [illegible] day of [illegible] A.D. 193[illegible]

The State of Texas County of [illegible] I, [illegible] County Clerk of said County do hereby certify that the above license is duly registered in the office of the County Clerk of the County of [illegible] State of Texas. Witness my hand and official seal this [illegible] day of [illegible]

Secretary. President. The State Board of Embalming.

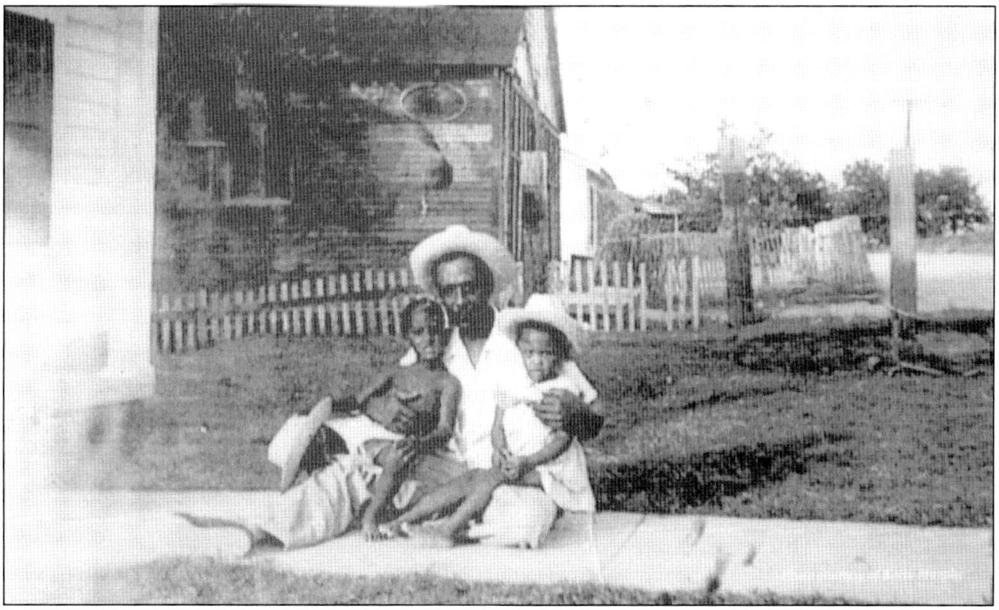

Simon Peter Stinnett sits on the front sidewalk of his Fulton Street home with grandchildren Garry and Charlotte Murphy. The frame building in the background was the Old Café, a popular gathering place for Van Alstyne's African American citizens. (Courtesy of Van Alstyne Historical Society.)

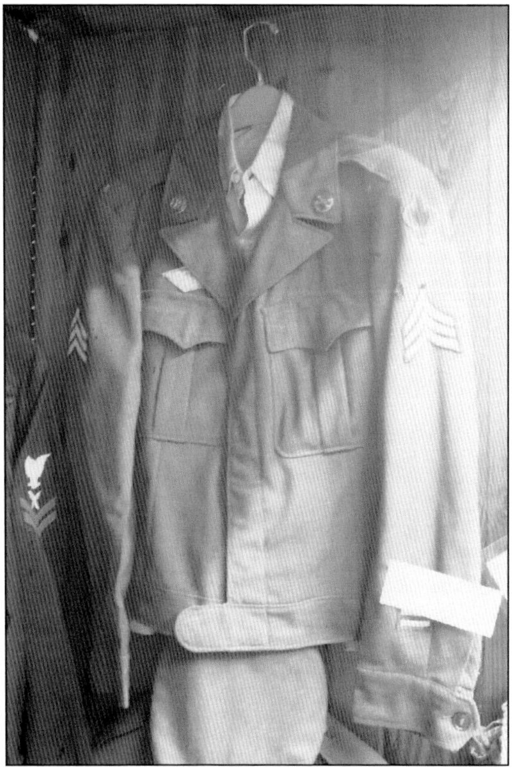

During World War II, 16 million men entered the US armed forces, including 830,000 Texans. More than 22,000 Texans lost their lives, a sad but courageous number that included at least 27 men from Van Alstyne. The Van Alstyne Historical Museum exhibits this infantry uniform worn by Sgt. Robert Hynds, son of World War I veteran Henry Hynds. (Photograph by the author.)

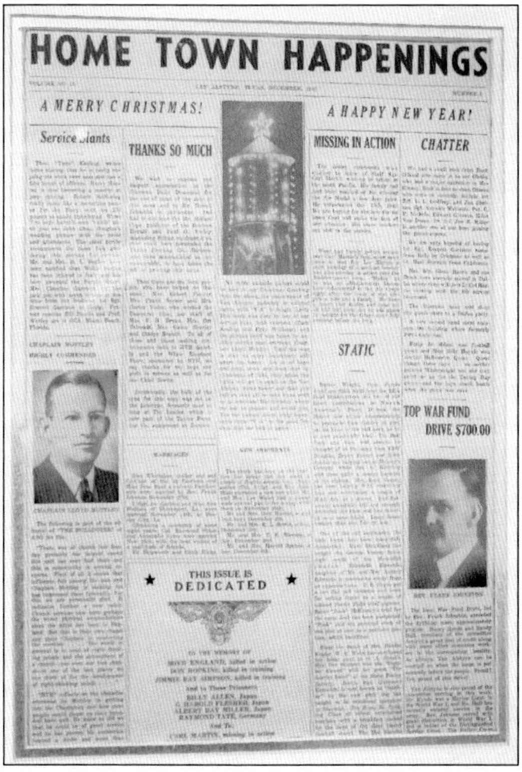

HOME TOWN HAPPENINGS

A MERRY CHRISTMAS!

A HAPPY NEW YEAR!

Service Slants

THANKS SO MUCH

MISSING IN ACTION

CHATTER

STATIC

TOP WAR FUND DRIVE $700.00

THIS ISSUE IS DEDICATED

In December 1942, Robert Fielder, who had written letters to several servicemen, began sending out a newsletter, *Home Town Happenings*. Postage was paid by donations, and there were 34 issues, the last of which was in the final months of the war, September 1945. (Courtesy of First Christian Church.)

On July 4, 1946, Van Alstyne staged a homecoming parade and picnic for servicemen who had returned to town during recent months. Leading the parade astride white horses were Stone Marshall (pictured at right) and Bill Stewart, both of whom had finished the war as German POWs. (Courtesy of Van Alstyne Historical Society.)

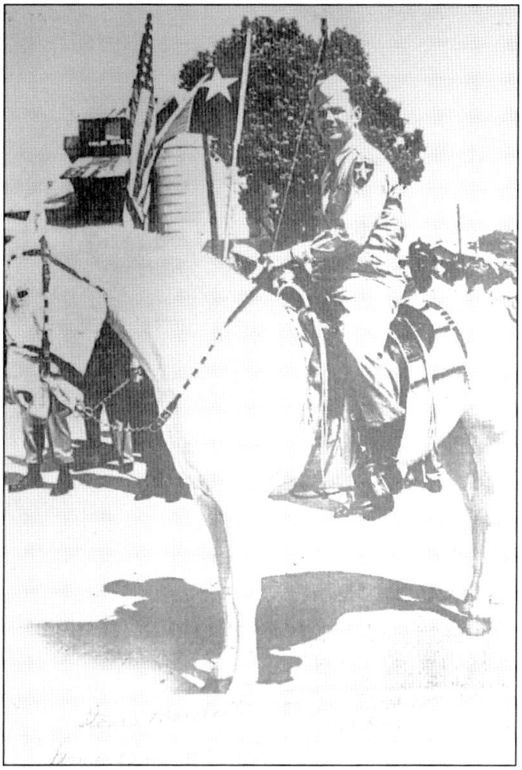

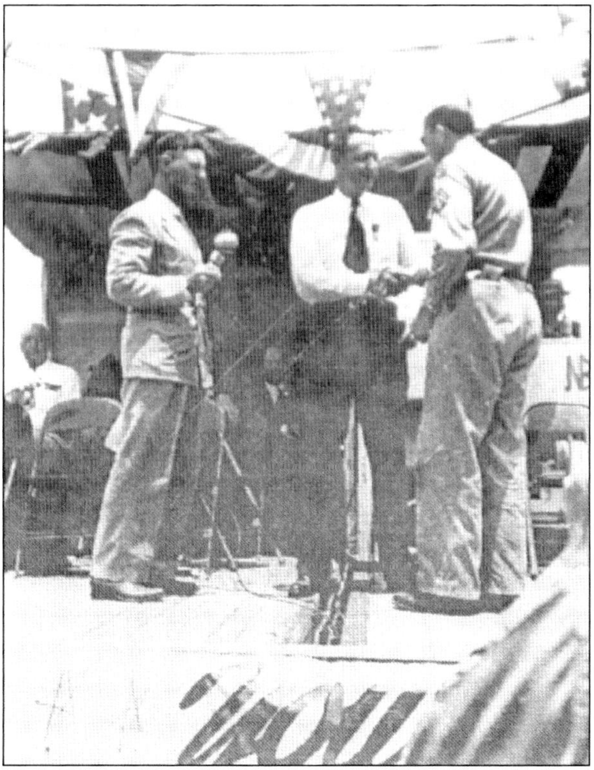

Welcoming returning veteran Randolph Hall at the July 4 Homecoming is Robert Fielder and, at left with microphone, Henry Hynds. A key community leader, Hynds served as mayor, chairman of the school board, board chairman of the First Christian Church, manager of the Van Alstyne Cemetery Foundation, and chairman of the Van Alstyne Housing Authority. He was a member of the chamber of commerce, Masonic lodge, American Legion, area Boy Scout council, and, during World War II, the Selective Service Board. (Courtesy of Van Alstyne Historical Society.)

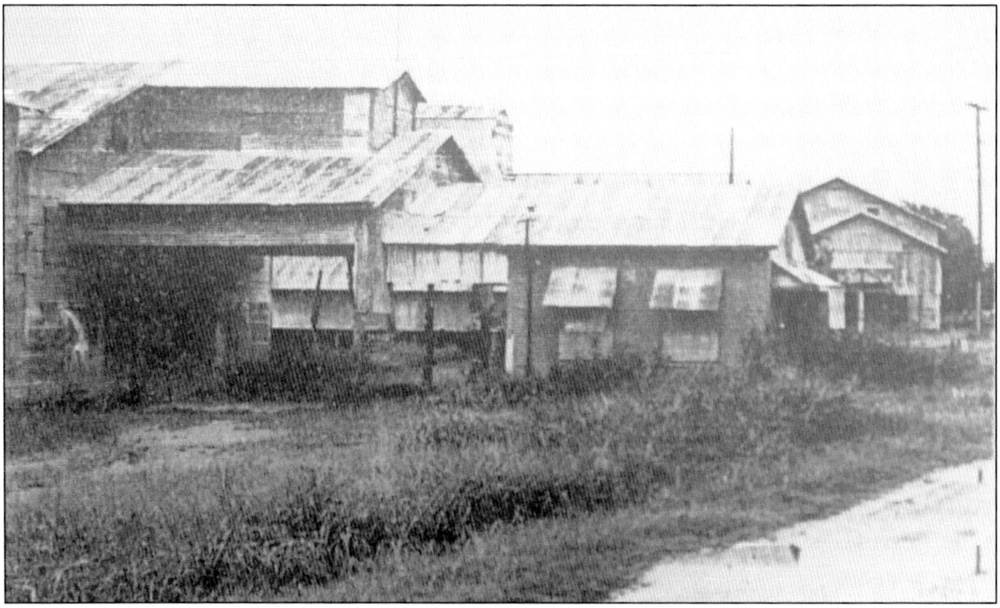

During the postwar years, area cotton production began a long decline. Van Alstyne's cotton gins closed one by one. The last gin shut down in 1957, although some of the buildings, such as the one above, were used for storage. When the Van Alstyne Cotton Oil Mill closed, the large complex of buildings began to deteriorate. Today, few remains are left of the structure that long provided employment to Van Alstyne men. (Both, courtesy Van Alstyne Historical Society.)

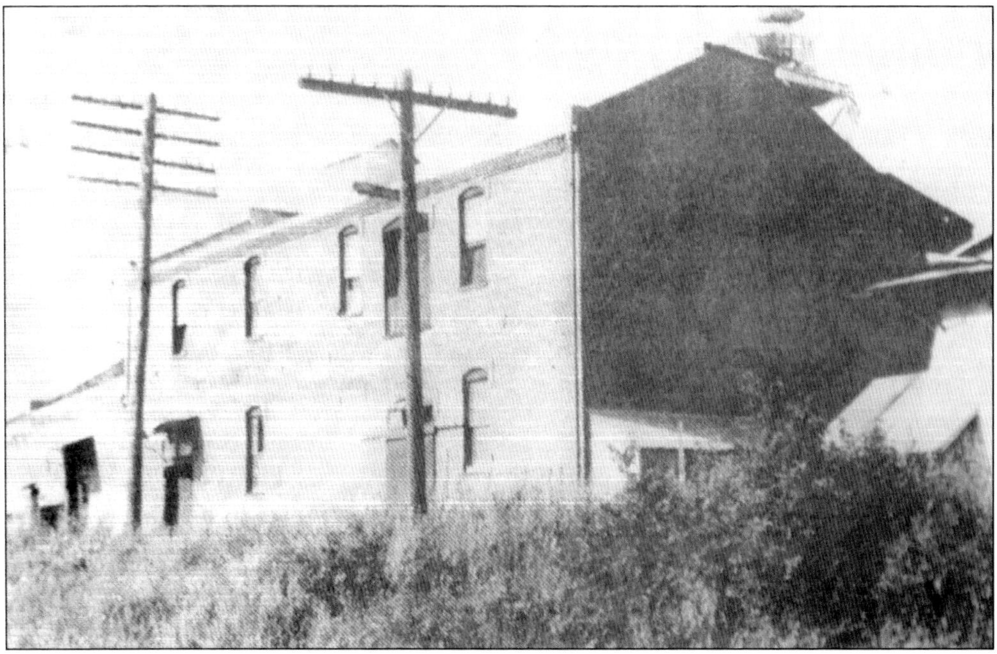

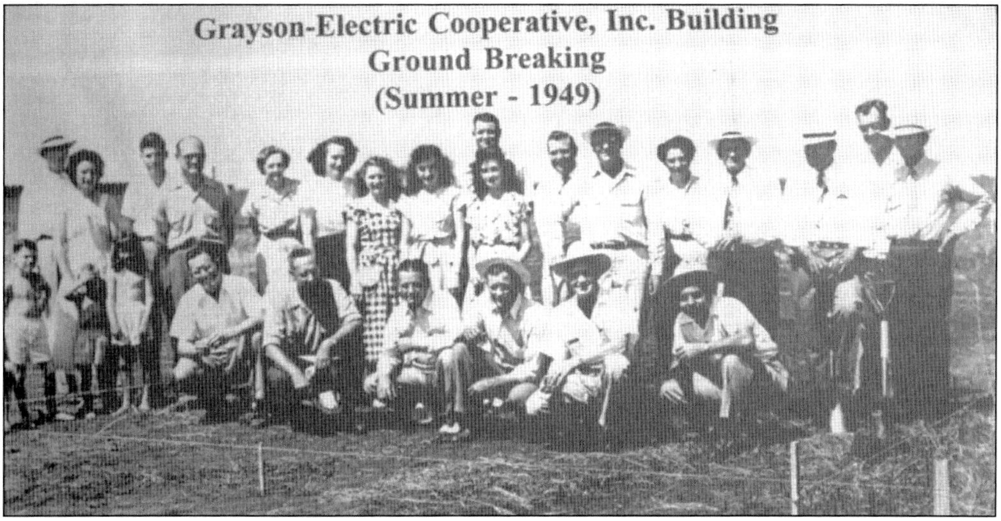

Van Alstyne had enjoyed electrical service for decades, but there was a significant upgrade in 1949, when ground was broken for a new building to house the local headquarters of the Grayson-Electric Cooperative, Inc. (Courtesy of Van Alstyne Historical Society.)

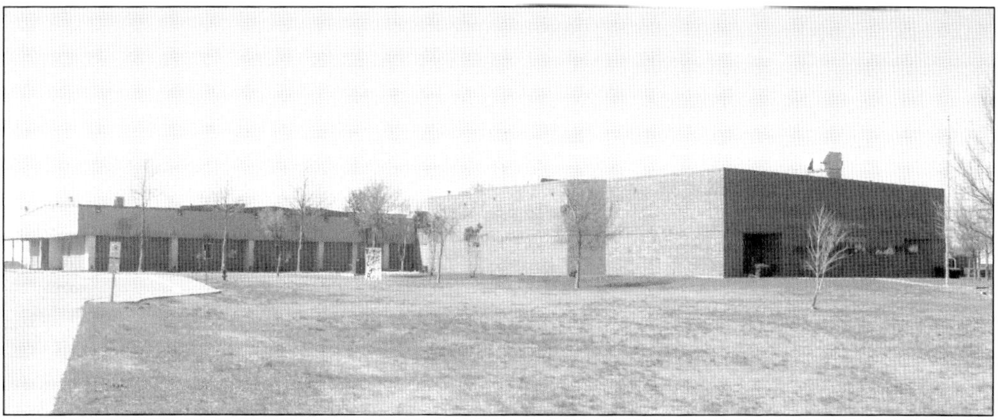

A spacious, modern high school opened on the north edge of Van Alstyne in 1972. School buildings had all been clustered on the old Columbia College campus, although the football stadium was a couple of blocks to the north. The new Van Alstyne High School stood north of the stadium and was an enormous source of pride of the community. (Photograph by the author.)

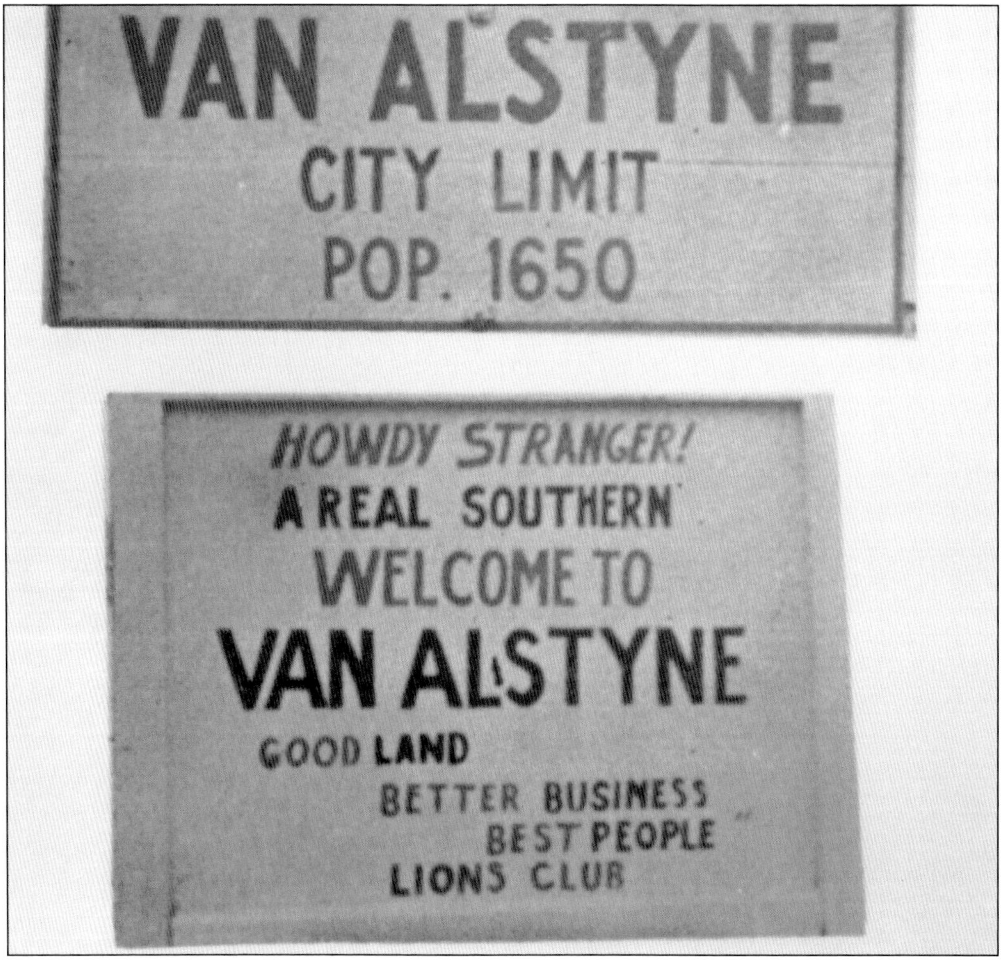

Van Alstyne ended the 20th century as it had begun, a mainstay of small town life and values. But noticeable growth was under way, and the new century would see more expansion and change. (Courtesy of Van Alstyne Historical Society.)

Seven

Into the 21st Century

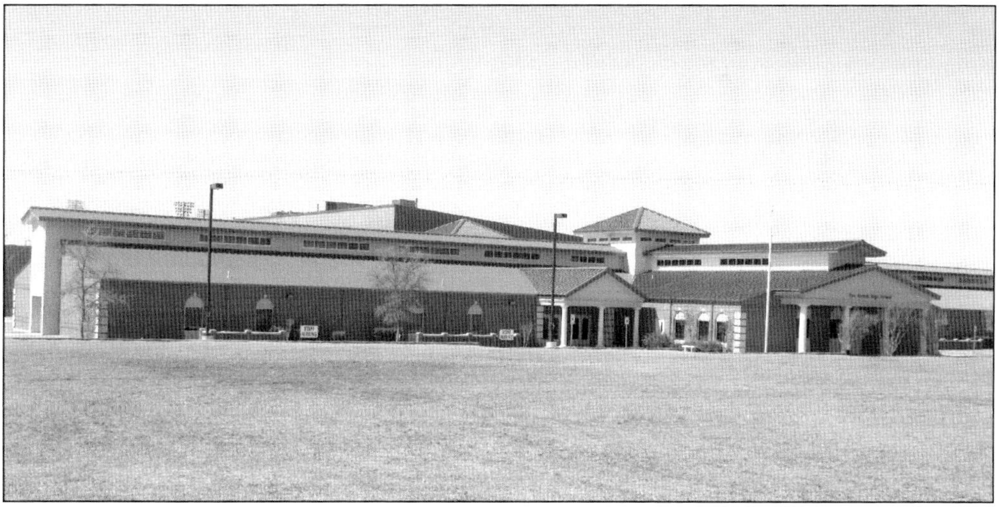

In 2003, Van Alstyne High School relocated to a splendid new campus on the northern outskirts of town. VAHS was just beginning its second century after beginning its first century in the old Columbia College building. In 1910, VAHS moved to Van Alstyne's first brick school. In 1954, VAHS opened classes in a modern single-story building on the north part of the campus. The next move was also to the north, into a new brick facility, which became the Van Alstyne Middle School when VAHS began operations in the impressive new school built in 2003. (Photograph by the author.)

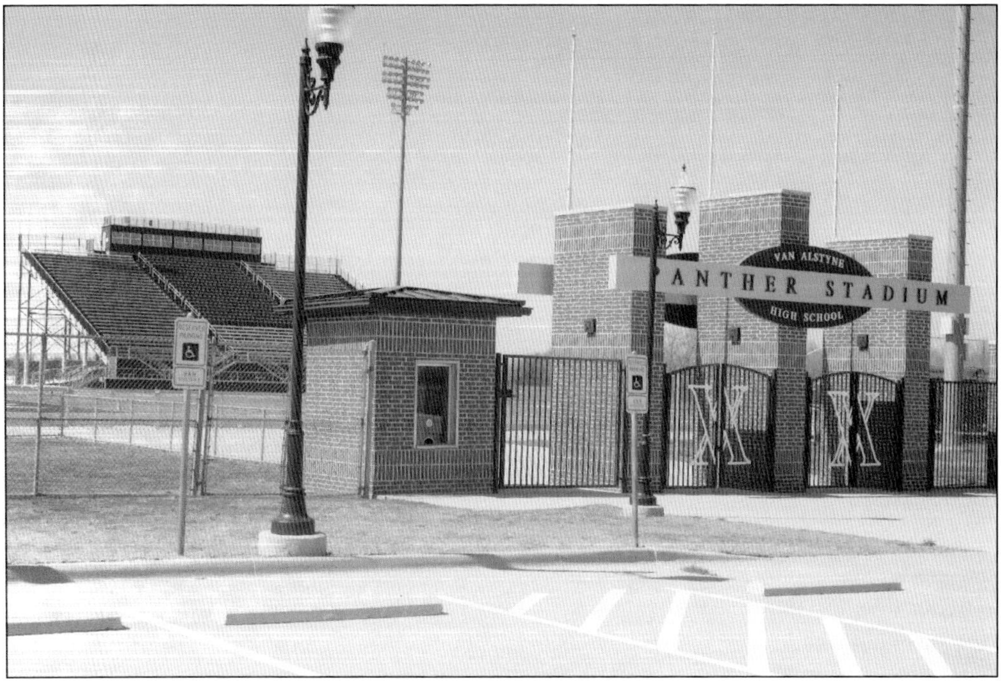

A new football stadium was erected behind the new VAHS. Panther Stadium can readily be expanded when needed. (Photograph by the author.)

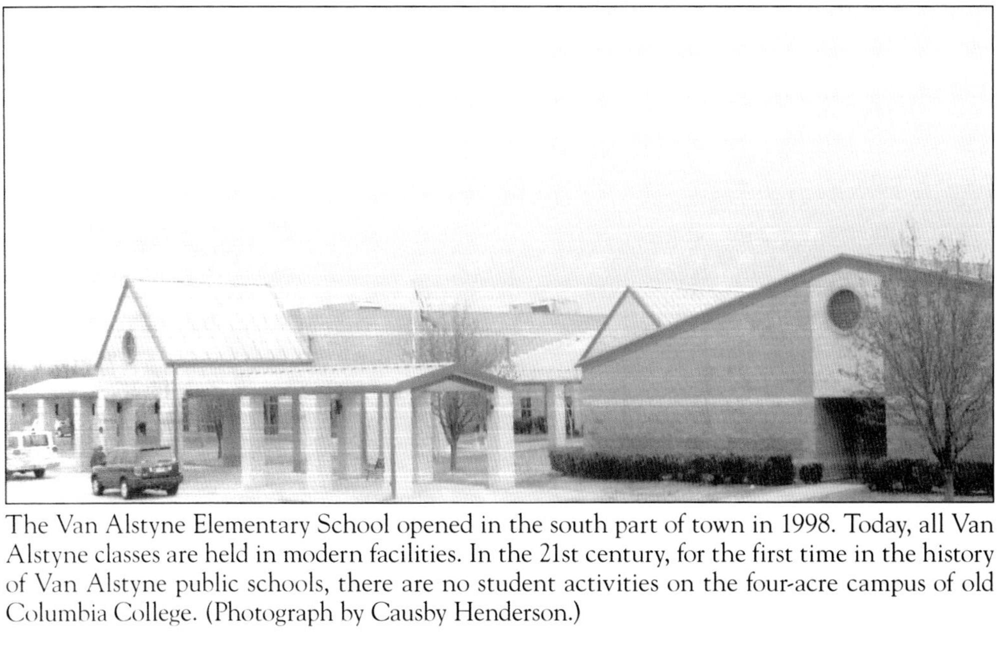

The Van Alstyne Elementary School opened in the south part of town in 1998. Today, all Van Alstyne classes are held in modern facilities. In the 21st century, for the first time in the history of Van Alstyne public schools, there are no student activities on the four-acre campus of old Columbia College. (Photograph by Causby Henderson.)

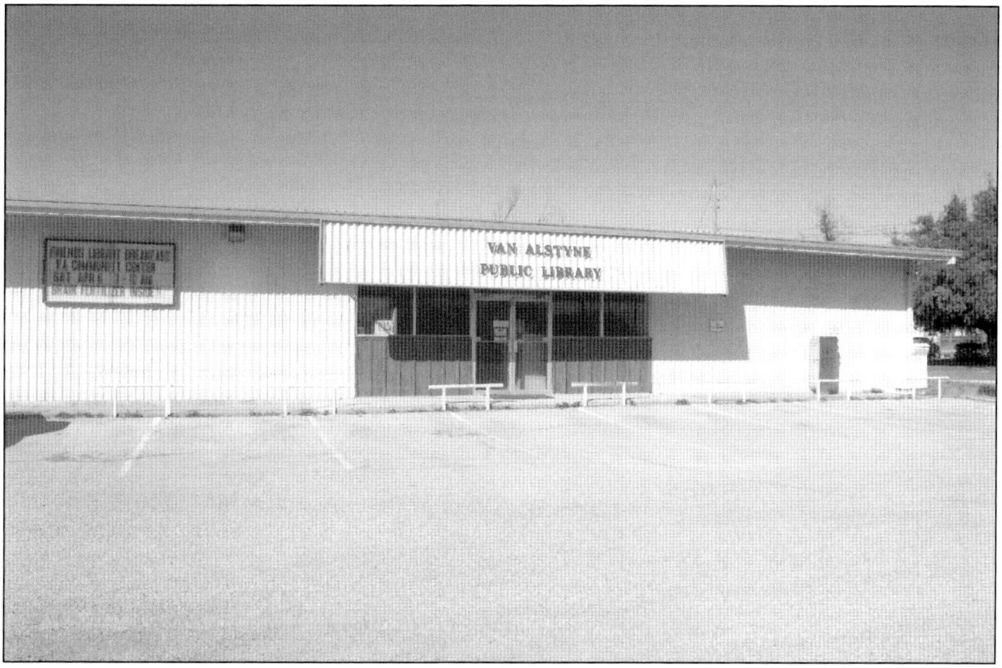

The Van Alstyne Public Library was founded in 1970. Presided over by a highly competent and helpful staff, the library provides all of the customary services and houses an outstanding archival collection of local history. (Photograph by the author.)

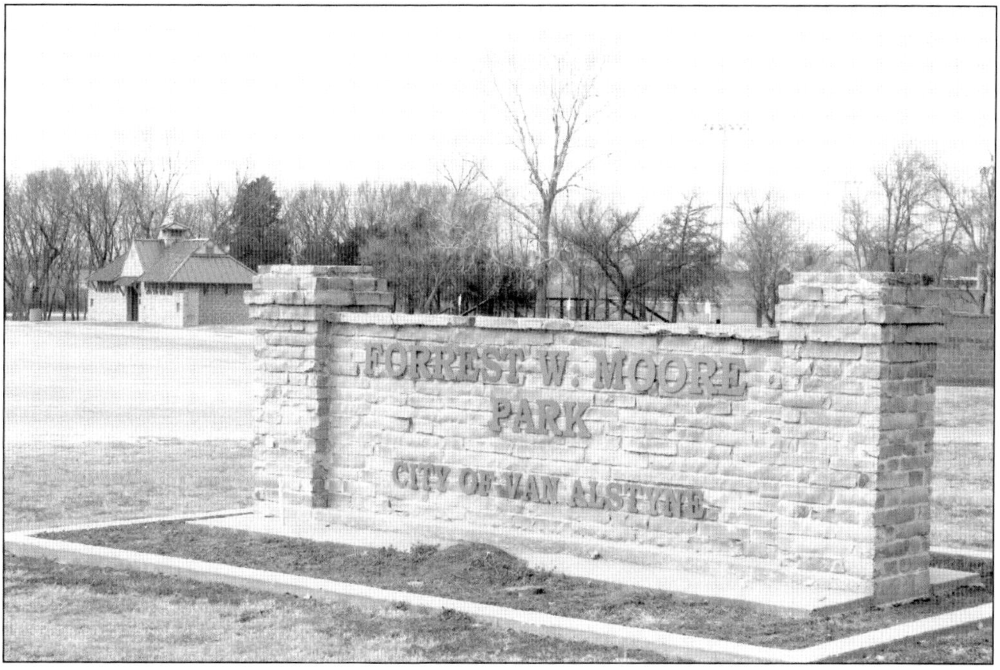

Forrest H. Moore Park is a beautiful community park that stretches across a large area south of the elementary school. The park offers a scenic nature trail, tennis courts, picnicking, baseball and softball diamonds, and open grassy areas. Forrest H. Moore Park will be a major asset to Van Alstyne in the 21st century. (Photograph by the author.)

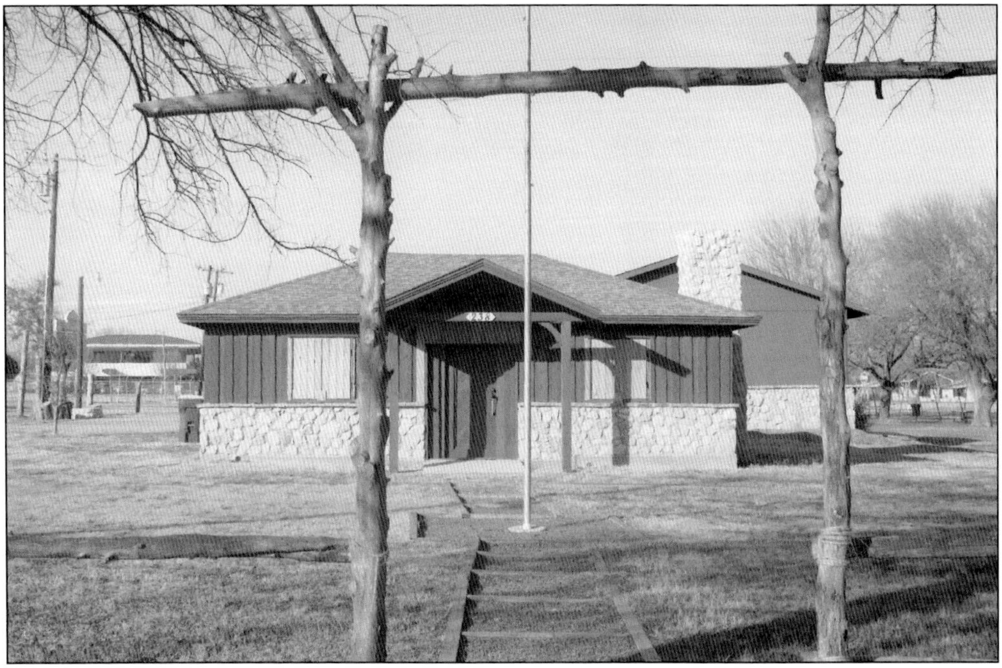

Van Alstyne's Boy Scout troop celebrated its centennial in 2013, the year this book was written and published. The Boy Scouts began the second century of their existence by moving into a rustic new lodge located just south of the old football stadium. (Photograph by the author.)

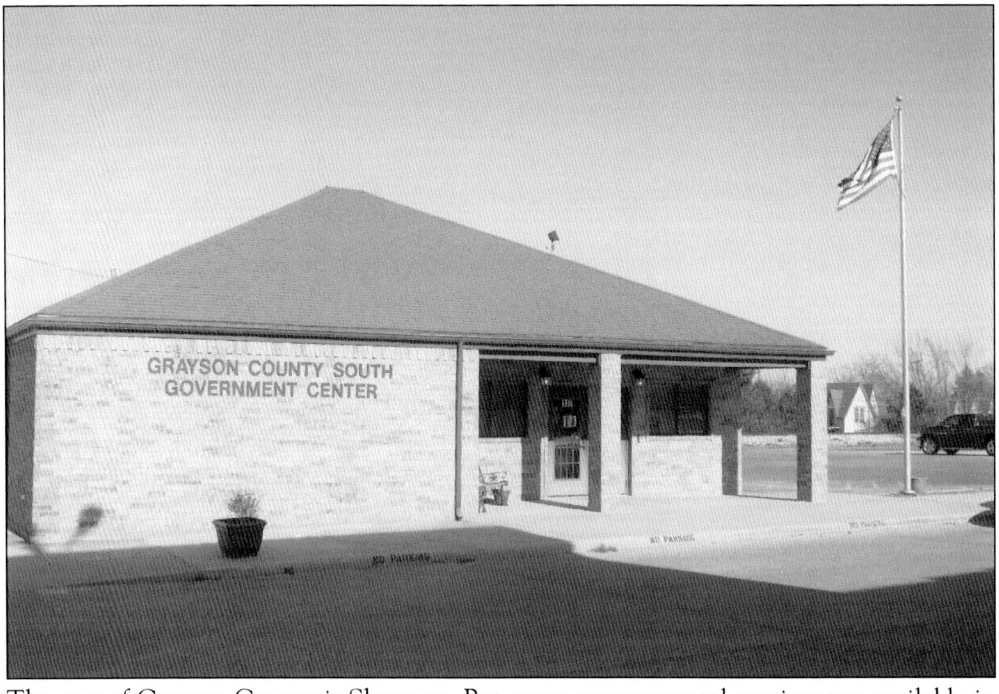

The seat of Grayson County is Sherman. But many governmental services are available in downtown Van Alstyne at the brick Grayson County South Government Center. (Photograph by the author.)

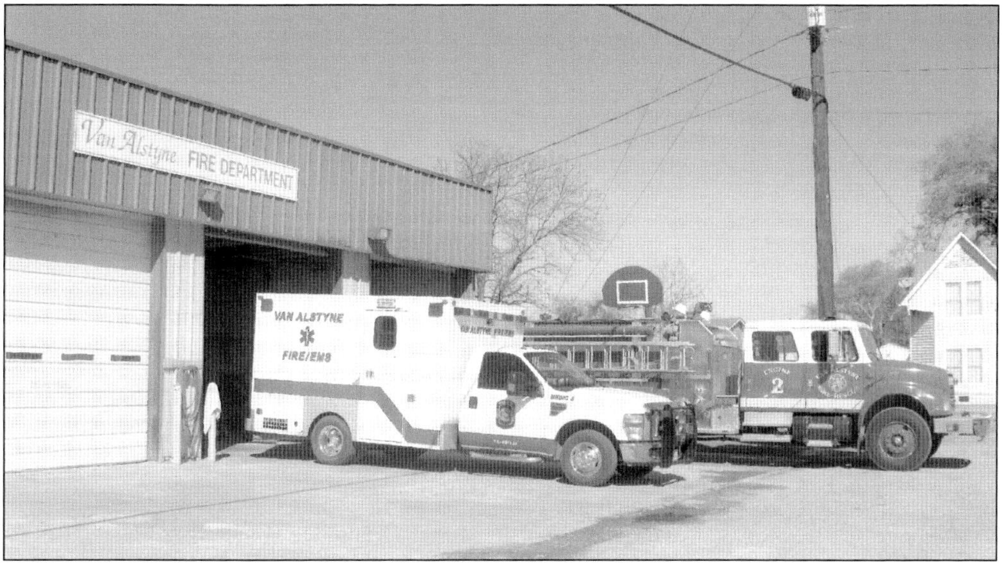

The Van Alstyne Fire Department (VAFD) entered the 20th century with 12 volunteer members and a hand-drawn wagon that carried 800 feet of hose, according to a 1901 Sanborn Fire Insurance map. But in the 21st century, the VAFD boasts a small fleet of emergency vehicles, highly trained responders, and an impressive array of modern equipment. (Photograph by the author.)

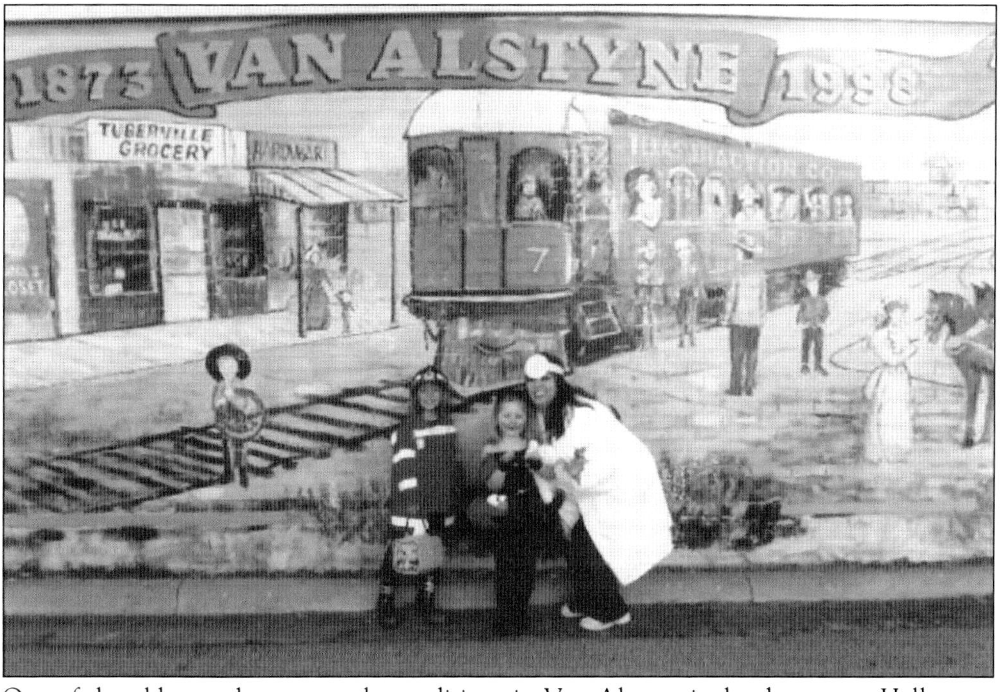

One of the oldest and most popular traditions in Van Alstyne is the downtown Halloween celebration. Children in costume go from business to business to collect goodies. There is a haunted house, firemen allow children to climb around on fire trucks, and there is wholesome fun at the downtown Baptist and Methodist churches. This costumed trio (elementary teacher Causby Henderson and daughters Bailey and Kendall) poses in front of the historic town mural near the post office. (Photograph by Dusty Henderson.)

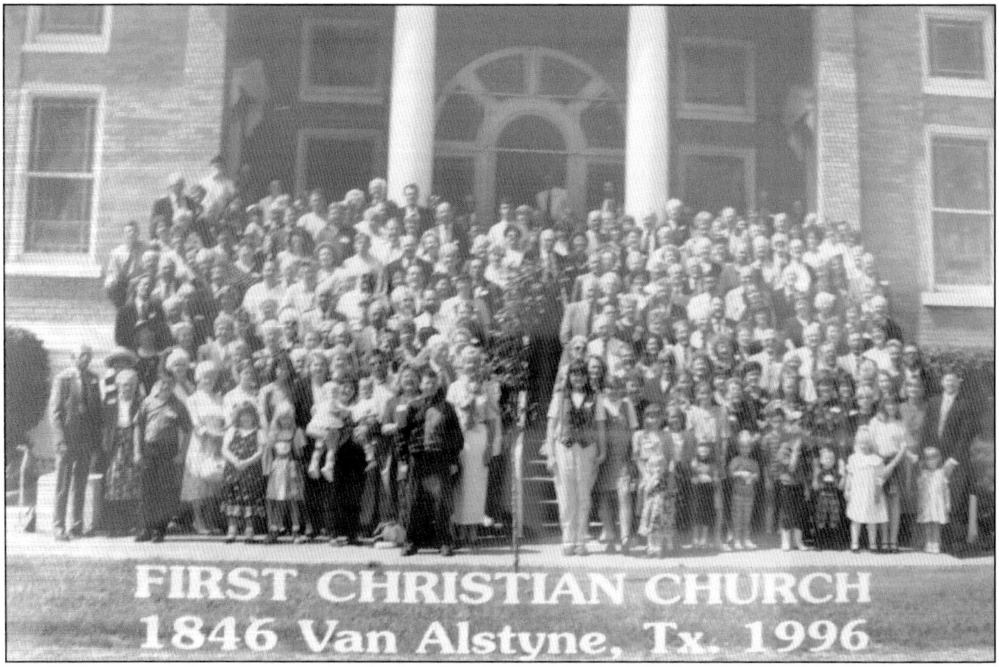

In 1996, a large crowd gathered at the First Christian Church to celebrate the congregation's 150th anniversary. A few years later, the historic church launched a decade-long expansion and renovation program, which included the Motley Building, erected behind the sanctuary, and an elevator and shaft attached to the north side of the church. Interior improvements included a basement chapel with a closed-circuit TV. The $650,000 program has already been paid. (Courtesy of First Christian Church.)

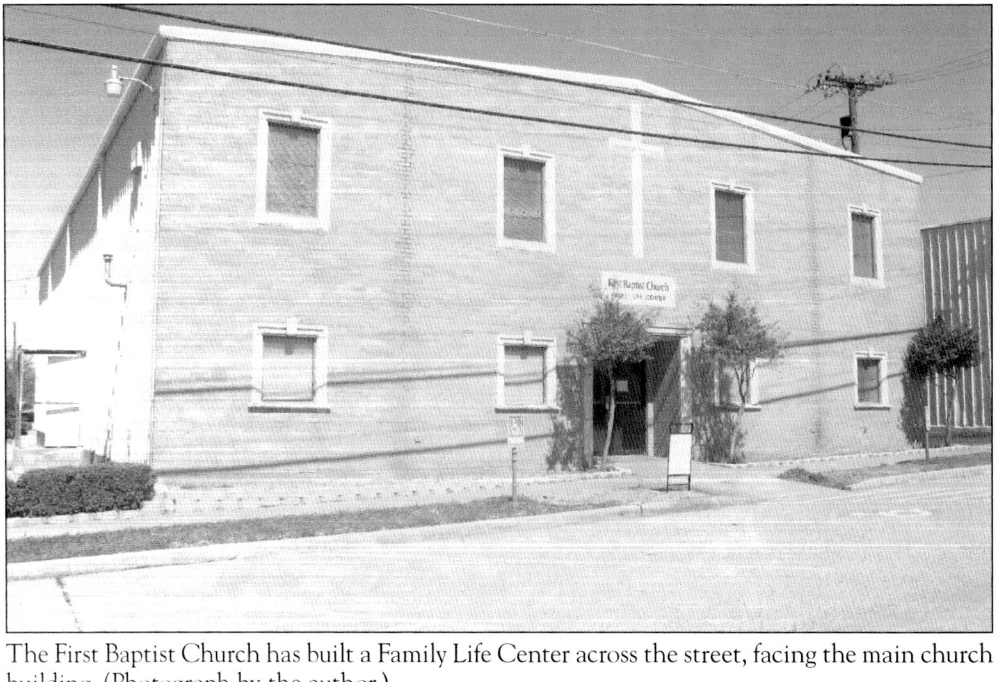

The First Baptist Church has built a Family Life Center across the street, facing the main church building. (Photograph by the author.)

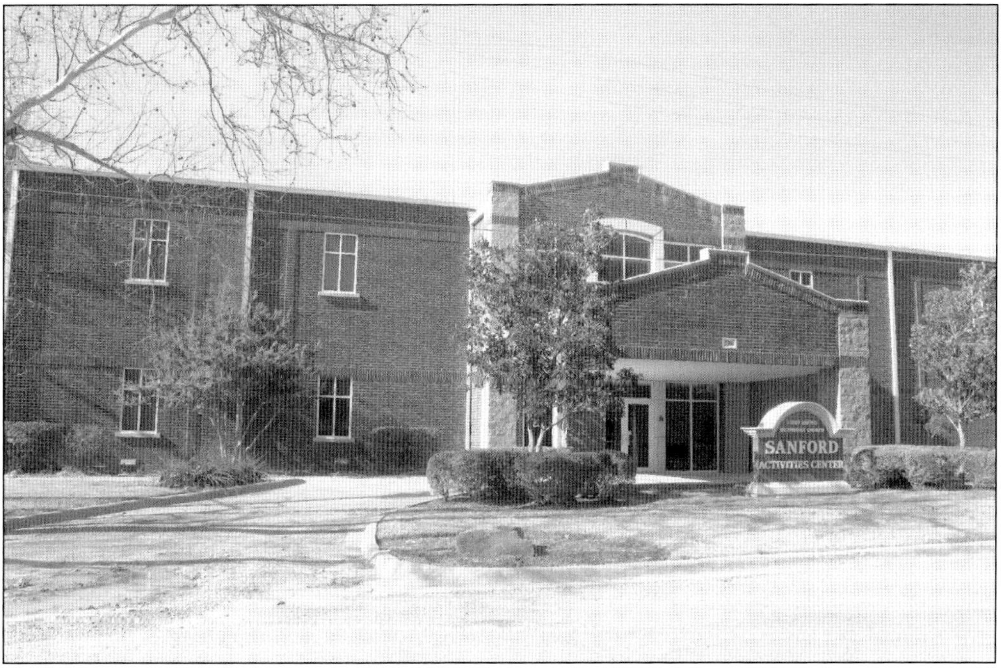

Behind the First Methodist Church and facing south is the large, impressive Sanford Activities Center. Among numerous other activities at the Sanford building, the Wee School, a Christian-based preschool, is held Monday through Thursday. (Photograph by the author.)

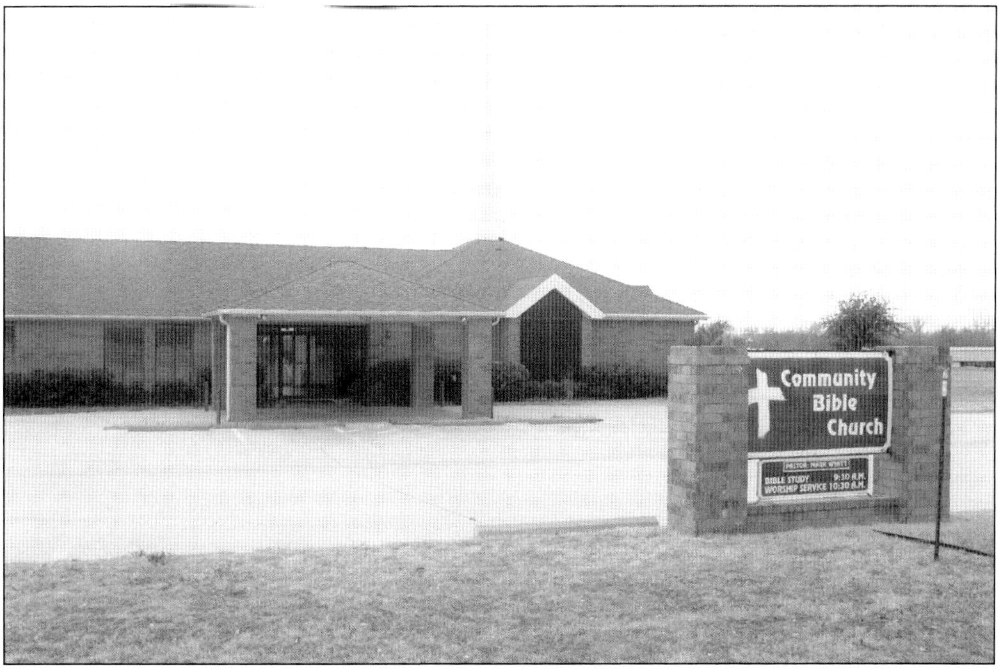

Representative of the newer churches in Van Alstyne is the Community Bible Church, located on Highway 5 at the south end of town. (Photograph by the author.)

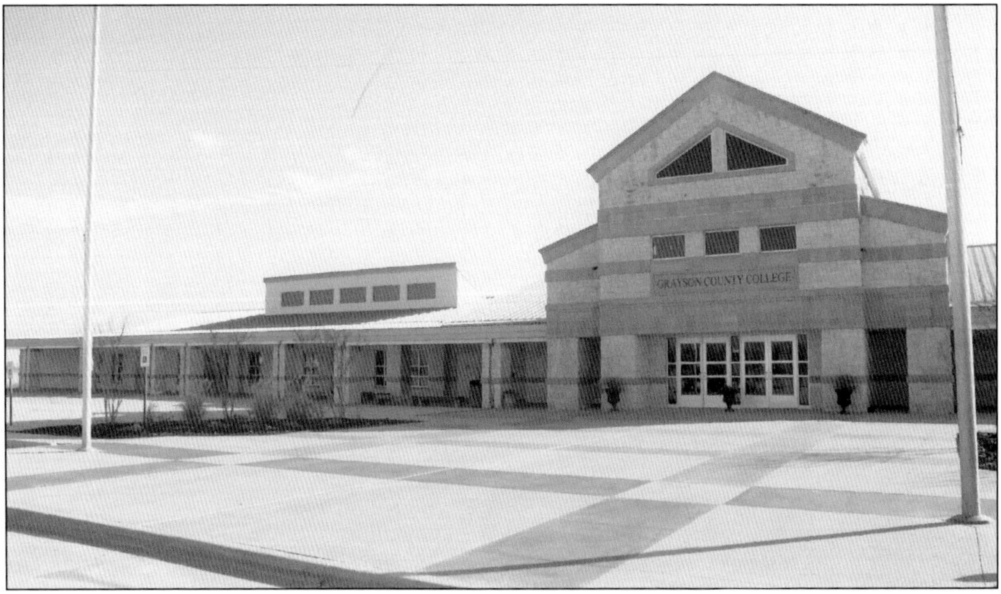

After Columbia College closed in 1905, nearly a century passed without an institution of higher learning in Van Alstyne. But in 2004, Grayson College Campus South opened at a location west of highway 75. Freshmen and sophomore courses are offered, including dual-credit classes to high school students. (Photograph by the author.)

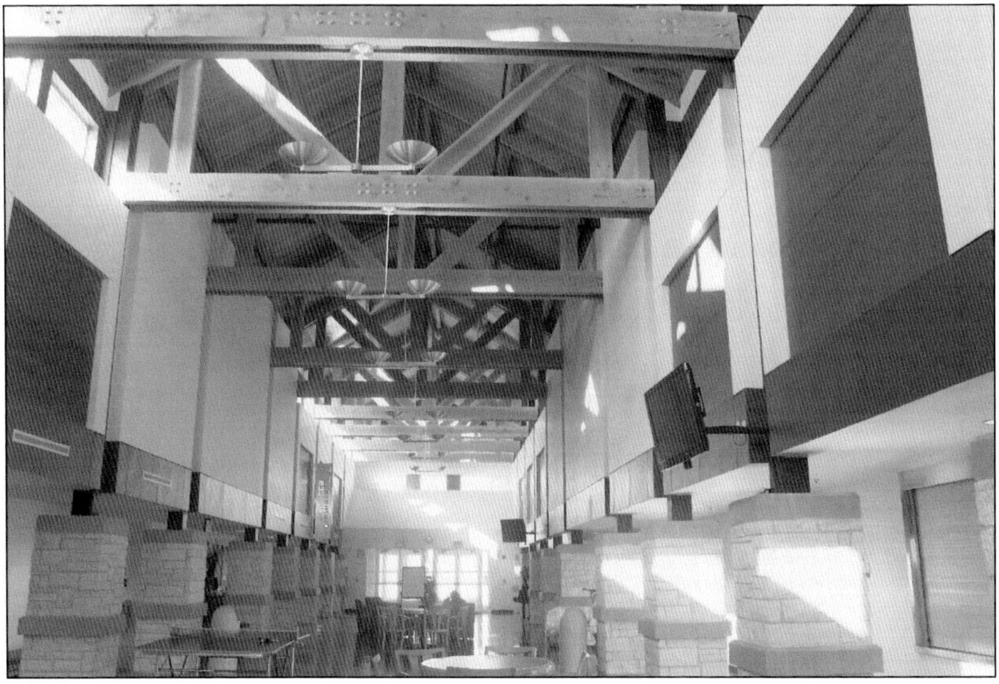

The main hall is impressive, and classrooms and offices are first-class college facilities. Recently, ground was broken next door for a $4-million technology building scheduled for completion in the fall of 2014. In conjunction with Southeastern Oklahoma State University, an array of new programs will be offered to area students. The 21st century offers exciting promise for higher education in Van Alstyne. (Photograph by the author.)

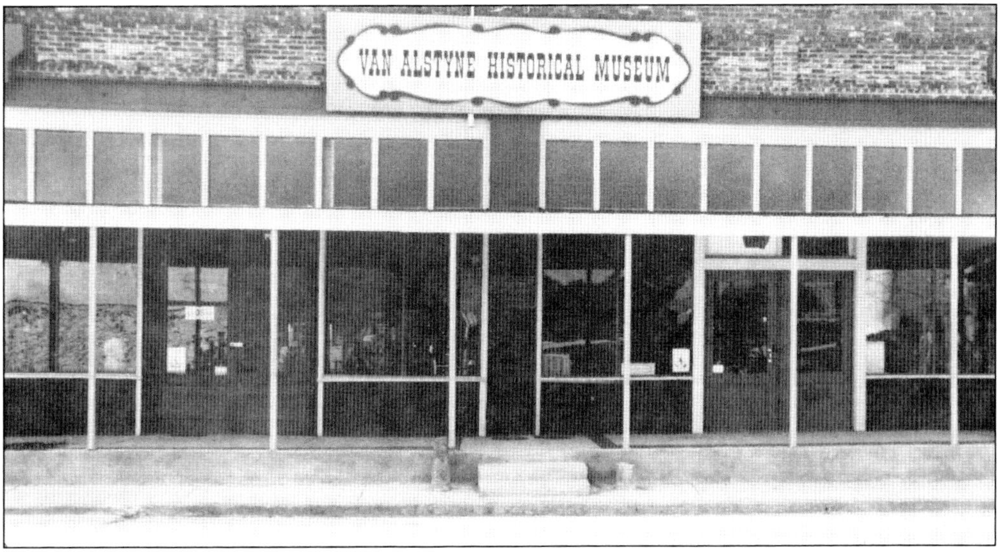

In 1973, the Van Alstyne Historical Society opened the Van Alstyne Historical Museum downtown on East Jefferson Street in a building donated by Robert and Dorothy Fielder. Operated by community-minded volunteers, the museum is a window to Van Alstyne's past. (Photograph by the author.)

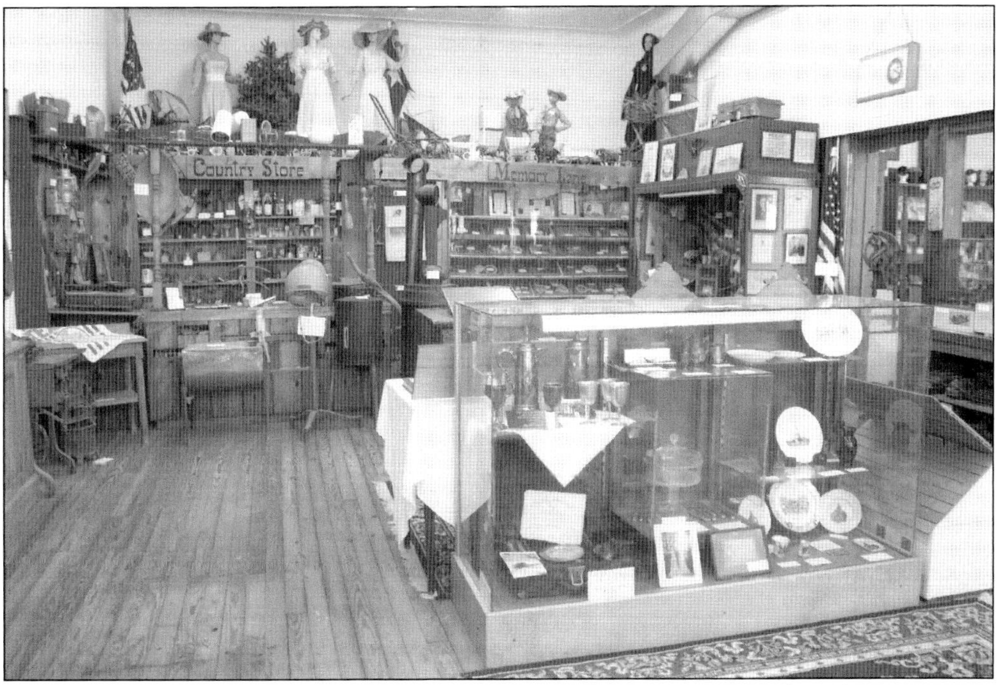

There are two large rooms in the Van Alstyne Historical Museum. Donors have been generous, and the rooms are filled with a rich collection of artifacts. A visit to the museum is a visit to Van Alstyne in an earlier time. (Photograph by the author.)